THE PRESENTATION OF SELF
IN EVERYDAY LIFE

THE PRESENTATION OF SELF
IN EVERYDAY LIFE

Erving Goffman

ANCHOR BOOKS
DOUBLEDAY
NEW YORK LONDON TORONTO SYDNEY AUCKLAND

AN ANCHOR BOOK
PUBLISHED BY DOUBLEDAY
a division of Bantam Doubleday Dell Publishing Group, Inc.
1540 Broadway, New York, New York 10036

ANCHOR BOOKS, DOUBLEDAY, and the portrayal
of an anchor are trademarks of Doubleday, a division of
Bantam Doubleday Dell Publishing Group, Inc.

The Anchor Books edition is the first publication
of this revised edition of *The Presentation of Self
in Everyday Life*.

ISBN 0-385-09402-7

Library of Congress Catalog Card Number 59–9138

Masks are arrested expressions and admirable echoes of feeling, at once faithful, discreet, and superlative. Living things in contact with the air must acquire a cuticle, and it is not urged against cuticles that they are not hearts; yet some philosophers seem to be angry with images for not being things, and with words for not being feelings. Words and images are like shells, no less integral parts of nature than are the substances they cover, but better addressed to the eye and more open to observation. I would not say that substance exists for the sake of appearance, or faces for the sake of masks, or the passions for the sake of poetry and virtue. Nothing arises in nature for the sake of anything else; all these phases and products are involved equally in the round of existence. . . .

George Santayana[1]

[1] *Soliloquies in England and Later Soliloquies* (New York: Scribner's, 1922), pp. 131–32.

ACKNOWLEDGMENTS

The report presented here was developed in connection with a study of interaction undertaken for the Department of Social Anthropology and the Social Sciences Research Committee of the University of Edinburgh and a study of social stratification supported by a Ford Foundation grant directed by Professor E. A. Shils at the University of Chicago. I am grateful to these sources of guidance and support. I would like to express thanks to my teachers C. W. M. Hart, W. L. Warner, and E. C. Hughes. I want, too, to thank Elizabeth Bott, James Littlejohn, and Edward Banfield, who helped me at the beginning of the study, and fellow students of occupations at the University of Chicago who helped me later. Without the collaboration of my wife, Angelica S. Goffman, this report would not have been written.

PREFACE

I mean this report to serve as a sort of handbook detailing one sociological perspective from which social life can be studied, especially the kind of social life that is organized within the physical confines of a building or plant. A set of features will be described which together form a framework that can be applied to any concrete social establishment, be it domestic, industrial, or commercial.

The perspective employed in this report is that of the theatrical performance; the principles derived are dramaturgical ones. I shall consider the way in which the individual in ordinary work situations presents himself and his activity to others, the ways in which he guides and controls the impression they form of him, and the kinds of things he may and may not do while sustaining his performance before them. In using this model I will attempt not to make light of its obvious inadequacies. The stage presents things that are make-believe; presumably life presents things that are real and sometimes not well rehearsed. More important, perhaps, on the stage one player presents himself in the guise of a character to characters projected by other players; the audience constitutes a third party to the interaction—one that is essential and yet, if the stage performance were real, one that would not be there. In real life, the three parties are compressed into two; the part one individual plays is tailored to the parts played by the others present, and yet these others also constitute the audience. Still other inadequacies in this model will be considered later.

The illustrative materials used in this study are of mixed status: some are taken from respectable researches where qualified generalizations are given concerning reliably recorded regularities; some are taken from informal memoirs written by colorful people; many fall in between. In addi-

tion, frequent use is made of a study of my own of a
Shetland Island crofting (subsistence farming) community.[1] The justification for this approach (as I take to be
the justification for Simmel's also) is that the illustrations
together fit into a coherent framework that ties together
bits of experience the reader has already had and provides
the student with a guide worth testing in case-studies of
institutional social life.

The framework is presented in logical steps. The introduction is necessarily abstract and may be skipped.

[1] Reported in part in E. Goffman, "Communication Conduct
in an Island Community" (unpublished Ph.D. dissertation, Department of Sociology, University of Chicago, 1953). The community hereafter will be called "Shetland Isle."

CONTENTS

INTRODUCTION

When an individual enters the presence of others, they commonly seek to acquire information about him or to bring into play information about him already possessed. They will be interested in his general socio-economic status, his conception of self, his attitude toward them, his competence, his trustworthiness, etc. Although some of this information seems to be sought almost as an end in itself, there are usually quite practical reasons for acquiring it. Information about the individual helps to define the situation, enabling others to know in advance what he will expect of them and what they may expect of him. Informed in these ways, the others will know how best to act in order to call forth a desired response from him.

For those present, many sources of information become accessible and many carriers (or "sign-vehicles") become available for conveying this information. If unacquainted with the individual, observers can glean clues from his conduct and appearance which allow them to apply their previous experience with individuals roughly similar to the one before them or, more important, to apply untested stereotypes to him. They can also assume from past experience that only individuals of a particular kind are likely to be found in a given social setting. They can rely on what the individual says about himself or on documentary evidence he provides as to who and what he is. If they know, or know of, the individual by virtue of experience prior to the interaction, they can rely on assumptions as to the persistence and generality of psychological traits as a means of predicting his present and future behavior.

However, during the period in which the individual is in the immediate presence of the others, few events may occur which directly provide the others with the conclusive information they will need if they are to direct wisely their own activity. Many crucial facts lie beyond the time and place of interaction or lie concealed within it. For example, the "true" or "real" attitudes, beliefs, and emotions of the individual can be ascertained only indirectly, through his avowals or through what appears to be involuntary expressive behavior. Similarly, if the individual offers the others a product or service, they will often find that during the interaction there will be no time and place immediately available for eating the pudding that the proof can be found in. They will be forced to accept some events as conventional or natural signs of something not directly available to the senses. In Ichheiser's terms,[1] the individual will have to act so that he intentionally or unintentionally *expresses* himself, and the others will in turn have to be *impressed* in some way by him._

The expressiveness of the individual (and therefore his capacity to give impressions) appears to involve two radically different kinds of sign activity: the expression that he *gives,* and the expression that he *gives off.* The first involves verbal symbols or their substitutes which he uses admittedly and solely to convey the information that he and the others are known to attach to these symbols. This is communication in the traditional and narrow sense. The second involves a wide range of action that others can treat as symptomatic of the actor, the expectation being that the action was performed for reasons other than the information conveyed in this way. As we shall have to see, this distinction has an only initial validity. The individual does of course intentionally convey misinformation by means of both of these types of communication, the first involving deceit, the second feigning.

Taking communication in both its narrow and broad sense, one finds that when the individual is in the immediate presence of others, his activity will have a promissory character. The others are likely to find that they must accept the individual on faith, offering him a just return

[1] Gustav Ichheiser, "Misunderstandings in Human Relations," Supplement to *The American Journal of Sociology,* LV (September, 1949), pp. 6–7.

while he is present before them in exchange for something whose true value will not be established until after he has left their presence. (Of course, the others also live by inference in their dealings with the physical world, but it is only in the world of social interaction that the objects about which they make inferences will purposely facilitate and hinder this inferential process.) The security that they justifiably feel in making inferences about the individual will vary, of course, depending on such factors as the amount of information they already possess about him, but no amount of such past evidence can entirely obviate the necessity of acting on the basis of inferences. As William I. Thomas suggested:

> It is also highly important for us to realize that we do not as a matter of fact lead our lives, make our decisions, and reach our goals in everyday life either statistically or scientifically. We live by inference. I am, let us say, your guest. You do not know, you cannot determine scientifically, that I will not steal your money or your spoons. But inferentially I will not, and inferentially you have me as a guest.[2]

Let us now turn from the others to the point of view of the individual who presents himself before them. He may wish them to think highly of him, or to think that he thinks highly of them, or to perceive how in fact he feels toward them, or to obtain no clear-cut impression; he may wish to ensure sufficient harmony so that the interaction can be sustained, or to defraud, get rid of, confuse, mislead, antagonize, or insult them. Regardless of the particular objective which the individual has in mind and of his motive for having this objective, it will be in his interests to control the conduct of the others, especially their responsive treatment of him.[3] This control is achieved largely by influenc-

[2] Quoted in E. H. Volkart, editor, *Social Behavior and Personality*, Contributions of W. I. Thomas to Theory and Social Research (New York: Social Science Research Council, 1951), p. 5.

[3] Here I owe much to an unpublished paper by Tom Burns of the University of Edinburgh. He presents the argument that in

ing the definition of the situation which the others come to formulate, and he can influence this definition by expressing himself in such a way as to give them the kind of impression that will lead them to act voluntarily in accordance with his own plan. Thus, when an individual appears in the presence of others, there will usually be some reason for him to mobilize his activity so that it will convey an impression to others which it is in his interests to convey. Since a girl's dormitory mates will glean evidence of her popularity from the calls she receives on the phone, we can suspect that some girls will arrange for calls to be made, and Willard Waller's finding can be anticipated:

> It has been reported by many observers that a girl who is called to the telephone in the dormitories will often allow herself to be called several times, in order to give all the other girls ample opportunity to hear her paged.[4]

Of the two kinds of communication—expressions given and expressions given off—this report will be primarily concerned with the latter, with the more theatrical and contextual kind, the non-verbal, presumably unintentional kind, whether this communication be purposely engineered or not. As an example of what we must try to examine, I would like to cite at length a novelistic incident in which Preedy, a vacationing Englishman, makes his first appearance on the beach of his summer hotel in Spain:

> But in any case he took care to avoid catching anyone's eye. First of all, he had to make it clear to those potential companions of his holiday that they were of no concern to him whatsoever. He stared through them, round

---

all interaction a basic underlying theme is the desire of each participant to guide and control the responses made by the others present. A similar argument has been advanced by Jay Haley in a recent unpublished paper, but in regard to a special kind of control, that having to do with defining the nature of the relationship of those involved in the interaction.

[4] Willard Waller, "The Rating and Dating Complex," *American Sociological Review*, II, p. 730.

them, over them—eyes lost in space. The beach might have been empty. If by chance a ball was thrown his way, he looked surprised; then let a smile of amusement lighten his face (Kindly Preedy), looked round dazed to see that there *were* people on the beach, tossed it back with a smile to himself and not a smile *at* the people, and then resumed carelessly his nonchalant survey of space.

But it was time to institute a little parade, the parade of the Ideal Preedy. By devious handlings he gave any who wanted to look a chance to see the title of his book—a Spanish translation of Homer, classic thus, but not daring, cosmopolitan too—and then gathered together his beach-wrap and bag into a neat sand-resistant pile (Methodical and Sensible Preedy), rose slowly to stretch at ease his huge frame (Big-Cat Preedy), and tossed aside his sandals (Carefree Preedy, after all).

The marriage of Preedy and the sea! There were alternative rituals. The first involved the stroll that turns into a run and a dive straight into the water, thereafter smoothing into a strong splashless crawl towards the horizon. But of course not really to the horizon. Quite suddenly he would turn on to his back and thrash great white splashes with his legs, somehow thus showing that he could have swum further had he wanted to, and then would stand up a quarter out of water for all to see who it was.

The alternative course was simpler, it avoided the cold-water shock and it avoided the risk of appearing too high-spirited. The point was to appear to be so used to the sea, the Mediterranean, and this particular beach, that one might as well be in the sea as out of it. It involved a slow stroll down and into the edge of the water—not even noticing his toes were wet, land and water all the same to *him!*—with his eyes up at the sky gravely surveying portents, invisible to others, of the weather (Local Fisherman Preedy).[5]

[5] William Sansom, *A Contest of Ladies* (London: Hogarth, 1956), pp. 230–32.

The novelist means us to see that Preedy is improperly concerned with the extensive impressions he feels his sheer bodily action is giving off to those around him. We can malign Preedy further by assuming that he has acted merely in order to give a particular impression, that this is a false impression, and that the others present receive either no impression at all, or, worse still, the impression that Preedy is affectedly trying to cause them to receive this particular impression. But the important point for us here is that the kind of impression Preedy thinks he is making is in fact the kind of impression that others correctly and incorrectly glean from someone in their midst.

I have said that when an individual appears before others his actions will influence the definition of the situation which they come to have. Sometimes the individual will act in a thoroughly calculating manner, expressing himself in a given way solely in order to give the kind of impression to others that is likely to evoke from them a specific response he is concerned to obtain. Sometimes the individual will be calculating in his activity but be relatively unaware that this is the case. Sometimes he will intentionally and consciously express himself in a particular way, but chiefly because the tradition of his group or social status require this kind of expression and not because of any particular response (other than vague acceptance or approval) that is likely to be evoked from those impressed by the expression. Sometimes the traditions of an individual's role will lead him to give a well-designed impression of a particular kind and yet he may be neither consciously nor unconsciously disposed to create such an impression. The others, in their turn, may be suitably impressed by the individual's efforts to convey something, or may misunderstand the situation and come to conclusions that are warranted neither by the individual's intent nor by the facts. In any case, in so far as the others act *as if* the individual had conveyed a particular impression, we may take a functional or pragmatic view and say that the individual has "effectively" projected a given definition of the situation and "effectively" fostered the understanding that a given state of affairs obtains.

There is one aspect of the others' response that bears special comment here. Knowing that the individual is likely to present himself in a light that is favorable to him, the others may divide what they witness into two parts; a part that is relatively easy for the individual to manipulate at will, being chiefly his verbal assertions, and a part in regard to which he seems to have little concern or control, being chiefly derived from the expressions he gives off. The others may then use what are considered to be the ungovernable aspects of his expressive behavior as a check upon the validity of what is conveyed by the governable aspects. In this a fundamental asymmetry is demonstrated in the communication process, the individual presumably being aware of only one stream of his communication, the witnesses of this stream and one other. For example, in Shetland Isle one crofter's wife, in serving native dishes to a visitor from the mainland of Britain, would listen with a polite smile to his polite claims of liking what he was eating; at the same time she would take note of the rapidity with which the visitor lifted his fork or spoon to his mouth, the eagerness with which he passed food into his mouth, and the gusto expressed in chewing the food, using these signs as a check on the stated feelings of the eater. The same woman, in order to discover what one acquaintance (A) "actually" thought of another acquaintance (B), would wait until B was in the presence of A but engaged in conversation with still another person (C). She would then covertly examine the facial expressions of A as he regarded B in conversation with C. Not being in conversation with B, and not being directly observed by him, A would sometimes relax usual constraints and tactful deceptions, and freely express what he was "actually" feeling about B. This Shetlander, in short, would observe the unobserved observer.

Now given the fact that others are likely to check up on the more controllable aspects of behavior by means of the less controllable, one can expect that sometimes the individual will try to exploit this very possibility, guiding the impression he makes through behavior felt to be reliably

informing.[6] For example, in gaining admission to a tight
social circle, the participant observer may not only wear an
accepting look while listening to an informant, but may also
be careful to wear the same look when observing the informant talking to others; observers of the observer will
then not as easily discover where he actually stands. A
specific illustration may be cited from Shetland Isle. When
a neighbor dropped in to have a cup of tea, he would
ordinarily wear at least a hint of an expectant warm smile
as he passed through the door into the cottage. Since lack
of physical obstructions outside the cottage and lack of
light within it usually made it possible to observe the visitor
unobserved as he approached the house, islanders sometimes took pleasure in watching the visitor drop whatever
expression he was manifesting and replace it with a sociable
one just before reaching the door. However, some visitors,
in appreciating that this examination was occurring, would
blindly adopt a social face a long distance from the house,
thus ensuring the projection of a constant image.

This kind of control upon the part of the individual rein-
states the symmetry of the communication process, and sets
the stage for a kind of information game—a potentially in-
finite cycle of concealment, discovery, false revelation, and
rediscovery. It should be added that since the others are
likely to be relatively unsuspicious of the presumably un-
guided aspect of the individual's conduct, he can gain much
by controlling it. The others of course may sense that the
individual is manipulating the presumably spontaneous aspects of his behavior, and seek in this very act of manipulation some shading of conduct that the individual has not
managed to control. This again provides a check upon the
individual's behavior, this time his presumably uncalculated
behavior, thus re-establishing the asymmetry of the communication process. Here I would like only to add the suggestion that the arts of piercing an individual's effort at

[6] The widely read and rather sound writings of Stephen Potter
are concerned in part with signs that can be engineered to give
a shrewd observer the apparently incidental cues he needs to
discover concealed virtues the gamesman does not in fact possess.

calculated unintentionality seem better developed than our capacity to manipulate our own behavior, so that regardless of how many steps have occurred in the information game, the witness is likely to have the advantage over the actor, and the initial asymmetry of the communication process is likely to be retained.

When we allow that the individual projects a definition of the situation when he appears before others, we must also see that the others, however passive their role may seem to be, will themselves effectively project a definition of the situation by virtue of their response to the individual and by virtue of any lines of action they initiate to him. Ordinarily the definitions of the situation projected by the several different participants are sufficiently attuned to one another so that open contradiction will not occur. I do not mean that there will be the kind of consensus that arises when each individual present candidly expresses what he really feels and honestly agrees with the expressed feelings of the others present. This kind of harmony is an optimistic ideal and in any case not necessary for the smooth working of society. Rather, each participant is expected to suppress his immediate heartfelt feelings, conveying a view of the situation which he feels the others will be able to find at least temporarily acceptable. The maintenance of this surface of agreement, this veneer of consensus, is facilitated by each participant concealing his own wants behind statements which assert values to which everyone present feels obliged to give lip service. Further, there is usually a kind of division of definitional labor. Each participant is allowed to establish the tentative official ruling regarding matters which are vital to him but not immediately important to others, e.g., the rationalizations and justifications by which he accounts for his past activity. In exchange for this courtesy he remains silent or non-committal on matters important to others but not immediately important to him. We have then a kind of interactional *modus vivendi*. Together the participants contribute to a single over-all definition of the situation which involves not so much a real agreement as to what exists but rather a real agreement as to whose claims concerning what issues will be temporarily honored. Real agreement will also exist concerning the desirability of avoiding an open conflict of definitions of the situation.[7] I will refer to this level of agreement as a "working consensus." It is to be understood that the working consensus established in one interaction setting will be quite different in content from the working consensus established in a different type of setting. Thus, between two friends at lunch, a reciprocal show of affection, respect, and concern for the other is maintained. In service occupations, on the other hand, the specialist often maintains an image of disinterested involvement in the problem of the client, while the client responds with a show of respect for the competence and integrity of the specialist. Regardless of such differences in content, however, the general form of these working arrangements is the same.

In noting the tendency for a participant to accept the definitional claims made by the others present, we can appreciate the crucial importance of the information that the individual *initially* possesses or acquires concerning his fellow participants, for it is on the basis of this initial information that the individual starts to define the situation and starts to build up lines of responsive action. The individual's initial projection commits him to what he is proposing to be and requires him to drop all pretenses of being other things. As the interaction among the participants progresses, additions and modifications in this initial informational state will of course occur, but it is essential that these later developments be related without contradiction to, and even built up from, the initial positions taken by the several partic-

---

[7] An interaction can be purposely set up as a time and place for voicing differences in opinion, but in such cases participants must be careful to agree not to disagree on the proper tone of voice, vocabulary, and degree of seriousness in which all arguments are to be phrased, and upon the mutual respect which disagreeing participants must carefully continue to express toward one another. This debaters' or academic definition of the situation may also be invoked suddenly and judiciously as a way of translating a serious conflict of views into one that can be handled within a framework acceptable to all present.

ipants. It would seem that an individual can more easily make a choice as to what line of treatment to demand from and extend to the others present at the beginning of an encounter than he can alter the line of treatment that is being pursued once the interaction is underway.

In everyday life, of course, there is a clear understanding that first impressions are important. Thus, the work adjustment of those in service occupations will often hinge upon a capacity to seize and hold the initiative in the service relation, a capacity that will require subtle aggressiveness on the part of the server when he is of lower socio-economic status than his client. W. F. Whyte suggests the waitress as an example:

> The first point that stands out is that the waitress who bears up under pressure does not simply respond to her customers. She acts with some skill to control their behavior. The first question to ask when we look at the customer relationship is, "Does the waitress get the jump on the customer, or does the customer get the jump on the waitress?" The skilled waitress realizes the crucial nature of this question. . . .
>
> The skilled waitress tackles the customer with confidence and without hesitation. For example, she may find that a new customer has seated himself before she could clear off the dirty dishes and change the cloth. He is now leaning on the table studying the menu. She greets him, says, "May I change the cover, please?" and, without waiting for an answer, takes his menu away from him so that he moves back from the table, and she goes about her work. The relationship is handled politely but firmly, and there is never any question as to who is in charge.[8]

When the interaction that is initiated by "first impressions" is itself merely the initial interaction in an extended series of interactions involving the same participants, we speak of "getting off on the right foot" and feel that it is crucial that

[8] W. F. Whyte, "When Workers and Customers Meet," Chap. VII, *Industry and Society*, ed. W. F. Whyte (New York: McGraw-Hill, 1946), pp. 132–33.

we do so. Thus, one learns that some teachers take the
following view:

> You can't ever let them get the upper hand on you or
> you're through. So I start out tough. The first day I get a
> new class in, I let them know who's boss . . . You've got
> to start off tough, then you can ease up as you go along.
> If you start out easy-going, when you try to get tough,
> they'll just look at you and laugh.[9]

Similarly, attendants in mental institutions may feel that if
the new patient is sharply put in his place the first day on
the ward and made to see who is boss, much future difficulty will be prevented.[10]

Given the fact that the individual effectively projects a
definition of the situation when he enters the presence of
others, we can assume that events may occur within the
interaction which contradict, discredit, or otherwise throw
doubt upon this projection. When these disruptive events
occur, the interaction itself may come to a confused and
embarrassed halt. Some of the assumptions upon which
the responses of the participants had been predicated become untenable, and the participants find themselves
lodged in an interaction for which the situation has been
wrongly defined and is now no longer defined. At such
moments the individual whose presentation has been discredited may feel ashamed while the others present may
feel hostile, and all the participants may come to feel ill at
ease, nonplussed, out of countenance, embarrassed, experiencing the kind of anomy that is generated when the minute social system of face-to-face interaction breaks down.

In stressing the fact that the initial definition of the
situation projected by an individual tends to provide a plan
for the co-operative activity that follows—in stressing this

[9] Teacher interview quoted by Howard S. Becker, "Social
Class Variations in the Teacher-Pupil Relationship," *Journal
of Educational Sociology*, XXV, p. 459.

[10] Harold Taxel, "Authority Structure in a Mental Hospital
Ward" (unpublished Master's thesis, Department of Sociology,
University of Chicago, 1953).

action point of view—we must not overlook the crucial fact
that any projected definition of the situation also has a
distinctive moral character. It is this moral character of
projections that will chiefly concern us in this report. Society is organized on the principle that any individual who
possesses certain social characteristics has a moral right to
expect that others will value and treat him in an appropriate way. Connected with this principle is a second, namely
that an individual who implicitly or explicitly signifies that
he has certain social characteristics ought in fact to be
what he claims he is. In consequence, when an individual
projects a definition of the situation and thereby makes
an implicit or explicit claim to be a person of a particular kind, he automatically exerts a moral demand upon
the others, obliging them to value and treat him in the
manner that persons of his kind have a right to expect.
He also implicitly forgoes all claims to be things he does
not appear to be[11] and hence forgoes the treatment that
would be appropriate for such individuals. The others find,
then, that the individual has informed them as to what is
and as to what they *ought* to see as the "is."

One cannot judge the importance of definitional disruptions by the frequency with which they occur, for apparently they would occur more frequently were not constant
precautions taken. We find that preventive practices are
constantly employed to avoid these embarrassments and
that corrective practices are constantly employed to compensate for discrediting occurrences that have not been
successfully avoided. When the individual employs these
strategies and tactics to protect his own projections, we
may refer to them as "defensive practices"; when a participant employs them to save the definition of the situation
projected by another, we speak of "protective practices" or

[11] This role of the witness in limiting what it is the individual
can be has been stressed by Existentialists, who see it as a basic
threat to individual freedom. See Jean-Paul Sartre, *Being and
Nothingness*, trans. by Hazel E. Barnes (New York: Philosoph-
ical Library, 1956), p. 365 ff.

"tact." Together, defensive and protective practices comprise the techniques employed to safeguard the impression fostered by an individual during his presence before others. It should be added that while we may be ready to see that no fostered impression would survive if defensive practices were not employed, we are less ready perhaps to see that few impressions could survive if those who received the impression did not exert tact in their reception of it.

In addition to the fact that precautions are taken to prevent disruption of projected definitions, we may also note that an intense interest in these disruptions comes to play a significant role in the social life of the group. Practical jokes and social games are played in which embarrassments which are to be taken unseriously are purposely engineered.[12] Fantasies are created in which devastating exposures occur. Anecdotes from the past—real, embroidered, or fictitious—are told and retold, detailing disruptions which occurred, almost occurred, or occurred and were admirably resolved. There seems to be no grouping which does not have a ready supply of these games, reveries, and cautionary tales, to be used as a source of humor, a catharsis for anxieties, and a sanction for inducing individuals to be modest in their claims and reasonable in their projected expectations. The individual may tell himself through dreams of getting into impossible positions. Families tell of the time a guest got his dates mixed and arrived when neither the house nor anyone in it was ready for him. Journalists tell of times when an all-too-meaningful misprint occurred, and the paper's assumption of objectivity or decorum was humorously discredited. Public servants tell of times a client ridiculously misunderstood form instructions, giving answers which implied an unanticipated and bizarre definition of the situation.[13] Seamen, whose home away from home is rigorously he-man, tell stories of coming back home and inadvertently asking mother to "pass the

[12] Goffman, op. cit., pp. 319–27.
[13] Peter Blau, "Dynamics of Bureaucracy" (Ph.D. dissertation, Department of Sociology, Columbia University, forthcoming, University of Chicago Press), pp. 127–29.

fucking butter."[14] Diplomats tell of the time a near-sighted queen asked a republican ambassador about the health of his king.[15]

To summarize, then, I assume that when an individual appears before others he will have many motives for trying to control the impression they receive of the situation. This report is concerned with some of the common techniques that persons employ to sustain such impressions and with some of the common contingencies associated with the employment of these techniques. The specific content of any activity presented by the individual participant, or the role it plays in the interdependent activities of an on-going social system, will not be at issue; I shall be concerned only with the participant's dramaturgical problems of presenting the activity before others. The issues dealt with by stage-craft and stage management are sometimes trivial but they are quite general; they seem to occur everywhere in social life, providing a clear-cut dimension for formal sociological analysis.

It will be convenient to end this introduction with some definitions that are implied in what has gone before and required for what is to follow. For the purpose of this report, interaction (that is, face-to-face interaction) may be roughly defined as the reciprocal influence of individuals upon one another's actions when in one another's immediate physical presence. An interaction may be defined as all the interaction which occurs throughout any one occasion when a given set of individuals are in one another's continuous presence; the term "an encounter" would do as well. A "performance" may be defined as all the activity of a given participant on a given occasion which serves to influence in any way any of the other participants. Taking a particular participant and his performance as a basic point of reference, we may refer to those who contribute

14 Walter M. Beattie, Jr., "The Merchant Seaman" (unpublished M.A. Report, Department of Sociology, University of Chicago, 1950), p. 35.

15 Sir Frederick Ponsonby, *Recollections of Three Reigns* (New York: Dutton, 1952), p. 46.

the other performances as the audience, observers, or co-participants. The pre-established pattern of action which is unfolded during a performance and which may be presented or played through on other occasions may be called a "part" or "routine."[16] These situational terms can easily be related to conventional structural ones. When an individual or performer plays the same part to the same audience on different occasions, a social relationship is likely to arise. Defining social role as the enactment of rights and duties attached to a given status, we can say that a social role will involve one or more parts and that each of these different parts may be presented by the performer on a series of occasions to the same kinds of audience or to an audience of the same persons.

[16] For comments on the importance of distinguishing between a routine of interaction and any particular instance when this routine is played through, see John von Neumann and Oskar Morgenstern, *The Theory of Games and Economic Behaviour* (2nd ed.; Princeton: Princeton University Press, 1947), p. 49.

Chapter I

PERFORMANCES

Belief in the Part One is Playing

When an individual plays a part he implicitly requests his observers to take seriously the impression that is fostered before them. They are asked to believe that the character they see actually possesses the attributes he appears to possess, that the task he performs will have the consequences that are implicitly claimed for it, and that, in general, matters are what they appear to be. In line with this, there is the popular view that the individual offers his performance and puts on his show "for the benefit of other people." It will be convenient to begin a consideration of performances by turning the question around and looking at the individual's own belief in the impression of reality that he attempts to engender in those among whom he finds himself.

At one extreme, one finds that the performer can be fully taken in by his own act; he can be sincerely convinced that the impression of reality which he stages is the real reality. When his audience is also convinced in this way about the show he puts on—and this seems to be the typical case—then for the moment at least, only the sociologist or the socially disgruntled will have any doubts about the "realness" of what is presented.

At the other extreme, we find that the performer may not be taken in at all by his own routine. This possibility is understandable, since no one is in quite as good an observational position to see through the act as the person who puts it on. Coupled with this, the performer may be moved to guide the conviction of his audience only as a means to other ends, having no ultimate concern in the conception that they have of him or of the situation. When the individual has no belief in his own act and no ultimate concern with the beliefs of his audience, we may call him cynical, reserving the term "sincere" for individuals who believe in the impression fostered by their own performance. It should be understood that the cynic, with all his professional disinvolvement, may obtain unprofessional pleasures from his masquerade, experiencing a kind of gleeful spiritual aggression from the fact that he can toy at will with something his audience must take seriously.[1]

It is not assumed, of course, that all cynical performers are interested in deluding their audiences for purposes of what is called "self-interest" or private gain. A cynical individual may delude his audience for what he considers to be their own good, or for the good of the community, etc. For illustrations of this we need not appeal to sadly enlightened showmen such as Marcus Aurelius or Hsun Tzŭ. We know that in service occupations practitioners who may otherwise be sincere are sometimes forced to delude their customers because their customers show such a heartfelt demand for it. Doctors who are led into giving placebos, filling station attendants who resignedly check and recheck tire pressures for anxious women motorists, shoe clerks who sell a shoe that fits but tell the customer it is the size she wants to hear—these are cynical performers whose audiences will not allow them to be sincere. Similarly, it seems that sympathetic patients in mental wards will sometimes feign bizarre symptoms so that student nurses will not be subjected to a disappointingly sane performance.[2] So also,

---

[1] Perhaps the real crime of the confidence man is not that he takes money from his victims but that he robs all of us of the belief that middle-class manners and appearance can be sustained only by middle class people. A disabused professional can be cynically hostile to the service relation his clients expect him to extend to them. the confidence man is in a position to hold the whole "legit" world in this contempt.

[2] See Taxel, op. cit., p. 4. Harry Stack Sullivan has suggested that the tact of institutionalized performers can operate in the other direction, resulting in a kind of noblesse-oblige sanity.

when inferiors extend their most lavish reception for visiting superiors, the selfish desire to win favor may not be the chief motive; the inferior may be tactfully attempting to put the superior at ease by simulating the kind of world the superior is thought to take for granted.

I have suggested two extremes: an individual may be taken in by his own act or be cynical about it. These extremes are something a little more than just the ends of a continuum. Each provides the individual with a position which has its own particular securities and defenses, so there will be a tendency for those who have traveled close to one of these poles to complete the voyage. Starting with lack of inward belief in one's role, the individual may follow the natural movement described by Park:

> It is probably no mere historical accident that the word person, in its first meaning, is a mask. It is rather a recognition of the fact that everyone is always and everywhere, more or less consciously, playing a role . . . It is in these roles that we know each other; it is in these roles that we know ourselves.[8]

> In a sense, and in so far as this mask represents the conception we have formed of ourselves—the role we are striving to live up to—this mask is our truer self, the self we would like to be. In the end, our conception of our role becomes second nature and an integral part of our

---

See his "Socio-Psychiatric Research," *American Journal of Psychiatry*, X, pp. 987–88.
"A study of 'social recoveries' in one of our large mental hospitals some years ago taught me that patients were often released from care because they had learned not to manifest symptoms to the environing persons; in other words, had integrated enough of the personal environment to realize the prejudice opposed to their delusions. It seemed almost as if they grew wise enough to be tolerant of the imbecility surrounding them, having finally discovered that it was stupidity and not malice. They could then secure satisfaction from contact with others, while discharging a part of their cravings by psychotic means."

[8] Robert Ezra Park, *Race and Culture* (Glencoe, Ill.: The Free Press, 1950), p. 249.

personality. We come into the world as individuals, achieve character, and become persons.[4]

This may be illustrated from the community life of Shetland.[5] For the last four or five years the island's tourist hotel has been owned and operated by a married couple of crofter origins. From the beginning, the owners were forced to set aside their own conceptions as to how life ought to be led, displaying in the hotel a full round of middle-class services and amenities. Lately, however, it appears that the managers have become less cynical about the performance that they stage; they themselves are becoming middle class and more and more enamored of the selves their clients impute to them.

Another illustration may be found in the raw recruit who initially follows army etiquette in order to avoid physical punishment and eventually comes to follow the rules so that his organization will not be shamed and his officers and fellow soldiers will respect him.

As suggested, the cycle of disbelief-to-belief can be followed in the other direction, starting with conviction or insecure aspiration and ending in cynicism. Professions which the public holds in religious awe often allow their recruits to follow the cycle in this direction, and often recruits follow it in this direction not because of a slow realization that they are deluding their audience—for by ordinary social standards the claims they make may be quite valid—but because they can use this cynicism as a means of insulating their inner selves from contact with the audience. And we may even expect to find typical careers of faith, with the individual starting out with one kind of involvement in the performance he is required to give, then moving back and forth several times between sincerity and cynicism before completing all the phases and turning-points of self-belief for a person of his station. Thus, students of medical schools suggest that idealistically oriented beginners in

[4] *Ibid.,* p. 250.
[5] Shetland Isle study.

medical school typically lay aside their holy aspirations for a period of time. During the first two years the students find that their interest in medicine must be dropped that they may give all their time to the task of learning how to get through examinations. During the next two years they are too busy learning about diseases to show much concern for the persons who are diseased. It is only after their medical schooling has ended that their original ideals about medical service may be reasserted.[6]

While we can expect to find natural movement back and forth between cynicism and sincerity, still we must not rule out the kind of transitional point that can be sustained on the strength of a little self-illusion. We find that the individual may attempt to induce the audience to judge him and the situation in a particular way, and he may seek this judgment as an ultimate end in itself, and yet he may not completely believe that he deserves the valuation of self which he asks for or that the impression of reality which he fosters is valid. Another mixture of cynicism and belief is suggested in Kroeber's discussion of shamanism:

> Next, there is the old question of deception. Probably most shamans or medicine men, the world over, help along with sleight-of-hand in curing and especially in exhibitions of power. This sleight-of-hand is sometimes deliberate; in many cases awareness is perhaps not deeper than the foreconscious. The attitude, whether there has been repression or not, seems to be as toward a pious fraud. Field ethnographers seem quite generally convinced that even shamans who know that they add fraud nevertheless also believe in their powers, and especially in those of other shamans: they consult them when they themselves or their children are ill.[7]

[6] H. S. Becker and Blanche Greer, "The Fate of Idealism in Medical School," *American Sociological Review*, 23, pp. 50–56.

[7] A. L. Kroeber, *The Nature of Culture* (Chicago: University of Chicago Press, 1952), p. 311.

Front

I have been using the term "performance" to refer to all the activity of an individual which occurs during a period marked by his continuous presence before a particular set of observers and which has some influence on the observers. It will be convenient to label as "front" that part of the individual's performance which regularly functions in a general and fixed fashion to define the situation for those who observe the performance. Front, then, is the expressive equipment of a standard kind intentionally or unwittingly employed by the individual during his performance. For preliminary purposes, it will be convenient to distinguish and label what seem to be the standard parts of front.

First, there is the "setting," involving furniture, décor, physical layout, and other background items which supply the scenery and stage props for the spate of human action played out before, within, or upon it. A setting tends to stay put, geographically speaking, so that those who would use a particular setting as part of their performance cannot begin their act until they have brought themselves to the appropriate place and must terminate their performance when they leave it. It is only in exceptional circumstances that the setting follows along with the performers; we see this in the funeral cortège, the civic parade, and the dream-like processions that kings and queens are made of. In the main, these exceptions seem to offer some kind of extra protection for performers who are, or who have momentarily become, highly sacred. These worthies are to be distinguished, of course, from quite profane performers of the peddler class who move their place of work between performances, often being forced to do so. In the matter of having one fixed place for one's setting, a ruler may be too sacred, a peddler too profane.

In thinking about the scenic aspects of front, we tend to think of the living room in a particular house and the small number of performers who can thoroughly identify themselves with it. We have given insufficient attention to assemblages of sign-equipment which large numbers of performers can call their own for short periods of time. It is characteristic of Western European countries, and no doubt a source of stability for them, that a large number of luxurious settings are available for hire to anyone of the right kind who can afford them. One illustration of this may be cited from a study of the higher civil servant in Britain:

> The question how far the men who rise to the top in the Civil Service take on the "tone" or "color" of a class other than that to which they belong by birth is delicate and difficult. The only definite information bearing on the question is the figures relating to the membership of the great London clubs. More than three-quarters of our high administrative officials belong to one or more clubs of high status and considerable luxury, where the entrance fee might be twenty guineas or more, and the annual subscription from twelve to twenty guineas. These institutions are of the upper class (not even of the upper-middle) in their premises, their equipment, the style of living practiced there, their whole atmosphere. Though many of the members would not be described as wealthy, only a wealthy man would unaided provide for himself and his family space, food and drink, service, and other amenities of life to the same standard as he will find at the Union, the Travellers', or the Reform.[1]

Another example can be found in the recent development of the medical profession where we find that it is increasingly important for a doctor to have access to the elaborate scientific stage provided by large hospitals, so that fewer and fewer doctors are able to feel that their setting is a place that they can lock up at night.[2]

If we take the term "setting" to refer to the scenic parts of expressive equipment, one may take the term "personal

[1] H. E. Dale, *The Higher Civil Service of Great Britain* (Oxford: Oxford University Press, 1941), p. 50.

[2] David Solomon, "Career Contingencies of Chicago Physicians" (unpublished Ph.D. dissertation, Department of Sociology, University of Chicago, 1952), p. 74.

front" to refer to the other items of expressive equipment, the items that we most intimately identify with the performer himself and that we naturally expect will follow the performer wherever he goes. As part of personal front we may include: insignia of office or rank; clothing; sex, age, and racial characteristics; size and looks; posture; speech patterns; facial expressions; bodily gestures; and the like. Some of these vehicles for conveying signs, such as racial characteristics, are relatively fixed and over a span of time do not vary for the individual from one situation to another. On the other hand, some of these sign vehicles are relatively mobile or transitory, such as facial expression, and can vary during a performance from one moment to the next.

It is sometimes convenient to divide the stimuli which make up personal front into "appearance" and "manner," according to the function performed by the information that these stimuli convey. "Appearance" may be taken to refer to those stimuli which function at the time to tell us of the performer's social statuses. These stimuli also tell us of the individual's temporary ritual state, that is, whether he is engaging in formal social activity, work, or informal recreation, whether or not he is celebrating a new phase in the season cycle or in his life-cycle. "Manner" may be taken to refer to those stimuli which function at the time to warn us of the interaction role the performer will expect to play in the oncoming situation. Thus a haughty, aggressive manner may give the impression that the performer expects to be the one who will initiate the verbal interaction and direct its course. A meek, apologetic manner may give the impression that the performer expects to follow the lead of others, or at least that he can be led to do so.

We often expect, of course, a confirming consistency between appearance and manner; we expect that the differences in social statuses among the interactants will be expressed in some way by congruent differences in the indications that are made of an expected interaction role. This type of coherence of front may be illustrated by the following description of the procession of a mandarin through a Chinese city:

Coming closely behind . . . the luxurious chair of the mandarin, carried by eight bearers, fills the vacant space in the street. He is mayor of the town, and for all practical purposes the supreme power in it. He is an ideal-looking official, for he is large and massive in appearance, whilst he has that stern and uncompromising look that is supposed to be necessary in any magistrate who would hope to keep his subjects in order. He has a stern and forbidding aspect, as though he were on his way to the execution ground to have some criminal decapitated. This is the kind of air that the mandarins put on when they appear in public. In the course of many years' experience, I have never once seen any of them, from the highest to the lowest, with a smile on his face or a look of sympathy for the people whilst he was being carried officially through the streets.[8]

But, of course, appearance and manner may tend to contradict each other, as when a performer who appears to be of higher estate than his audience acts in a manner that is unexpectedly equalitarian, or intimate, or apologetic, or when a performer dressed in the garments of a high position presents himself to an individual of even higher status.

In addition to the expected consistency between appearance and manner, we expect, of course, some coherence among setting, appearance, and manner.[4] Such coherence represents an ideal type that provides us with a means of stimulating our attention to and interest in exceptions. In this the student is assisted by the journalist, for exceptions to expected consistency among setting, appearance, and manner provide the piquancy and glamor of many careers and the salable appeal of many magazine articles. For example, a *New Yorker* profile on Roger Stevens (the real estate agent who engineered the sale of the Empire State Building) comments on the startling fact that Stevens has a

[8] J. Macgowan, *Sidelights on Chinese Life* (Philadelphia: Lippincott, 1908), p. 187.
[4] Cf. Kenneth Burke's comments on the "scene-act-agent ratio," *A Grammar of Motives* (New York: Prentice-Hall, 1945), pp. 6–9.

small house, a meager office, and no letterhead stationery.[5]

In order to explore more fully the relations among the several parts of social front. it will be convenient to consider here a significant characteristic of the information conveyed by front. namely, its abstractness and generality.

However specialized and unique a routine is, its social front, with certain exceptions will tend to claim facts that can be equally claimed and asserted of other, somewhat different routines. For example many service occupations offer their clients a performance that is illuminated with dramatic expressions of cleanliness. modernity. compe tence. and integrity. While in fact these abstract standards have a different significance in different occupational per formances the observer is encouraged to stress the abstract similarities For the observer this is a wonderful. though sometimes disastrous, convenience. Instead of having to maintain a different pattern of expectation and responsive treatment for each slightly different performer and per formance he can place the situation in a broad category around which it is easy for him to mobilize his past ex perience and stereo-typical thinking. Observers then need only be familiar with a small and hence manageable vocab ulary of fronts, and know how to respond to them, in order to orient themselves in a wide variety of situations. Thus in London the current tendency for chimney sweeps[6] and perfume clerks to wear white lab coats tends to provide the client with an understanding that the delicate tasks performed by these persons will be performed in what has become a standardized. clinical confidential manner.

There are grounds for believing that the tendency for a large number of different acts to be presented from behind a small number of fronts is a natural development in social organization. Radcliffe-Brown has suggested this in his claim that a "descriptive" kinship system which gives each person a unique place may work for very small communi-

[5] E. J. Kahn, Jr., "Closings and Openings," *The New Yorker*, February 13 and 20, 1954.

[6] See Mervyn Jones, "White as a Sweep," *The New Statesman and Nation*, December 6, 1952.

ties, but, as the number of persons becomes large, clan segmentation becomes necessary as a means of providing a less complicated system of identifications and treatments.[7] We see this tendency illustrated in factories, barracks, and other large social establishments. Those who organize these establishments find it impossible to provide a special cafeteria, special modes of payment, special vacation rights, and special sanitary facilities for every line and staff status category in the organization, and at the same time they feel that persons of dissimilar status ought not to be indiscriminately thrown together or classified together. As a compromise, the full range of diversity is cut at a few crucial points, and all those within a given bracket are allowed or obliged to maintain the same social front in certain situations.

In addition to the fact that different routines may employ the same front, it is to be noted that a given social front tends to become institutionalized in terms of the abstract stereotyped expectations to which it gives rise, and tends to take on a meaning and stability apart from the specific tasks which happen at the time to be performed in its name. The front becomes a "collective representation" and a fact in its own right.

When an actor takes on an established social role, usually he finds that a particular front has already been established for it. Whether his acquisition of the role was primarily motivated by a desire to perform the given task or by a desire to maintain the corresponding front, the actor will find that he must do both.

Further, if the individual takes on a task that is not only new to him but also unestablished in the society, or if he attempts to change the light in which his task is viewed, he is likely to find that there are already several well-established fronts among which he must choose. Thus, when a task is given a new front we seldom find that the front it is given is itself new.

[7] A. R. Radcliffe-Brown, "The Social Organization of Australian Tribes," *Oceania*, I, 440.

Since fronts tend to be selected, not created, we may expect trouble to arise when those who perform a given task are forced to select a suitable front for themselves from among several quite dissimilar ones. Thus, in military organizations, tasks are always developing which (it is felt) require too much authority and skill to be carried out behind the front maintained by one grade of personnel and too little authority and skill to be carried out behind the front maintained by the next grade in the hierarchy. Since there are relatively large jumps between grades, the task will come to "carry too much rank" or to carry too little.

An interesting illustration of the dilemma of selecting an appropriate front from several not quite fitting ones may be found today in American medical organizations with respect to the task of administering anesthesia.[8] In some hospitals anesthesia is still administered by nurses behind the front that nurses are allowed to have in hospitals regardless of the tasks they perform—a front involving ceremonial subordination to doctors and a relatively low rate of pay. In order to establish anesthesiology as a speciality for graduate medical doctors, interested practitioners have had to advocate strongly the idea that administering anesthesia is a sufficiently complex and vital task to justify giving to those who perform it the ceremonial and financial reward given to doctors. The difference between the front maintained by a nurse and the front maintained by a doctor is great; many things that are acceptable for nurses are *infra dignitatem* for doctors. Some medical people have felt that a nurse "under-ranked" for the task of administering anesthesia and that doctors "over-ranked"; were there an established status midway between nurse and doctor, an easier solution to the problem could perhaps be found.[9]

[8] See the thorough treatment of this problem in Dan C. Lortie, "Doctors without Patients: The Anesthesiologist, a New Medical Specialty" (unpublished Master's thesis, Department of Sociology, University of Chicago, 1950). See also Mark Murphy's three-part Profile of Dr. Rovenstine, "Anesthesiologist," *The New Yorker*, October 25, November 1, and November 8, 1947.

[9] In some hospitals the intern and the medical student perform tasks that are beneath a doctor and above a nurse. Presumably

Similarly, had the Canadian Army had a rank halfway between lieutenant and captain, two and a half pips instead of two or three, then Dental Corps captains, many of them of a low ethnic origin, could have been given a rank that would perhaps have been more suitable in the eyes of the Army than the captaincies they were actually given.

I do not mean here to stress the point of view of a formal organization or a society; the individual, as someone who possesses a limited range of sign-equipment, must also make unhappy choices. Thus, in the crofting community studied by the writer, hosts often marked the visit of a friend by offering him a shot of hard liquor, a glass of wine, some home-made brew, or a cup of tea. The higher the rank or temporary ceremonial status of the visitor, the more likely he was to receive an offering near the liquor end of the continuum. Now one problem associated with this range of sign-equipment was that some crofters could not afford to keep a bottle of hard liquor, so that wine tended to be the most indulgent gesture they could employ. But perhaps a more common difficulty was the fact that certain visitors, given their permanent and temporary status at the time, outranked one potable and under-ranked the next one in line. There was often a danger that the visitor would feel just a little affronted or, on the other hand, that the host's costly and limited sign-equipment would be misused. In our middle classes a similar situation arises when a hostess has to decide whether or not to use the good silver, or which would be the more appropriate to wear, her best afternoon dress or her plainest evening gown.

I have suggested that social front can be divided into traditional parts, such as setting, appearance, and manner, and that (since different routines may be presented from behind the same front) we may not find a perfect fit between the specific character of a performance and the general socialized guise in which it appears to us. These two

---

such tasks do not require a large amount of experience and practical training, for while this intermediate status of doctor-in-training is a permanent part of hospitals, all those who hold it do so temporarily.

facts, taken together, lead one to appreciate that items in the social front of a particular routine are not only found in the social fronts of a whole range of routines but also that the whole range of routines in which one item of sign-equipment is found will differ from the range of routines in which another item in the same social front will be found. Thus, a lawyer may talk to a client in a social setting that he employs only for this purpose (or for a study), but the suitable clothes he wears on such occasions he will also employ, with equal suitability, at dinner with colleagues and at the theater with his wife. Similarly, the prints that hang on his wall and the carpet on his floor may be found in domestic social establishments. Of course, in highly cere-monial occasions, setting, manner, and appearance may all be unique and specific, used only for performances of a single type of routine, but such exclusive use of sign-equipment is the exception rather than the rule.

Dramatic Realization

While in the presence of others, the individual typically infuses his activity with signs which dramatically highlight and portray confirmatory facts that might otherwise remain unapparent or obscure. For if the individual's activity is to become significant to others, he must mobilize his activity so that it will express *during the interaction* what he wishes to convey. In fact, the performer may be required not only to express his claimed capacities during the interaction but also to do so during a split second in the interaction. Thus, if a baseball umpire is to give the impression that he is sure of his judgment, he must forgo the moment of thought which might make him sure of his judgment; he must give an instantaneous decision so that the audience will be sure that he is sure of his judgment.[1]

It may be noted that in the case of some statuses drama-tization presents no problem, since some of the acts which

[1] See Babe Pinelli, as told to Joe King, *Mr. Ump* (Philadel-phia: Westminster Press, 1953), p. 75.

are instrumentally essential for the completion of the core task of the status are at the same time wonderfully adapted, from the point of view of communication, as means of vividly conveying the qualities and attributes claimed by the performer. The roles of prizefighters, surgeons, violinists, and policemen are cases in point. These activities allow for so much dramatic self-expression that exemplary practitioners—whether real or fictional—become famous and are given a special place in the commercially organized fantasies of the nation.

In many cases, however, dramatization of one's work does constitute a problem. An illustration of this may be cited from a hospital study where the medical nursing staff is shown to have a problem that the surgical nursing staff does not have:

> The things which a nurse does for post-operative patients on the surgical floor are frequently of recognizable importance, even to patients who are strangers to hospital activities. For example, the patient sees his nurse changing bandages, swinging orthopedic frames into place, and can realize that these are purposeful activities. Even if she cannot be at his side, he can respect her purposeful activities.

> Medical nursing is also highly skilled work. . . . The physician's diagnosis must rest upon careful observation of symptoms over time where the surgeon's are in larger part dependent on visible things. The lack of visibility creates problems on the medical. A patient will see his nurse stop at the next bed and chat for a moment or two with the patient there. He doesn't know that she is observing the shallowness of the breathing and color and tone of the skin. He thinks she is just visiting. So, alas, does his family who may thereupon decide that these nurses aren't very impressive. If the nurse spends more time at the next bed than at his own, the patient may feel slighted. . . . The nurses are "wasting time" unless

they are darting about doing some visible thing such as administering hypodermics.[2]

Similarly, the proprietor of a service establishment may find it difficult to dramatize what is actually being done for clients because the clients cannot "see" the overhead costs of the service rendered them. Undertakers must therefore charge a great deal for their highly visible product—a coffin that has been transformed into a casket—because many of the other costs of conducting a funeral are ones that cannot be readily dramatized.[8] Merchants, too, find that they must charge high prices for things that look intrinsically expensive in order to compensate the establishment for expensive things like insurance, slack periods, etc., that never appear before the customers' eyes.

The problem of dramatizing one's work involves more than merely making invisible costs visible. The work that must be done by those who fill certain statuses is often so poorly designed as an expression of a desired meaning, that if the incumbent would dramatize the character of his role, he must divert an appreciable amount of his energy to do so. And this activity diverted to communication will often require different attributes from the ones which are being dramatized. Thus to furnish a house so that it will express simple quiet dignity, the householder may have to race to auction sales, haggle with antique dealers, and doggedly canvass all the local shops for proper wallpaper and curtain materials. To give a radio talk that will sound genuinely informal, spontaneous, and relaxed, the speaker may have to design his script with painstaking care, testing one phrase after another, in order to follow the content, language, rhythm, and pace of everyday talk.[4] Similarly, a *Vogue*

2 Edith Lentz, "A Comparison of Medical and Surgical Floors" (Mimeo: New York State School of Industrial and Labor Relations. Cornell University, 1954), pp. 2–3.

8 Material on the burial business used throughout this report is taken from Robert W. Habenstein, "The American Funeral Director" (unpublished Ph.D. dissertation, Department of Sociology, University of Chicago, 1954). I owe much to Mr. Habenstein's analysis of a funeral as a performance.

4 John Hilton, "Calculated Spontaneity," *Oxford Book of English Talk* (Oxford: Clarendon Press, 1953), pp. 399–404.

model, by her clothing, stance, and facial expression, is able expressively to portray a cultivated understanding of the book she poses in her hand; but those who trouble to express themselves so appropriately will have very little time left over for reading. As Sartre suggested: "The attentive pupil who wishes to *be* attentive, his eyes riveted on the teacher, his ears open wide, so exhausts himself in playing the attentive role that he ends up by no longer hearing anything."[5] And so individuals often find themselves with the dilemma of expression *versus* action. Those who have the time and talent to perform a task well may not, because of this, have the time or talent to make it apparent that they are performing well. It may be said that some organizations resolve this dilemma by officially delegating the dramatic function to a specialist who will spend his time expressing the meaning of the task and spend no time actually doing it.

If we alter our frame of reference for a moment and turn from a particular performance to the individuals who present it, we can consider an interesting fact about the round of different routines which any group or class of individuals helps to perform. When a group or class is examined, one finds that the members of it tend to invest their egos primarily in certain routines, giving less stress to the other ones which they perform. Thus a professional man may be willing to take a very modest role in the street, in a shop, or in his home, but, in the social sphere which encompasses his display of professional competency, he will be much concerned to make an effective showing. In mobilizing his behavior to make a showing, he will be concerned not so much with the full round of the different routines he performs but only with the one from which his occupational reputation derives. It is upon this issue that some writers have chosen to distinguish groups with aristocratic habits (whatever their social status) from those of middle-class character. The aristocratic habit, it has been said, is one that mobilizes all the minor activities of life which fall out-

[5] Sartre, *op. cit.*, p. 60.

side the serious specialities of other classes and injects into these activities an expression of character, power, and high rank.

> By what important accomplishments is the young noble-man instructed to support the dignity of his rank, and to render himself worthy of that superiority over his fellow-citizens, to which the virtue of his ancestors had raised them: Is it by knowledge, by industry, by patience, by self-denial, or by virtue of any kind? As all his words, as all his motions are attended to, he learns a habitual regard to every circumstance of ordinary behavior, and studies to perform all those small duties with the most exact propriety. As he is conscious of how much he is observed, and how much mankind are disposed to favor all his inclinations, he acts, upon the most indifferent occasions, with that freedom and elevation which the thought of this naturally inspires. His air, his manner, his deportment, all mark that elegant, and graceful sense of his own superiority, which those who are born to inferior stations can hardly ever arrive at. These are the arts by which he proposes to make mankind more easily submit to his authority, and to govern their inclinations according to his own pleasure: and in this he is seldom disappointed. These arts, supported by rank and pre-eminence, are, upon ordinary occasions, sufficient to govern the world.[6]

If such virtuosi actually exist, they would provide a suitable group in which to study the techniques by which activity is transformed into a show.

Idealization

It was suggested earlier that a performance of a routine presents through its front some rather abstract claims upon the audience, claims that are likely to be presented to them during the performance of other routines. This constitutes

[6] Adam Smith, *The Theory of Moral Sentiments* (London: Henry Bohn, 1853), p. 75.

one way in which a performance is "socialized," molded, and modified to fit into the understanding and expectations of the society in which it is presented. I want to consider here another important aspect of this socialization process—the tendency for performers to offer their observers an impression that is idealized in several different ways.

The notion that a performance presents an idealized view of the situation is, of course, quite common. Cooley's view may be taken as an illustration:

> If we never tried to seem a little better than we are, how could we improve or "train ourselves from the outside inward?" And the same impulse to show the world a better or idealized aspect of ourselves finds an organized expression in the various professions and classes, each of which has to some extent a cant or pose, which its members assume unconsciously, for the most part, but which has the effect of a conspiracy to work upon the credulity of the rest of the world. There is a cant not only of theology and of philanthropy, but also of law, medicine, teaching, even of science—perhaps especially of science, just now, since the more a particular kind of merit is recognized and admired, the more it is likely to be assumed by the unworthy.[1]

Thus, when the individual presents himself before others, his performance will tend to incorporate and exemplify the officially accredited values of the society, more so, in fact, than does his behavior as a whole.

To the degree that a performance highlights the common official values of the society in which it occurs, we may look upon it, in the manner of Durkheim and Radcliffe-Brown, as a ceremony—as an expressive rejuvenation and reaffirmation of the moral values of the community. Furthermore, in so far as the expressive bias of performances comes to be accepted as reality, then that which is accepted at the moment as reality will have some of the characteristics of a celebration. To stay in one's room away from

[1] Charles H. Cooley, *Human Nature and the Social Order* (New York: Scribner's, 1922), pp. 352-53.

the place where the party is given, or away from where the practitioner attends his client, is to stay away from where reality is being performed. The world, in truth, is a wedding.

One of the richest sources of data on the presentation of idealized performances is the literature on social mobility. In most societies there seems to be a major or general system of stratification, and in most stratified societies there is an idealization of the higher strata and some aspiration on the part of those in low places to move to higher ones. (One must be careful to appreciate that this involves not merely a desire for a prestigeful place but also a desire for a place close to the sacred center of the common values of the society.) Commonly we find that upward mobility involves the presentation of proper performances and that efforts to move upward and efforts to keep from moving downward are expressed in terms of sacrifices made for the maintenance of front. Once the proper sign-equipment has been obtained and familiarity gained in the management of it, then this equipment can be used to embellish and illumine one's daily performances with a favorable social style.

Perhaps the most important piece of sign-equipment associated with social class consists of the status symbols through which material wealth is expressed. American society is similar to others in this regard but seems to have been singled out as an extreme example of wealth-oriented class structure—perhaps because in America the license to employ symbols of wealth and financial capacity to do so are so widely distributed. Indian society, on the other hand, has sometimes been cited not only as one in which mobility occurs in terms of caste groups, not individuals, but also as one in which performances tend to establish favorable claims regarding non-material values. A recent student of India, for example, has suggested the following:

> The caste system is far from a rigid system in which the position of each component is fixed for all time. Movement has always been possible, and especially so in

the middle regions of the hierarchy. A low caste was able, in a generation or two, to rise to a higher position in the hierarchy by adopting vegetarianism and teetotalism, and by Sanskritizing its ritual and pantheon. In short, it took over, as far as possible, the customs, rites, and beliefs of the Brahmins, and the adoption of the Brahminic way of life by a low caste seems to have been frequent, though theoretically forbidden. . . .

The tendency of the lower castes to imitate the higher has been a powerful factor in the spread of Sanskritic ritual and customs, and in the achievement of a certain amount of cultural uniformity, not only throughout the caste scale but over the entire length and breadth of India.[2]

In fact, of course, there are many Hindu circles whose members are much concerned with injecting an expression of wealth, luxury, and class status into the performance of their daily round and who think too little of ascetic purity to bother affecting it. Correspondingly, there have always been influential groups in America whose members have felt that some aspect of every performance ought to play down the expression of sheer wealth in order to foster the impression that standards regarding birth, culture, or moral earnestness are the ones that prevail.

Perhaps because of the orientation upward found in major societies today, we tend to assume that the expressive stresses in a performance necessarily claim for the performer a higher class status than might otherwise be accorded him. For example, we are not surprised to learn the following details of past domestic performances in Scotland:

> One thing is fairly certain: the average laird and his family lived far more frugally in the ordinary way than they did when they were entertaining visitors. They would rise to a great occasion and serve dishes reminiscent of the banquets of the medieval nobility; but, like those same nobles, between the festivities they would

[2] M. N. Srinivas, *Religion and Society Among the Coorgs of South India* (Oxford: Oxford University Press, 1952), p. 30.

"keep secret house," as the saying used to be, and live on the plainest of fare. The secret was well guarded. Even Edward Burt, with all his knowledge of the Highlanders, found it very difficult to describe their everyday meals. All he could say definitely was that whenever they entertained an Englishman they provided far too much food; "and," he remarked, "it has often been said they will ransack all their tenants rather than we should think meanly of their housekeeping; but I have heard it from many whom they have employed . . . that, although they have been attended at dinner by five or six servants, yet, with all that state, they have often dined upon oatmeal varied several ways, pickled herring, or other such cheap and indifferent diet."[3]

In fact, however, many classes of persons have had many different reasons for exercising systematic modesty and for underplaying any expressions of wealth, capacity, spiritual strength, or self-respect.

The ignorant, shiftless, happy-go-lucky manner which Negroes in the Southern states sometimes felt obliged to affect during interaction with whites illustrates how a performance can play up ideal values which accord to the performer a lower position than he covertly accepts for himself. A modern version of this masquerade can be cited:

Where there is actual competition above the unskilled levels for jobs usually thought of as "white jobs" some Negroes will of their own choice accept symbols of lower status while performing work of higher rank. Thus a shipping clerk will take the title and pay of a messenger; a nurse will permit herself to be called a domestic; and a chiropodist will enter the homes of white persons by the back door at night.[4]

[3] Marjorie Plant, *The Domestic Life of Scotland in the Eighteenth Century* (Edinburgh: Edinburgh University Press, 1952), pp. 96–97.

[4] Charles Johnson, *Patterns of Negro Segregation* (New York: Harper Bros., 1943), p. 273.

American college girls did, and no doubt do, play down their intelligence, skills, and determinativeness when in the presence of datable boys, thereby manifesting a profound psychic discipline in spite of their international reputation for flightiness.[5] These performers are reported to allow their boy friends to explain things to them tediously that they already know; they conceal proficiency in mathematics from their less able consorts; they lose ping-pong games just before the ending:

> "One of the nicest techniques is to spell long words incorrectly once in a while. My boy friend seems to get a great kick out of it and writes back, 'Honey, you certainly don't know how to spell.'"[6]

Through all of this the natural superiority of the male is demonstrated, and the weaker role of the female affirmed.

Similarly, I have been told by Shetlanders that their grandfathers used to refrain from improving the appearance of the cottage lest the laird take such improvements as a sign that increased rents could be extracted from them. This tradition has lingered just a little in connection with a show of poverty that is sometimes played out before the Shetland assistance officer. More important, there are male islanders today who have long since given up the subsistence farming and stringent pattern of endless work, few comforts, and a diet of fish and potatoes, traditionally the islander's lot. Yet these men frequently wear in public places the fleece-lined leather jerkin and high rubber boots that are notoriously symbolic of crofter status. They present themselves to the community as persons with no "side" who are loyal to the social status of their fellow islanders. It is a part they play with sincerity, warmth, the appropriate dialect, and a great command. Yet in the seclusion provided by their own kitchens this loyalty is relaxed, and they enjoy some of the middle-class modern comforts to which they have become accustomed.

[5] Mirra Komarovsky, "Cultural Contradictions and Sex Roles," *American Journal of Sociology*, LII, pp. 186–88.
[6] *Ibid.*, p. 187.

The same kind of negative idealization was common, of course, during the Depression in America, when a household's state of poverty was sometimes overcommunicated for the benefit of visiting welfare agents, demonstrating that wherever there is a means test there is likely to be a poverty show:

> An investigator for the D.P.C. reported some interesting experiences in this connection. She is Italian but is light-skinned and fair-haired and decidedly un-Italian looking. Her main work has been the investigation of Italian families on the F.E.R.A. The fact that she did not look Italian has caused her to overhear conversations in Italian, indicating the attitude of the clients toward relief. For example, while sitting in the front room talking to the wife, the wife will call out to a child to come and see the investigator, but she will warn the child to put on his old shoes first. Or she will hear the mother or father tell someone in the back of the house to put away the wine or the food before the investigator comes into the house.[7]

A further instance may be quoted from a recent study of the junk business, in which data are provided on the kind of impression that practitioners feel it is opportune for them to foster.

> . . . the junk peddler is vitally interested in keeping information as to the true financial value of "junk" from the general public. He wishes to perpetuate the myth that junk is valueless and that the individuals who deal in it are "down and out" and should be pitied.[8]

Such impressions have an idealized aspect, for if the performer is to be successful he must offer the kind of scene that realizes the observers' extreme stereotypes of hapless poverty.

[7] E. Wight Bakke, *The Unemployed Worker* (New Haven: Yale University Press, 1940), p. 371.
[8] J. B. Ralph, "The Junk Business and the Junk Peddler" (unpublished M.A. Report, Department of Sociology, University of Chicago, 1950), p. 26.

As further illustration of such idealized routines there are perhaps none with so much sociological charm as the performances maintained by street beggars. In Western society, however, since the turn of this century, the scenes that beggars stage seem to have declined in dramatic merit. Today we hear less of the "clean family dodge" in which a family appears in tattered but incredibly clean clothes, the faces of children glistening from a layer of soap that has been polished with a soft cloth. We no longer see the performances in which a half-naked man chokes over a dirty crust of bread that he is apparently too weak to swallow, or the scene in which a tattered man chases a sparrow from a piece of bread, wipes the morsel slowly on his coat sleeve, and, apparently oblivious to the audience that is now around him, attempts to eat it. Rare, too, has become the "ashamed beggar" who meekly implores with his eyes what his delicate sensibilities apparently prevent him from saying. Incidentally, the scenes presented by beggars have been variously called, in English, grifts, dodges, lays, rackets, lurks, pitches, and capers—providing us with terms well suited to describe performances that have greater legality and less art.[9]

If an individual is to give expression to ideal standards during his performance, then he will have to forgo or conceal action which is inconsistent with these standards. When this inappropriate conduct is itself satisfying in some way, as is often the case, then one commonly finds it indulged in secretly; in this way the performer is able to forgo his cake and eat it too. For example, in American society we find that eight-year-old children claim lack of interest in the television programs that are directed to five- and six-year-olds, but sometimes surreptitiously watch them.[10] We also find that middle-class housewives some-

[9] For details on beggars see Henry Mayhew, *London Labour and the London Poor* (4 vols.; London: Griffin, Bohn), I (1861), pp. 415–17, and IV (1862), pp. 404–38.

[10] Unpublished research reports of Social Research, Inc., Chicago. I am grateful to Social Research, Inc., for permission to use these and other of their data in this report.

times employ—in a secret and surreptitious way—cheap substitutes for coffee, ice cream, or butter; in this way they can save money, or effort, or time, and still maintain an impression that the food they serve is of high quality.[11] The same women may leave *The Saturday Evening Post* on their living room end table but keep a copy of *True Romance* ("It's something the cleaning woman must have left around") concealed in their bedroom.[12] It has been suggested that the same sort of behavior, which we may refer to as "secret consumption" can be found among the Hindus.

> They conform to all their customs, while they are seen, but they are not so scrupulous when in their retirement.[18]
>
> I have been credibly informed that some Brahmins in small companies, have gone very secretly to the houses of Sudras whom they could depend on, to partake of meat and strong liquors, which they indulged in without scruple.[14]
>
> The secret use of intoxicating drink is still less uncommon than that of interdicted food, because it is less difficult to conceal. Yet it is a thing unheard of to meet a Brahmin drunk in public.[15]

It may be added that recently the Kinsey reports have added new impetus to the study and analysis of secret consumption.[16]

[11] Unpublished research reports of Social Research, Inc.

[12] Reported by Professor W. L. Warner of the University of Chicago, in seminar, 1951.

[18] Abbé J. A. Dubois, *Character, Manners, and Customs of the People of India* (2 vols.; Philadelphia: M'Carey & Son, 1818), I, p. 235.

[14] *Ibid.*, p. 237.

[15] *Ibid.*, p. 238.

[16] As Adam Smith suggested, *op. cit.*, p. 88, virtues as well as vices may be concealed:

"Vain men often give themselves airs of a fashionable profligacy, which, in their hearts, they do not approve of, and of which, perhaps, they are really not guilty. They desire to be

It is important to note that when an individual offers a performance he typically conceals something more than inappropriate pleasures and economies. Some of these matters for concealment may be suggested here.

First, in addition to secret pleasures and economies, the performer may be engaged in a profitable form of activity that is concealed from his audience and that is incompatible with the view of his activity which he hopes they will obtain. The model here is to be found with hilarious clarity in the cigar-store–bookie-joint, but something of the spirit of these establishments can be found in many places. A surprising number of workers seem to justify their jobs to themselves by the tools that can be stolen, or the food supplies that can be resold, or the traveling that can be enjoyed on company time, or the propaganda that can be distributed, or the contacts that can be made and properly influenced, etc.[17] In all such cases, place of work and official activity come to be a kind of shell which conceals the spirited life of the performer.

Secondly, we find that errors and mistakes are often corrected before the performance takes place, while telltale signs that errors have been made and corrected are themselves concealed. In this way an impression of infallibility, so important in many presentations, is maintained. There is a famous remark that doctors bury their mistakes. Another example is found in a recent dissertation on social interaction in three government offices, which suggests that officers disliked dictating reports to a stenographer because they liked to go back over their reports and correct the

---

praised for what they themselves do not think praiseworthy, and are ashamed of unfashionable virtues, which they sometimes practice in secret, and for which they have secretly some degree of real veneration."

[17] Two recent students of the social service worker suggest the term "outside racket" to refer to secret sources of income available to the Chicago Public Case Worker. See Earl Bogdanoff and Arnold Glass, *The Sociology of the Public Case Worker in an Urban Area* (unpublished Master's Report, Department of Sociology, University of Chicago, 1953).

flaws before a stenographer, let alone a superior, saw the reports.[18]

Thirdly, in those interactions where the individual presents a product to others, he will tend to show them only the end product, and they will be led into judging him on the basis of something that has been finished, polished, and packaged. In some cases, if very little effort was actually required to complete the object, this fact will be concealed. In other cases, it will be the long, tedious hours of lonely labor that will be hidden. For example, the urbane style affected in some scholarly books can be instructively compared with the feverish drudgery the author may have endured in order to complete the index on time, or with the squabbles he may have had with his publisher in order to increase the size of the first letter of his last name as it appears on the cover of his book.

A fourth discrepancy between appearances and over-all reality may be cited. We find that there are many performances which could not have been given had not tasks been done which were physically unclean, semi-illegal, cruel, and degrading in other ways; but these disturbing facts are seldom expressed during a performance. In Hughes's terms, we tend to conceal from our audience all evidence of "dirty work," whether we do this work in private or allocate it to a servant, to the impersonal market, to a legitimate specialist, or to an illegitimate one.

Closely connected with the notion of dirty work is a fifth discrepancy between appearance and actual activity. If the activity of an individual is to embody several ideal standards, and if a good showing is to be made, it is likely then that some of these standards will be sustained in public by the private sacrifice of some of the others. Often, of course, the performer will sacrifice those standards whose loss can be concealed and will make this sacrifice in order to maintain standards whose inadequate application cannot be concealed. Thus, during times of rationing, if a *restaurateur*, grocer, or butcher is to maintain his customary

[18] Blau, *op. cit.*, p. 184.

show of variety, and affirm his customers' image of him,
then concealable sources of illegal supply may be his solution. So, too, if a service is judged on the basis of speed
and quality, quality is likely to fall before speed because
poor quality can be concealed but not slow service. Similarly, if attendants in a mental ward are to maintain order
and at the same time not hit patients, and if this combination of standards is difficult to maintain, then the unruly
patient may be "necked" with a wet towel and choked into
submission in a way that leaves no visible evidence of mistreatment.[19] Absence of mistreatment can be faked, not
order:

> Those rules, regulations, and orders which are most
> easily enforced are those which leave tangible evidence
> of having been either obeyed or disobeyed, such as rules
> pertaining to the cleaning of the ward, locking doors,
> the use of intoxicating liquors while on duty, the use of
> restraints, etc.[20]

Here it would be incorrect to be too cynical. Often we find
that if the principal ideal aims of an organization are to
be achieved, then it will be necessary at times to by-pass
momentarily other ideals of the organization, while maintaining the impression that these other ideals are still in
force. In such cases, a sacrifice is made not for the most
visible ideal but rather for the most legitimately important
one. An illustration is provided in a paper on naval bureaucracy:

> This characteristic [group-imposed secrecy] is not en-
> tirely attributable, by any means, to the fear of the
> members that unsavory elements will be brought to
> light. While this fear always plays some role in keeping
> off the record the "inside picture" of any bureaucracy,
> it is to one of the features of the informal structure itself

[19] Robert H. Willoughby, "The Attendant in the State Mental
Hospital" (unpublished Master's thesis, Department of Sociology, University of Chicago, 1953), p. 44.
[20] Ibid., pp. 45–46.

that more importance must be assigned. For the informal structure serves the very significant role of providing a *channel of circumvention* of the formally prescribed rules and methods of procedure. No organization feels that it can afford to publicize those methods (by which certain problems are solved, it is important to note) which are antithetical to the officially sanctioned and, in this case, strongly sanctioned methods dear to the traditions of the group.[21]

Finally, we find performers often foster the impression that they had ideal motives for acquiring the role in which they are performing, that they have ideal qualifications for the role, and that it was not necessary for them to suffer any indignities, insults, and humiliations, or make any tacitly understood "deals," in order to acquire the role. (While this general impression of sacred compatability between the man and his job is perhaps most commonly fostered by members of the higher professions, a similar element is found in many of the lesser ones.) Reinforcing these ideal impressions there is a kind of "rhetoric of training," whereby labor unions, universities, trade associations, and other licensing bodies require practitioners to absorb a mystical range and period of training, in part to maintain a monopoly, but in part to foster the impression that the licensed practitioner is someone who has been reconstituted by his learning experience and is now set apart from other men. Thus, one student suggests about pharmacists that they feel that the four-year university course required for license is "good for the profession" but that some admit that a few months' training is all that is really needed.[22] It may be added that the American Army during World War II innocently treated trades such as pharmacy and watch-repairing in a purely instrumental way and trained efficient practitioners in five or six weeks to the horror of established

[21] Charles Hunt Page, "Bureaucracy's Other Face," *Social Forces*, XXV, p. 90.

[22] Anthony Weinlein, "Pharmacy as a Profession in Wisconsin" (unpublished Master's thesis, Department of Sociology, University of Chicago, 1943), p. 89.

members of these callings. And so we find that clergymen give the impression that they entered the church because of a call of felt vocation, in America tending to conceal their interest in moving up socially, in Britain tending to conceal their interest in not moving too far down. And again, clergymen tend to give the impression that they have chosen their current congregation because of what they can offer it spiritually and not, as may in fact be the case, because the elders offered a good house or full payment of moving expenses. Similarly, medical schools in America tend to recruit their students partly on the basis of ethnic origins, and certainly patients consider this factor in choosing their doctors; but in the actual interaction between doctor and patient the impression is allowed to develop that the doctor is a doctor purely because of special aptitudes and special training. Similarly, executives often project an air of competency and general grasp of the situation, blinding themselves and others to the fact that they hold their jobs partly because they look like executives, not because they can work like executives:

> Few executives realize how critically important their physical appearance may be to an employer. Placement expert Ann Hoff observes that employers now seem to be looking for an ideal "Hollywood type." One company rejected a candidate because he had "teeth that were too square" and others have been disqualified because their ears stuck out, or they drank and smoked too heavily during an interview. Racial and religious requirements also are often frankly stipulated by employers.[23]

Performers may even attempt to give the impression that their present poise and proficiency are something they have always had and that they have never had to fumble their way through a learning period. In all of this the performer may receive tacit assistance from the establishment in which he is to perform. Thus, many schools and institutions

[23] Perrin Stryker, "How Executives Get Jobs," *Fortune*, August 1953, p. 182.

announce stiff entrance qualifications and examinations, but may in fact reject very few applicants. For example, a mental hospital may require prospective attendants to submit to a Rorschach examination and a long interview, but hire all comers.[24]

Interestingly enough, when the significance of unofficial qualifications becomes a scandal or political issue, then a few individuals who are obtrusively lacking in the informal qualifications may be admitted with fanfare and given a highly visible role as evidence of fair play. An impression of legitimacy is thus created.[25]

I have suggested that a performer tends to conceal or underplay those activities, facts, and motives which are incompatible with an idealized version of himself and his products. In addition, a performer often engenders in his audience the belief that he is related *to them* in a more ideal way than is always the case. Two general illustrations may be cited.

First, individuals often foster the impression that the routine they are presently performing is their only routine or at least their most essential one. As previously suggested, the audience, in their turn, often assume that the character projected before them is all there is to the individual who acts out the projection for them. As suggested in the well-known quotation from William James:

. . . we may practically say that he has as many different social selves as there are distinct *groups* of persons about whose opinion he cares. He generally shows a different side of himself to each of these different groups. Many a youth who is demure enough before his parents and teachers, swears and swaggers like a pirate among his "tough" young friends. We do not show ourselves to our children as to our club companions, to our customers

---

[24] Willoughby, *op. cit.*, pp. 22–23.
[25] See, for example, William Kornhauser, "The Negro Union Official: A Study of Sponsorship and Control," *American Journal of Sociology*, LVII, pp. 443–52, and Scott Greer, "Situated Pressures and Functional Role of Ethnic Labor Leaders," *Social Forces*, XXXII, pp. 41–45.

as to the laborers we employ, to our own masters and employers as to our intimate friends.[26]

As both effect and enabling cause of this kind of commitment to the part one is currently performing, we find that "audience segregation" occurs; by audience segregation the individual ensures that those before whom he plays one of his parts will not be the same individuals before whom he plays a different part in another setting. Audience segregation as a device for protecting fostered impressions will be considered later. Here I would like only to note that even if performers attempted to break down this segregation, and the illusion that is fostered by it, audiences would often prevent such action. The audience can see a great saving of time and emotional energy in the right to treat the performer at occupational face value, as if the performer were all and only what his uniform claimed him to be.[27] Urban life would become unbearably sticky for some if every contact between two individuals entailed a sharing of personal trials, worries, and secrets. Thus if a man wants to be served a restful dinner, he may seek the service of a waitress rather than a wife.

Secondly, performers tend to foster the impression that their current performance of their routine and their relationship to their current audience have something special and unique about them. The routine character of the performance is obscured (the performer himself is typically unaware of just how routinized his performance really is) and the spontaneous aspects of the situation are stressed. The medical performer provides an obvious example. As one writer suggests:

> . . . he must simulate a memory. The patient, conscious of the unique importance of the events occurring within him, remembers everything and, in his delight in telling the doctor about it, suffers from "complete recall." The

[26] William James, *The Philosophy of William James* (Modern Library ed.; New York: Random House, n. d.), pp. 128–29.

[27] I am grateful to Warren Peterson for this and other suggestions.

patient can't believe that the doctor doesn't remember too, and his pride is deeply wounded if the latter allows him to perceive that he doesn't carry in the forefront of his mind precisely what kind of tablets he prescribed on his last visit, how many of them to be taken and when.[28]

Similarly, as a current study of Chicago doctors suggests, a general practitioner presents a specialist to a patient as the best choice on technical grounds, but in fact the specialist may have been chosen partly because of collegial ties with the referring doctor, or because of a split-fee arrangement, or because of some other clearly defined *quid pro quo* between the two medical men.[29] In our commercial life this characteristic of performances has been exploited and maligned under the rubric "personalized service"; in other areas of life we make jokes about "the bedside manner" or "the glad hand." (We often neglect to mention that as performers in the role of client we tactfully uphold this personalizing effect by attempting to give the impression that we have not "shopped" for the service and would not consider obtaining it elsewhere.) Perhaps it is our guilt that has directed our attention to these areas of crass "pseudo-*gemeinschaft*," for there is hardly a performance, in whatever area of life, which does not rely on the personal touch to exaggerate the uniqueness of the transactions between performer and audience. For example, we feel a slight disappointment when we hear a close friend, whose spontaneous gestures of warmth we felt were our own preserve, talk intimately with another of his friends (especially one whom we do not know). An explicit statement of this theme is given in a nineteenth-century American guide to manners:

If you have paid a compliment to one man, or have used toward him any expression of particular civility, you should not show the same conduct to any other person in his presence. For example, if a gentleman comes to

[28] C. E. M. Joad, "On Doctors," *The New Statesman and Nation*, March 7, 1953, pp. 255–56.
[29] Solomon, *op. cit.*, p. 146.

your house and you tell him with warmth and interest that you "are glad to see him," he will be pleased with the attention, and will probably thank you; but if he hears you say the same thing to twenty other people, he will not only perceive that your courtesy was worth nothing, but he will feel some resentment at having been imposed on.[30]

Maintenance of Expressive Control

It has been suggested that the performer can rely upon his audience to accept minor cues as a sign of something important about his performance. This convenient fact has an inconvenient implication. By virtue of the same sign-accepting tendency, the audience may misunderstand the meaning that a cue was designed to convey, or may read an embarrassing meaning into gestures or events that were accidental, inadvertent, or incidental and not meant by the performer to carry any meaning whatsoever.

In response to these communication contingencies, performers commonly attempt to exert a kind of synecdochic responsibility, making sure that as many as possible of the minor events in the performance, however instrumentally inconsequential these events may be, will occur in such a way as to convey either no impression or an impression that is compatible and consistent with the over-all definition of the situation that is being fostered. When the audience is known to be secretly skeptical of the reality that is being impressed upon them, we have been ready to appreciate their tendency to pounce on trifling flaws as a sign that the whole show is false; but as students of social life we have been less ready to appreciate that even sympathetic audiences can be momentarily disturbed, shocked, and weakened in their faith by the discovery of a picayune discrepancy in the impressions presented to them. Some of these minor accidents and "unmeant gestures" happen to be so aptly designed to give an impression that con-

[30] *The Canons of Good Breeding: or the Handbook of the Man of Fashion* (Philadelphia: Lee and Blanchard, 1839), p. 87.

tradicts the one fostered by the performer that the audience cannot help but be startled from a proper degree of involvement in the interaction, even though the audience may realize that in the last analysis the discordant event is really meaningless and ought to be completely overlooked. The crucial point is not that the fleeting definition of the situation caused by an unmeant gesture is itself so blameworthy but rather merely that it is *different* from the definition officially projected. This difference forces an acutely embarrassing wedge between the official projection and reality, for it is part of the official projection that it is the only possible one under the circumstances. Perhaps, then, we should not analyze performances in terms of mechanical standards, by which a large gain can offset a small loss, or a large weight a smaller one. Artistic imagery would be more accurate, for it prepares us for the fact that a single note off key can disrupt the tone of an entire performance.

In our society, some unmeant gestures occur in such a wide variety of performances and convey impressions that are in general so incompatible with the ones being fostered that these inopportune events have acquired collective symbolic status. Three rough groupings of these events may be mentioned. First, a performer may accidentally convey incapacity, impropriety, or disrespect by momentarily losing muscular control of himself. He may trip, stumble, fall; he may belch, yawn, make a slip of the tongue, scratch himself, or be flatulent; he may accidentally impinge upon the body of another participant. Secondly, the performer may act in such a way as to give the impression that he is too much or too little concerned with the interaction. He may stutter, forget his lines, appear nervous, or guilty, or self-conscious; he may give way to inappropriate outbursts of laughter, anger, or other kinds of affect which momentarily incapacitate him as an interactant; he may show too much serious involvement and interest, or too little. Thirdly, the performer may allow his presentation to suffer from inadequate dramaturgical direction. The setting may not have been put in order, or may have become readied for the wrong performance, or may become deranged during the performance; unforeseen contingencies may cause improper timing of the performer's arrival or departure or may cause embarrassing lulls to occur during the interaction.[1]

Performances differ, of course, in the degree of item-by-item expressive care required of them. In the case of some cultures foreign to us, we are ready to see a high degree of expressive coherence. Granet, for example, suggests this of filial performances in China:

> Their fine toilet is in itself a homage. Their good deportment will be accounted an offering of respect. In the presence of parents, gravity is requisite: one must therefore be careful not to belch, to sneeze, to cough, to yawn, to blow one's nose nor to spit. Every expectoration would run the risk of soiling the paternal sanctity. It would be a crime to show the lining of one's garments. To show the father that one is treating him as a chief, one ought always to stand in his presence, the eyes right, the body upright upon the two legs, never daring to lean upon any object, nor to bend, nor to stand on one foot. It is thus that with the low and humble voice which becomes a follower, one comes night and morning to pay homage. After which, one waits for orders.[2]

[1] One way of handling inadvertent disruptions is for the interactants to laugh at them as a sign that the expressive implications of the disruptions have been understood but not taken seriously. Assuming this, Bergson's essay on laughter can be taken as a description of the ways in which we expect the performer to adhere to human capacities for movement, of the tendency for the audience to impute these capacities to the performer from the start of the interaction, and of the ways in which this effective projection is disrupted when the performer moves in a non-human fashion. Similarly, Freud's essays on wit and the psychopathology of everyday life can be taken, at one level, as a description of the ways in which we expect performers to have achieved certain standards of tact, modesty, and virtue, and as a description of ways in which these effective projections can be discredited by slips that are hilarious to the layman but symptomatic to analysts.

[2] Marcel Granet, *Chinese Civilization*, trans. Innes and Brailsford (London: Kegan Paul, 1930), p. 328.

We are also ready to see that in scenes in our own culture involving high personages in symbolically important actions, consistency, too, will be demanded. Sir Frederick Ponsonby, late Equerry at the British Court, writes:

> When I attended a "Court" I was always struck by the incongruous music the band played, and determined to do what I could to have this remedied. The majority of the Household, being quite unmusical, clamored for popular airs. . . . I argued that these popular airs robbed the ceremony of all dignity. A presentation at Court was often a great event in a lady's life, but if she went past the King and Queen to the tune of "His nose was redder than it was," the whole impression was spoilt. I maintained that minuets and old-fashioned airs, operatic music with a "mysterious" touch, were what was wanted.[3]
>
> I also took up the question of the music played by the band of the guard of honor at investitures and wrote to the Senior Bandmaster, Captain Rogan, on the subject. What I disliked was seeing eminent men being knighted while comic songs were being played by the band outside; also when the Home Secretary was reading out impressively some particularly heroic deed which had been performed by a man who was to receive the Albert Medal, the band outside played a two-step, which robbed the whole ceremony of any dignity. I suggested operatic music of a dramatic nature being played, and he entirely agreed. . . .[4]

Similarly, at middle-class American funerals, a hearse driver, decorously dressed in black and tactfully located at the outskirts of the cemetery during the service, may be allowed to smoke, but he is likely to shock and anger the bereaved if he happens to flick his cigarette stub into a bush, letting it describe an elegant arc, instead of circumspectly dropping it at his feet.[5]

[3] Ponsonby, *op. cit.*, pp. 182–83.
[4] *Ibid.*, p. 183.
[5] Habenstein, *op. cit.*

In addition to our appreciation of the consistency required on sacred occasions, we readily appreciate that during secular conflicts, especially high-level conflicts, each protagonist will have to watch his own conduct carefully lest he give the opposition a vulnerable point at which to direct criticism. Thus, Dale, in discussing the work contingencies of higher civil servants, suggests:

> An even closer scrutiny [than that accorded to statements] is applied to drafts of official letters: for an incorrect statement or an unhappy phrase in a letter of which the substance is perfectly harmless and the subject unimportant may cover the Department with confusion if it happens to be seized on by one of the many persons to whom the most trivial mistake of a Government Department is a dainty dish to set before the public. Three or four years of this discipline during the still receptive years from twenty-four to twenty-eight suffuse the mind and character permanently with a passion for precise facts and close inferences, and with a grim distrust of vague generalities.[6]

In spite of our willingness to appreciate the expressive requirements of these several kinds of situations, we tend to see these situations as special cases; we tend to blind ourselves to the fact that everyday secular performances in our own Anglo-American society must often pass a strict test of aptness, fitness, propriety, and decorum. Perhaps this blindness is partly due to the fact that as performers we are often more conscious of the standards which we might have applied to our activity but have not than of the standards we unthinkingly apply. In any case, as students we must be ready to examine the dissonance created by a misspelled word, or by a slip that is not quite concealed by a skirt; and we must be ready to appreciate why a near-sighted plumber, to protect the impression of rough strength that is *de rigueur* in his profession, feels it necessary to sweep his spectacles into his pocket when the house-

6 Dale, *op. cit.*, p. 81.

wife's approach changes his work into a performance, or why a television repairman is advised by his public relations counsels that the screws he fails to put back into the set should be kept alongside his own so that the unreplaced parts will not give an improper impression. In other words, we must be prepared to see that the impression of reality fostered by a performance is a delicate, fragile thing that can be shattered by very minor mishaps.

The expressive coherence that is required in performances points out a crucial discrepancy between our all-too-human selves and our socialized selves. As human beings we are presumably creatures of variable impulse with moods and energies that change from one moment to the next. As characters put on for an audience, however, we must not be subject to ups and downs. As Durkheim suggested, we do not allow our higher social activity "to follow in the trail of our bodily states, as our sensations and our general bodily consciousness do."[7] A certain bureaucratization of the spirit is expected so that we can be relied upon to give a perfectly homogeneous performance at every appointed time. As Santayana suggests, the socialization process not only transfigures, it fixes:

> But whether the visage we assume be a joyful or a sad one, in adopting and emphasizing it we define our sovereign temper. Henceforth, so long as we continue under the spell of this self-knowledge, we do not merely live but act; we compose and play our chosen character, we wear the buskin of deliberation, we defend and idealize our passions, we encourage ourselves eloquently to be what we are, devoted or scornful or careless or austere; we soliloquize (before an imaginary audience) and we wrap ourselves gracefully in the mantle of our inalienable part. So draped, we solicit applause and expect to die amid a universal hush. We profess to live up to the fine sentiments we have uttered, as we try to believe in the religion we profess. The greater our difficulties the

[7] Emile Durkheim, *The Elementary Forms of the Religious Life,* trans. J. W. Swain (London: Allen & Unwin, 1926), p. 272.

greater our zeal. Under our published principles and plighted language we must assiduously hide all the inequalities of our moods and conduct, and this without hypocrisy, since our deliberate character is more truly ourself than is the flux of our involuntary dreams. The portrait we paint in this way and exhibit as our true person may well be in the grand manner, with column and curtain and distant landscape and finger pointing to the terrestrial globe or to the Yorick-skull of philosophy; but if this style is native to us and our art is vital, the more it transmutes its model the deeper and truer art it will be. The severe bust of an archaic sculpture, scarcely humanizing the block, will express a spirit far more justly than the man's dull morning looks or casual grimaces. Everyone who is sure of his mind, or proud of his office, or anxious about his duty assumes a tragic mask. He deputes it to be himself and transfers to it almost all his vanity. While still alive and subject, like all existing things, to the undermining flux of his own substance, he has crystallized his soul into an idea, and more in pride than in sorrow he has offered up his life on the altar of the Muses. Self-knowledge, like any art or science, renders its subject-matter in a new medium, the medium of ideas, in which it loses its old dimensions and its old place. Our animal habits are transmuted by conscience into loyalties and duties, and we become "persons" or masks.[8]

Through social discipline, then, a mask of manner can be held in place from within. But, as Simone de Beauvoir suggests, we are helped in keeping this pose by clamps that are tightened directly on the body, some hidden, some showing:

Even if each woman dresses in conformity with her status, a game is still being played: artifice, like art, belongs to the realm of the imaginary. It is not only that girdle, brassiere, hair-dye, make-up disguise body and face; but that the least sophisticated of women, once

[8] Santayana, op. cit., pp. 133–34.

she is "dressed," does not present *herself* to observation; she is, like the picture or the statue, or the actor on the stage, an agent through whom is suggested someone not there that is, the character she represents, but is not. It is this identification with something unreal, fixed, perfect as the hero of a novel, as a portrait or a bust, that gratifies her; she strives to identify herself with this figure and thus to seem to herself to be stabilized, justified in her splendor.[9]

Misrepresentation

It was suggested earlier that an audience is able to orient itself in a situation by accepting performed cues on faith, treating these signs as evidence of something greater than or different from the sign-vehicles themselves. If this tendency of the audience to accept signs places the performer in a position to be misunderstood and makes it necessary for him to exercise expressive care regarding everything he does when before the audience, so also this sign-accepting tendency puts the audience in a position to be duped and misled, for there are few signs that cannot be used to attest to the presence of something that is not really there. And it is plain that many performers have ample capacity and motive to misrepresent the facts; only shame, guilt, or fear prevent them from doing so.

As members of an audience it is natural for us to feel that the impression the performer seeks to give may be true or false, genuine or spurious, valid or "phony." So common is this doubt that, as suggested we often give special attention to features of the performance that cannot be readily manipulated, thus enabling ourselves to judge the reliability of the more misrepresentable cues in the performance. (Scientific police work and projective testing are extreme examples of the application of this tendency.) And if we grudgingly allow certain symbols of status to establish a performer's right to a given treatment, we are always ready

[9] Simone de Beauvoir, *The Second Sex*, trans. H. M. Parshley (New York: Knopf, 1953), p. 533.

to pounce on chinks in his symbolic armor in order to discredit his pretensions.

When we think of those who present a false front or "only" a front, of those who dissemble, deceive, and defraud, we think of a discrepancy between fostered appearances and reality. We also think of the precarious position in which these performers place themselves, for at any moment in their performance an event may occur to catch them out and baldly contradict what they have openly avowed, bringing them immediate humiliation and sometimes permanent loss of reputation. We often feel that it is just these terrible eventualities, which arise from being caught out *flagrante delicto* in a patent act of misrepresentation, that an honest performer is able to avoid. This common-sense view has limited analytical utility.

Sometimes when we ask whether a fostered impression is true or false we really mean to ask whether or not the performer is authorized to give the performance in question, and are not primarily concerned with the actual performance itself. When we discover that someone with whom we have dealings is an impostor and out-and-out fraud, we are discovering that he did not have the right to play the part he played, that he was not an accredited incumbent of the relevant status. We assume that the impostor's performance, in addition to the fact that it misrepresents him, will be at fault in other ways, but often his masquerade is discovered before we can detect any other difference between the false performance and the legitimate one which it simulates. Paradoxically, the more closely the impostor's performance approximates to the real thing, the more intensely we may be threatened, for a competent performance by someone who proves to be an impostor may weaken in our minds the moral connection between legitimate authorization to play a part and the capacity to play it. (Skilled mimics, who admit all along that their intentions are unserious, seem to provide one way in which we can "work through" some of these anxieties.)

The social definition of impersonation, however, is not itself a very consistent thing. For example, while it is felt to be an inexcusable crime against communication to impersonate someone of sacred status, such as a doctor or a priest, we are often less concerned when someone impersonates a member of a disesteemed, non-crucial, profane status, such as that of a hobo or unskilled worker. When a disclosure shows that we have been participating with a performer who has a higher status than he led us to believe, there is good Christian precedent for our reacting with wonderment and chagrin rather than with hostility. Mythology and our popular magazines, in fact, are full of romantic stories in which the villain and the hero both make fraudulent claims that are discredited in the last chapter, the villain proving not to have a high status, the hero proving not to have a low one.

Further, while we may take a harsh view of performers such as confidence men who knowingly misrepresent every fact about their lives, we may have some sympathy for those who have but one fatal flaw and who attempt to conceal the fact that they are, for example, ex-convicts, deflowered, epileptic, or racially impure, instead of admitting their fault and making an honorable attempt to live it down. Also, we distinguish between impersonation of a specific, concrete individual, which we usually feel is quite inexcusable, and impersonation of category membership, which we may feel less strongly about. So, too, we often feel differently about those who misrepresent themselves to forward what they feel are the just claims of a collectivity, or those who misrepresent themselves accidentally or for a lark, than about those who misrepresent themselves for private psychological or material gain.

Finally, since there are senses in which the concept of "a status" is not clear-cut, so there are senses in which the concept of impersonation is not clear either. For example, there are many statuses in which membership obviously is not subject to formal ratification. Claims to be a law graduate can be established as valid or invalid, but claims to be a friend, a true believer, or a music-lover can be confirmed or disconfirmed only more or less. Where standards of competence are not objective, and where *bona fide* practitioners are not collectively organized to protect their mandate, an individual may style himself an expert and be penalized by nothing stronger than sniggers.

All of these sources of confusion are instructively illustrated in the variable attitude we have toward the handling of age and sexual status. It is a culpable thing for a fifteen-year-old boy who drives a car or drinks in a tavern to represent himself as being eighteen, but there are many social contexts in which it would be improper for a woman not to misrepresent herself as being more youthful and sexually attractive than is really the case. When we say a particular woman is not really as well-formed as she appears to be and that the same woman is not really a physician although she appears to be, we are using different conceptions of the term "really." Further, modifications of one's personal front that are considered misrepresentative one year may be considered merely decorative a few years later, and this dissensus may be found at any one time between one subgroup in our society and others. For example, very recently the concealment of gray hair by dyeing has come to be considered acceptable, although there still are sectors of the populace which consider this to be impermissible.[1] It is felt to be all right for immigrants to impersonate native Americans in dress and in patterns of decorum but it is still a doubtful matter to Americanize one's name[2] or one's nose.[3]

Let us try another approach to the understanding of misrepresentation. An "open," "flat," or barefaced lie may be defined as one for which there can be unquestionable evidence that the teller knew he lied and willfully did so. A claim to have been at a particular place at a particular time, when this was not the case, is an example. (Some

[1] See, for example, "Tintair," *Fortune*, November 1951, p. 102.
[2] See, for example, H. L. Mencken, *The American Language* (4th ed.; New York: Knopf, 1936), pp. 474–525.
[3] See, for example, "Plastic Surgery," *Ebony*, May 1949, and F. C. Macgregor and B. Schaffner, "Screening Patients for Nasal Plastic Operations: Some Sociological and Psychiatric Considerations," *Psychosomatic Medicine*, XII, pp. 277–91.

kinds of impersonation, but not all, involve such lies, and many such lies do not involve impersonation.) Those caught out in the act of telling barefaced lies not only lose face during the interaction but may have their face destroyed, for it is felt by many audiences that if an individual can once bring himself to tell such a lie, he ought never again to be fully trusted. However, there are many "white lies," told by doctors, potential guests, and others, presumably to save the feelings of the audience that is lied to, and these kinds of untruths are not thought to be horrendous. (Such lies, meant to protect others rather than to defend the self, will be considered again later.) Further, in everyday life it is usually possible for the performer to create intentionally almost any kind of false impression without putting himself in the indefensible position of having told a clear-cut lie. Communication techniques such as innuendo, strategic ambiguity, and crucial omissions allow the misinformer to profit from lies without, technically, telling any. The mass media have their own version of this and demonstrate that by judicious camera angles and editing, a trickle of response to a celebrity can be transformed into a wild stream.[4]

Formal recognition has been given to the shadings between lies and truths and to the embarrassing difficulties caused by this continuum. Organizations such as real estate boards develop explicit codes specifying the degree to which doubtful impressions can be given by overstatement, understatement, and omissions.[5] The Civil Service in Britain apparently operates on a similar understanding:

> The rule here (as regards "statements which are intended or are likely to become public") is simple. Noth-

---

[4] A good illustration of this is given in a study of MacArthur's arrival at Chicago during the 1952 Republican National Convention. See K. and G. Lang, "The Unique Perspective of Television and its Effect: A Pilot Study," *American Sociological Review*, XVIII, pp. 3–12.

[5] See, for example, E. C. Hughes, "Study of a Secular Institution: The Chicago Real Estate Board" (unpublished Ph.D. dissertation, Department of Sociology, University of Chicago, 1928), p. 85.

ing may be said which is not true: but it is as unnecessary as it is sometimes undesirable, even in the public interest, to say everything relevant which is true; and the facts given may be arranged in any convenient order. It is wonderful what can be done within these limits by a skillful draftsman. It might be said, cynically, but with some measure of truth, that the perfect reply to an embarrassing question in the House of Commons is one that is brief, appears to answer the question completely, if challenged can be proved to be accurate in every word, gives no opening for awkward "supplementaries," and discloses really nothing.[6]

The law crosscuts many ordinary social niceties by introducing ones of its own. In American law, intent, negligence, and strict liability are distinguished; misrepresentation is held to be an intentional act, but one that can arise through word or deed, ambiguous statement or misleading literal truth, non-disclosure, or prevention of discovery.[7] Culpable non-disclosure is held to vary, depending on the area of life, there being one standard for the advertising business and another standard for professional counselors. Further, the law tends to hold that:

A representation made with an honest belief in its truth may still be negligent, because of lack of reasonable care in ascertaining the facts, or in the manner of expression, or absence of the skill and competence required by a particular business or profession.[8]

. . . the fact that the defendant was disinterested, that he had the best of motives, and that he thought he was doing the plaintiff a kindness, will not absolve him from liability so long as he did in fact intend to mislead.[9]

[6] Dale, *op. cit.*, p. 105.
[7] See William L. Prosser, *Handbook of the Law of Torts* (Hornbook Series; St. Paul, Minn.: West Publishing Co., 1941), pp. 701–76.
[8] *Ibid.*, p. 733.
[9] *Ibid.*, p. 728.

When we turn from outright impersonations and bare-faced lies to other types of misrepresentation, the common-sense distinction between true and false impressions becomes even less tenable. Charlatan professional activity of one decade sometimes becomes an acceptable legitimate occupation in the next.[10] We find that activities which are thought to be legitimate by some audiences in our society are thought to be rackets by others.

More important, we find that there is hardly a legitimate everyday vocation or relationship whose performers do not engage in concealed practices which are incompatible with fostered impressions. Although particular performances, and even particular parts or routines, may place a performer in a position of having nothing to hide, somewhere in the full round of his activities there will be something he cannot treat openly. The larger the number of matters and the larger the number of acting parts which fall within the domain of the role or relationship, the more likelihood, it would seem, for points of secrecy to exist. Thus in well-adjusted marriages, we expect that each partner may keep from the other secrets having to do with financial matters, past experiences, current flirtations indulgencies in "bad" or expensive habits, personal aspirations and worries, actions of children, true opinions held about relatives or mutual friends, etc.[11] With such strategically located points of reticence, it is possible to maintain a desirable *status quo* in the relationship without having to carry out rigidly the implications of this arrangement in all areas of life.

Perhaps most important of all, we must note that a false impression maintained by an individual in any one of his routines may be a threat to the whole relationship or role of which the routine is only one part, for a discreditable disclosure in one area of an individual's activity will throw

[10] See Harold D. McDowell, *Osteopathy: A Study of a Semi-orthodox Healing Agency and the Recruitment of its Clientele* (unpublished Master's thesis, Department of Sociology, University of Chicago, 1951).

[11] See, for example, David Dressler, "What Don't They Tell Each Other," *This Week*, September 13, 1953.

doubt on the many areas of activity in which he may have nothing to conceal. Similarly, if the individual has only one thing to conceal during a performance, and even if the likelihood of disclosure occurs only at a particular turn or phase in the performance, the performer's anxiety may well extend to the whole performance.

In previous sections of this chapter some general characteristics of performance were suggested: activity oriented towards work-tasks tends to be converted into activity oriented towards communication; the front behind which the routine is presented is also likely to be suitable for other, somewhat different routines and so is likely not to fit completely any particular routine; sufficient self-control is exerted so as to maintain a working consensus; an idealized impression is offered by accentuating certain facts and concealing others; expressive coherence is maintained by the performer taking more care to guard against minor disharmonies than the stated purpose of the performance might lead the audience to think was warranted. All of these general characteristics of performances can be seen as interaction constraints which play upon the individual and transform his activities into performances. Instead of merely doing his task and giving vent to his feelings, he will express the doing of his task and acceptably convey his feelings. In general, then, the representation of an activity will vary in some degree from the activity itself and therefore inevitably misrepresent it. And since the individual will be required to rely on signs in order to construct a representation of his activity, the image he constructs, however faithful to the facts, will be subject to all the disruptions that impressions are subject to.

While we could retain the common-sense notion that fostered appearances can be discredited by a discrepant reality, there is often no reason for claiming that the facts discrepant with the fostered impression are any more the real reality than is the fostered reality they embarrass. A cynical view of everyday performances can be as one-sided as the one that is sponsored by the performer. For many sociological issues it may not even be necessary to decide

which is the more real, the fostered impression or the one
the performer attempts to prevent the audience from receiving. The crucial sociological consideration, for this
report at least, is merely that impressions fostered in everyday performances are subject to disruption. We will want
to know what kind of impression of reality can shatter the
fostered impression of reality, and what reality really is
can be left to other students. We will want to ask, "What
are the ways in which a given impression can be discredited?" and this is not quite the same as asking, "What
are the ways in which the given impression is false?"

We come back, then, to a realization that while the performance offered by impostors and liars is quite flagrantly
false and differs in this respect from ordinary performances,
both are similar in the care their performers must exert in
order to maintain the impression that is fostered. Thus, for
example, we know that the formal code of British civil
servants[12] and of American baseball umpires[18] obliges
them not only to desist from making improper "deals" but
also to desist from innocent action which might possibly
give the (wrong) impression that they are making deals.
Whether an honest performer wishes to convey the truth
or whether a dishonest performer wishes to convey a false-
hood, both must take care to enliven their performances
with appropriate expressions, exclude from their performances expressions that might discredit the impression being
fostered, and take care lest the audience impute unintended
meanings.[14] Because of these shared dramatic contingencies, we can profitably study performances that are quite
false in order to learn about ones that are quite honest.[15]

[12] Dale, *op. cit.*, p. 103.
[18] Pinelli, *op. cit.*, p. 100.
[14] One exception to this similarity should be mentioned, albeit
one that brings little credit to honest performers. As previously
suggested, ordinary legitimate performances tend to overstress
the degree to which a particular playing of a routine is unique.
Quite false performances, on the other hand, may accentuate a
sense of routinization in order to allay suspicion.
[15] There is a further reason for giving attention to performances and fronts that are flagrantly false. When we find that

Mystification

I have suggested ways in which the performance of an individual accentuates certain matters and conceals others. If we see perception as a form of contact and communion, then control over what is perceived is control over contact that is made, and the limitation and regulation of what is shown is a limitation and regulation of contact. There is a relation here between informational terms and ritual ones. Failure to regulate the information acquired by the audience involves possible disruption of the projected definition of the situation; failure to regulate contact involves possible ritual contamination of the performer.

It is a widely held notion that restrictions placed upon contact, the maintenance of social distance, provide a way in which awe can be generated and sustained in the audience—a way, as Kenneth Burke has said, in which the audience can be held in a state of mystification in regard to the performer. Cooley's statement may serve as an illustration:

> How far it is possible for a man to work upon others through a false idea of himself depends upon a variety of circumstances. As already pointed out, the man himself may be a mere incident with no definite relation to the idea of him, the latter being a separate product of the imagination. This can hardly be except where there is no immediate contact between leader and follower, and partly explains why authority, especially if it covers intrinsic personal weakness, has always a tendency to

---

fake television aerials are sold to persons who do not have sets, and packages of exotic travel labels to persons who have never left home and wire-wheel hub-cap attachments to motorists with ordinary cars, we have clear-cut evidence of the impressive function of presumably instrumental objects When we study the real thing, i.e., persons with real aerials and real sets, etc., it may be difficult in many cases to demonstrate conclusively the impressive function of what can be claimed as a spontaneous or instrumental act.

surround itself with forms and artificial mystery, whose object is to prevent familiar contact and so give the imagination a chance to idealize. . . . The discipline of armies and navies, for instance, very distinctly recognizes the necessity of those forms which separate superior from inferior, and so help to establish an unscrutinized ascendancy in the former. In the same way manners, as Professor Ross remarks in his work on Social Control, are largely used by men of the world as a means of self-concealment, and this self-concealment serves, among other purposes, that of preserving a sort of ascendancy over the unsophisticated.[1]

Ponsonby, in giving advice to the King of Norway, gives voice to the same theory:

One night King Haakon told me of his difficulties in face of the republican leanings of the opposition and how careful in consequence he had to be in all he did and said. He intended, he said, to go as much as possible among the people and thought it would be popular if, instead of going in a motor car, he and Queen Maud were to use the tramways.

I told him frankly that I thought this would be a great mistake as familiarity bred contempt. As a naval officer he would know that the captain of a ship never had his meals with the other officers but remained quite aloof. This was, of course, to stop any familiarity with them. I told him that he must get up on a pedestal and remain there. He could then step off occasionally and no harm would be done. The people didn't want a King with whom they could hob-nob but something nebulous like the Delphic oracle. The Monarchy was really the creation of each individual's brain. Every man liked to think what he would do, if he was King. People invested the Monarch with every conceivable virtue and talent. They were bound therefore to be disappointed if they saw him going about like an ordinary man in the street.[2]

[1] Cooley, *op. cit.*, p. 351.
[2] Ponsonby, *op. cit.*, p. 277.

The logical extreme implied in this kind of theory, whether it is in fact correct or not, is to prohibit the audience from looking at the performer at all, and at times when celestial qualities and powers have been claimed by a performer, this logical conclusion seems to have been put into effect.

Of course, in the matter of keeping social distance, the audience itself will often co-operate by acting in a respectful fashion, in awed regard for the sacred integrity imputed to the performer. As Simmel suggests:

> To act upon the second of these decisions corresponds to the feeling (which also operates elsewhere) that an ideal sphere lies around every human being. Although differing in size in various directions and differing according to the person with whom one entertains relations, this sphere cannot be penetrated, unless the personality value of the individual is thereby destroyed. A sphere of this sort is placed around man by his "honor." Language very poignantly designates an insult to one's honor as "coming too close": the radius of this sphere marks, as it were, the distance whose trespassing by another person insults one's honor.[3]

Durkheim makes a similar point:

> The human personality is a sacred thing; one does not violate it nor infringe its bounds, while at the same time the greatest good is in communion with others.[4]

It must be made quite clear, in contradiction to the implications of Cooley's remarks, that awe and distance are felt toward performers of equal and inferior status as well as (albeit not as much) toward performers of superordinate status.

Whatever their function for the audience, these inhibitions of the audience allow the performer some elbow room in building up an impression of his own choice and allow

---

[3] *The Sociology of Georg Simmel,* trans. and ed. Kurt H. Wolff (Glencoe, Ill.: The Free Press, 1950), p. 321.

[4] Emile Durkheim, *Sociology and Philosophy,* trans. D. F. Pocock (London: Cohen & West, 1953), p. 37.

him to function, for his own good or the audience's, as a protection or a threat that close inspection would destroy.

I would like, finally, to add that the matters which the audience leave alone because of their awe of the performer are likely to be the matters about which he would feel shame were a disclosure to occur. As Riezler has suggested, we have, then, a basic social coin, with awe on one side and shame on the other.[5] The audience senses secret mysteries and powers behind the performance, and the performer senses that his chief secrets are petty ones. As countless folk tales and initiation rites show, often the real secret behind the mystery is that there really is no mystery; the real problem is to prevent the audience from learning this too.

Reality and Contrivance

In our own Anglo-American culture there seems to be two common-sense models according to which we formulate our conceptions of behavior: the real, sincere, or honest performance; and the false one that thorough fabricators assemble for us, whether meant to be taken unseriously, as in the work of stage actors, or seriously, as in the work of confidence men. We tend to see real performances as something not purposely put together at all, being an unintentional product of the individual's unselfconscious response to the facts in his situation. And contrived performances we tend to see as something painstakingly pasted together, one false item on another, since there is no reality to which the items of behavior could be a direct response. It will be necessary to see now that these dichotomous conceptions are by way of being the ideology of honest performers, providing strength to the show they put on, but a poor analysis of it.

First, let it be said that there are many individuals who sincerely believe that the definition of the situation they habitually project is the real reality. In this report I do not

[5] Kurt Riezler, "Comment on the Social Psychology of Shame," *American Journal of Sociology*, XLVIII, p. 462 ff.

mean to question their proportion in the population but rather the structural relation of their sincerity to the performances they offer. If a performance is to come off, the witnesses by and large must be able to believe that the performers are sincere. This is the structural place of sincerity in the drama of events. Performers may be sincere —or be insincere but sincerely convinced of their own sincerity- but this kind of affection for one's part is not necessary for its convincing performance. There are not many French cooks who are really Russian spies, and perhaps there are not many women who play the part of wife to one man and mistress to another but these duplicities do occur, often being sustained successfully for long periods of time. This suggests that while persons usually are what they appear to be, such appearances could still have been managed. There is, then, a statistical relation between appearances and reality, not an intrinsic or necessary one. In fact, given the unanticipated threats that play upon a performance, and given the need (later to be discussed) to maintain solidarity with one's fellow performers and some distance from the witnesses, we find that a rigid incapacity to depart from one's inward view of reality may at times endanger one's performance. Some performances are carried off successfully with complete dishonesty, others with complete honesty; but for performances in general neither of these extremes is essential and neither, perhaps, is dramaturgically advisable.

The implication here is that an honest, sincere, serious performance is less firmly connected with the solid world than one might first assume. And this implication will be strengthened if we look again at the distance usually placed between quite honest performances and quite contrived ones. In this connection take, for example, the remarkable phenomenon of stage acting. It does take deep skill, long training, and psychological capacity to become a good stage actor. But this fact should not blind us to another one: that almost anyone can quickly learn a script well enough to give a charitable audience some sense of realness in what is being contrived before them. And it seems this is so because ordinary social intercourse is itself put together as a scene is put together, by the exchange of dramatically inflated actions, counteractions, and terminating replies. Scripts even in the hands of unpracticed players can come to life because life itself is a dramatically enacted thing. All the world is not, of course, a stage, but the crucial ways in which it isn't are not easy to specify.

The recent use of "psychodrama" as a therapeutic technique illustrates a further point in this regard. In these psychiatrically staged scenes patients not only act out parts with some effectiveness, but employ no script in doing so. Their own past is available to them in a form which allows them to stage a recapitulation of it. Apparently a part once played honestly and in earnest leaves the performer in a position to contrive a showing of it later. Further, the parts that significant others played to him in the past also seem to be available, allowing him to switch from being the person that he was to being the persons that others were for him. This capacity to switch enacted roles when obliged to do so could have been predicted; everyone apparently can do it. For in learning to perform our parts in real life we guide our own productions by not too consciously maintaining an incipient familiarity with the routine of those to whom we will address ourselves. And when we come to be able properly to manage a real routine we are able to do this in part because of "anticipatory socialization,"[1] having already been schooled in the reality that is just coming to be real for us.

When the individual does move into a new position in society and obtains a new part to perform, he is not likely to be told in full detail how to conduct himself, nor will the facts of his new situation press sufficiently on him from the start to determine his conduct without his further giving thought to it. Ordinarily he will be given only a few cues, hints, and stage directions, and it will be assumed that he already has in his repertoire a large number of bits and

[1] See R. K. Merton, *Social Theory and Social Structure* (Glencoe: The Free Press, revised and enlarged edition, 1957), p. 265 ff.

pieces of performances that will be required in the new setting. The individual will already have a fair idea of what modesty, deference, or righteous indignation looks like, and can make a pass at playing these bits when necessary. He may even be able to play out the part of a hypnotic subject[2] or commit a "compulsive" crime[3] on the basis of models for these activities that he is already familiar with.

A theatrical performance or a staged confidence game requires a thorough scripting of the spoken content of the routine; but the vast part involving "expression given off" is often determined by meager stage directions. It is expected that the performer of illusions will already know a good deal about how to manage his voice, his face, and his body, although he—as well as any person who directs him—may find it difficult indeed to provide a detailed verbal statement of this kind of knowledge. And in this, of course, we approach the situation of the straightforward man in the street. Socialization may not so much involve a learning of the many specific details of a single concrete part—often there could not be enough time or energy for this. What does seem to be required of the individual is that he learn enough pieces of expression to be able to "fill in" and manage, more or less, any part that he is likely to be given. The legitimate performances of everyday life are not "acted" or "put on" in the sense that the performer knows in advance just what he is going to do, and does this solely because of the effect it is likely to have. The expressions it is felt he is giving off will be especially "inaccessible" to him.[4] But as in the case of less legitimate performers, the incapacity of the ordinary individual to formulate in advance the movements of his eyes and body does not mean

[2] This view of hypnosis is neatly presented by T. R. Sarbin, "Contributions to Role-Taking Theory. I: Hypnotic Behavior," *Psychological Review*, 57, pp. 255–70.

[3] See D. R. Cressey, "The Differential Association Theory and Compulsive Crimes," *Journal of Criminal Law, Criminology and Police Science*, 45, pp. 29–40.

[4] This concept derives from T. R. Sarbin, "Role Theory," in Gardner Lindzey, *Handbook of Social Psychology* (Cambridge: Addison-Wesley, 1954), Vol. 1, pp. 235–36.

that he will not express himself through these devices in a way that is dramatized and pre-formed in his repertoire of actions. In short, we all act better than we know how.

When we watch a television wrestler gouge, foul, and snarl at his opponent we are quite ready to see that, in spite of the dust, he is, and knows he is, merely playing at being the "heavy," and that in another match he may be given the other role, that of clean-cut wrestler, and perform this with equal verve and proficiency. We seem less ready to see, however, that while such details as the number and character of the falls may be fixed beforehand, the details of the expressions and movements used do not come from a script but from command of an idiom, a command that is exercised from moment to moment with little calculation or forethought.

In reading of persons in the West Indies who become the "horse" or the one possessed of a voodoo spirit,[5] it is enlightening to learn that the person possessed will be able to provide a correct portrayal of the god that has entered him because of "the knowledge and memories accumulated in a life spent visiting congregations of the cult";[6] that the person possessed will be in just the right social relation to those who are watching; that possession occurs at just the right moment in the ceremonial undertakings, the possessed one carrying out his ritual obligations to the point of participating in a kind of skit with persons possessed at the time with other spirits. But in learning this, it is important to see that this contextual structuring of the horse's role still allows participants in the cult to believe that possession is a real thing and that persons are possessed at random by gods whom they cannot select.

And when we observe a young American middle-class girl playing dumb for the benefit of her boy friend, we are ready to point to items of guile and contrivance in her behavior. But like herself and her boy friend, we accept as an unperformed fact that this performer *is* a young

---

[5] See, for example, Alfred Métraux, "Dramatic Elements in Ritual Possession," *Diogenes*, 11, pp. 18–36.

[6] *Ibid.*, p. 24.

American middle-class girl. But surely here we neglect the greater part of the performance. It is commonplace to say that different social groupings express in different ways such attributes as age, sex, territory, and class status, and that in each case these bare attributes are elaborated by means of a distinctive complex cultural configuration of proper ways of conducting oneself. To *be* a given kind of person, then, is not merely to possess the required attributes, but also to sustain the standards of conduct and appearance that one's social grouping attaches thereto. The unthinking ease with which performers consistently carry off such standard-maintaining routines does not deny that a performance has occurred, merely that the participants have been aware of it.

A status, a position, a social place is not a material thing, to be possessed and then displayed; it is a pattern of appropriate conduct, coherent, embellished, and well articulated. Performed with ease or clumsiness, awareness or not, guile or good faith, it is none the less something that must be enacted and portrayed, something that must be realized. Sartre, here, provides a good illustration:

> Let us consider this waiter in the café. His movement is quick and forward, a little too precise, a little too rapid. He comes toward the patrons with a step a little too quick. He bends forward a little too eagerly; his voice, his eyes express an interest a little too solicitous for the order of the customer. Finally there he returns, trying to imitate in his walk the inflexible stiffness of some kind of automaton while carrying his tray with the recklessness of a tightrope-walker by putting it in a perpetually unstable, perpetually broken equilibrium which he perpetually re-establishes by a light movement of the arm and hand. All his behavior seems to us a game. He applies himself to chaining his movements as if they were mechanisms, the one regulating the other; his gestures and even his voice seem to be mechanisms; he gives himself the quickness and pitiless rapidity of things. He is playing, he is amusing himself. But

what is he playing? We need not watch long before we can explain it: he is playing at being a waiter in a café. There is nothing there to surprise us. The game is a kind of marking out and investigation. The child plays with his body in order to explore it, to take inventory of it; the waiter in the café plays with his condition in order to *realize* it. This obligation is not different from that which is imposed on all tradesmen. Their condition is wholly one of ceremony. The public demands of them that they realize it as a ceremony; there is the dance of the grocer, of the tailor, of the auctioneer, by which they endeavor to persuade their clientele that they are nothing but a grocer, an auctioneer, a tailor. A grocer who dreams is offensive to the buyer, because such a grocer is not wholly a grocer. Society demands that he limit himself to his function as a grocer, just as the soldier at attention makes himself into a soldier-thing with a direct regard which does not see at all, which is not longer meant to see, since it is the rule and not the interest of the moment which determines the point he must fix his eyes on (the sight "fixed at ten paces"). There are indeed many precautions to imprison a man in what he is, as if we lived in perpetual fear that he might escape from it, that he might break away and suddenly elude his condition.[7]

[7] Sartre, *op. cit.*, p. 59.

Chapter II

TEAMS

In thinking about a performance it is easy to assume that the content of the presentation is merely an expressive extension of the character of the performer and to see the function of the performance in these personal terms. This is a limited view and can obscure important differences in the function of the performance for the interaction as a whole.

First, it often happens that the performance serves mainly to express the characteristics of the task that is performed and not the characteristics of the performer. Thus one finds that service personnel, whether in profession, bureaucracy, business, or craft, enliven their manner with movements which express proficiency and integrity, but, whatever this manner conveys about them, often its major purpose is to establish a favorable definition of their service or product. Further, we often find that the personal front of the performer is employed not so much because it allows him to present himself as he would like to appear but because his appearance and manner can do something for a scene of wider scope. It is in this light that we can understand how the sifting and sorting of urban life brings girls with good grooming and correct accent into the job of receptionist, where they can present a front for an organization as well as for themselves.

But most important of all, we commonly find that the definition of the situation projected by a particular participant is an integral part of a projection that is fostered and sustained by the intimate co-operation of more than one participant. For example, in a medical hospital the two staff internists may require the intern, as part of his training, to run through a patient's chart, giving an opinion about each recorded item. He may not appreciate that his show of relative ignorance comes in part from the staff studying up on the chart the night before; he is quite unlikely to appreciate that this impression is doubly ensured by the local team's tacit agreement allotting the work-up of half the chart to one staff person, the other half to the second staff person.[1] This teamwork ensures a good staff showing —providing, of course, that the right internist is able to take over the catechism at the right time.

Furthermore, it is often the case that each member of such a troupe or cast of players may be required to appear in a different light if the team's over-all effect is to be satisfactory. Thus if a household is to stage a formal dinner, someone in uniform or livery will be required as part of the working team. The individual who plays this part must direct at himself the social definition of a menial. At the same time the individual taking the part of hostess must direct at herself, and foster by her appearance and manner, the social definition of someone upon whom it is natural for menials to wait. This was strikingly demonstrated in the island tourist hotel studied by the writer (hereafter called "Shetland Hotel"). There an over-all impression of middle-class service was achieved by the management, who allocated to themselves the roles of middle-class host and hostess and to their employees that of domestics—although in terms of the local class structure the girls who acted as maids were of slightly higher status than the hotel owners who employed them. When hotel guests were absent, little nonsense about a maid-mistress status difference was allowed by the maids. Another example may be taken from middle-class family life. In our society, when husband and wife appear before new friends for an evening of sociability, the wife may demonstrate more respectful subordination to the will and opinion of her husband than she may bother

[1] Writer's unpublished study of a medical service.

to show when alone with him or when with old friends.
When she assumes a respectful role, he can assume a dominant one; and when each member of the marriage team
plays its special role, the conjugal unit, as a unit, can sustain the impression that new audiences expect of it. Race
etiquette in the South provides another example. Charles
Johnson's suggestion is that when few other whites are in
the region, a Negro may call his white fellow worker by
his first name, but when other whites approach it is understood that mistering will be reintroduced.[2] Business etiquette provides a similar example:

> When outsiders are present, the touch of businesslike
> formality is even more important. You may call your
> secretary "Mary" and your partner "Joe" all day, but
> when a stranger comes into your office you should refer
> to your associates as you would expect the stranger to
> address them: Miss or Mr. You may have a running joke
> with the switchboard operator, but you let it ride when
> you are placing a call in an outsider's hearing.[3]

> She [your secretary] wants to be called Miss or Mrs. in
> front of strangers; at least, she won't be flattered if your
> "Mary" provokes everyone else into addressing her with
> familiarity.[4]

I will use the term "performance team" or, in short, "team"
to refer to any set of individuals who co-operate in staging
a single routine.

Until now in this report we have taken the individual's
performance as the basic point of reference and have been
concerning ourselves with two levels of fact—the individual
and his performance on one hand and the full set of participants and the interaction as a whole on the other. For
the study of certain kinds and aspects of interaction, this
perspective would seem sufficient; anything that did not
fit this framework could be handled as a resolvable com-
plication of it. Thus co-operation between two performers

2 Charles S. Johnson, *op. cit.*, pp. 137–38.
3 *Esquire Etiquette* (Philadelphia: Lippincott, 1953), p. 6.
4 *Ibid.*, p. 15.

each of whom was ostensibly involved in presenting his own special performance could be analyzed as a type of collusion or "understanding" without altering the basic frame of reference. However in the case-study of particular social establishments, the co-operative activity of some of the participants seems too important to be handled merely as a variation on a previous theme. Whether the members of a team stage similar individual performances or stage dissimilar performances which fit together into a whole, an emergent team impression arises which can conveniently be treated as a fact in its own right, as a third level of fact located between the individual performance on one hand and the total interaction of participants on the other. It may even be said that if our special interest is the study of impression management, of the contingencies which arise in fostering an impression, and of the techniques for meeting these contingencies, then the team and the team-performance may well be the best units to take as the fundamental point of reference.[5] Given this point of reference, it is possible to assimilate such situations as two-person interaction into the framework by describing these situations as two-team interaction in which each team contains only one member. (Logically speaking, one could even say that an audience which was duly impressed by a particular social setting in which no other persons were present would be an audience witnessing a team-performance in which the team was one of no members.)

The concept of team allows us to think of performances that are given by one or more than one performer; it also covers another case. Earlier it was suggested that a performer may be taken in by his own act, convinced at the moment that the impression of reality which he fosters is the one and only reality. In such cases the performer comes to be his own audience; he comes to be performer and

[5] The use of the team (as opposed to the performer) as the fundamental unit I take from Von Neumann, *op. cit.*, especially p. 53, where bridge is analyzed as a game between two players, each of whom in some respects has two separate individuals to do the playing.

observer of the same show. Presumably he intracepts or incorporates the standards he attempts to maintain in the presence of others so that his conscience requires him to act in a socially proper way. It will have been necessary for the individual in his performing capacity to conceal from himself in his audience capacity the discreditable facts that he has had to learn about the performance; in everyday terms, there will be things he knows, or has known, that he will not be able to tell himself. This intricate maneuver of self-delusion constantly occurs; psychoanalysts have provided us with beautiful field data of this kind, under the headings of repression and dissociation.[6] Perhaps here we have a source of what has been called "self-distantiation," namely, that process by which a person comes to feel estranged from himself.[7]

When a performer guides his private activity in accordance with incorporated moral standards, he may associate these standards with a reference group of some kind, thus creating a non-present audience for his activity. This possibility leads us to consider a further one. The individual may privately maintain standards of behavior which he does not personally believe in, maintaining these standards because of a lively belief that an unseen audience is present who will punish deviations from these standards. In other words, an individual may be his own audience or may

[6] Individualistic modes of thought tend to treat processes such as self-deception and insincerity as characterological weaknesses generated within the deep recesses of the individual personality. It might be better to start from outside the individual and work inward than to start inside the individual and work out. We may say that the starting point for all that is to come later consists of the individual performer maintaining a definition of the situation before an audience. The individual automatically becomes insincere when he adheres to the obligation of maintaining a working consensus and participates in different routines or performs a given part before different audiences. Self-deception can be seen as something that results when two different roles, performer and audience, come to be compressed into the same individual.

[7] See Karl Mannheim, *Essays on the Sociology of Culture* (London: Routledge & Kegan Paul, 1956), p. 209.

imagine an audience to be present. (In all of this we see
the analytical difference between the concept of a team
and that of an individual performer.) This should make us
go on to see that a team itself may stage a performance
for an audience that is not present in the flesh to witness
the show. Thus, in some mental hospitals in America, un-
claimed deceased patients may be given a relatively elaborate funeral on the hospital grounds. No doubt this helps
to ensure the maintenance of minimal civilized standards
in a setting where back-ward conditions and the general
unconcern of society can threaten these standards. In any
case, on occasions when kinfolk do not appear, the hospital
minister, the hospital funeral director, and one or two other
functionaries may play out all the funeral roles themselves
and, with the dead patient now laid out, perform a demonstration of civilized regard for the dead before no one
present.

It is apparent that individuals who are members of the
same team will find themselves, by virtue of this fact, in an
important relationship to one another. Two basic components of this relationship may be cited.

First, it would seem that while a team-performance is
in progress, any member of the team has the power to give
the show away or to disrupt it by inappropriate conduct.
Each teammate is forced to rely on the good conduct and
behavior of his fellows, and they, in turn, are forced to rely
on him. There is then, perforce, a bond of reciprocal dependence linking teammates to one another. When members of a team have different formal statuses and rank in a
social establishment, as is often the case, then we can see
that the mutual dependence created by membership in the
team is likely to cut across structural or social cleavages in
the establishment and thus provide a source of cohesion
for the establishment. Where staff and line statuses tend to
divide an organization, performance teams may tend to
integrate the divisions.

Secondly, it is apparent that if members of a team must
co-operate to maintain a given definition of the situation
before their audience, they will hardly be in a position to

maintain that particular impression before one another. Accomplices in the maintenance of a particular appearance of things, they are forced to define one another as persons "in the know," as persons before whom a particular front cannot be maintained. Teammates, then, in proportion to the frequency with which they act as a team and the number of matters that fall within impressional protectiveness, tend to be bound by rights of what might be called "familiarity." Among teammates, the privilege of familiarity—which may constitute a kind of intimacy without warmth—need not be something of an organic kind, slowly developing with the passage of time spent together, but rather a formal relationship that is automatically extended and received as soon as the individual takes a place on the team.

In suggesting that teammates tend to be related to one another by bonds of reciprocal dependence and reciprocal familiarity, we must not confuse the type of group so formed with other types, such as an informal group or clique. A teammate is someone whose dramaturgical co-operation one is dependent upon in fostering a given definition of the situation; if such a person comes to be beyond the pale of informal sanctions and insists on giving the show away or forcing it to take a particular turn, he is none the less part of the team. In fact, it is just because he is part of the team that he can cause this kind of trouble. Thus the isolate in the factory who becomes a rate-buster is none the less part of the team, even if his productive activity embarrasses the impression the other workers are attempting to foster as to what constitutes a hard day's work. As an object of friendship he may be studiously ignored, but as a threat to the team's definition of the situation, he cannot be overlooked. Similarly, a girl at a party who is flagrantly accessible may be shunned by the other girls who are present, but in certain matters she is part of their team and cannot fail to threaten the definition they are collectively maintaining that girls are difficult sexual prizes. Thus while teammates are often persons who agree informally to guide their efforts in a certain way as a means of self-protection and by doing so constitute an informal group, this informal agreement is not a criterion for defining the concept of team.

The members of an informal clique, using this term in the sense of a small number of persons who join together for informal amusements, may also constitute a team, for it is likely that they will have to co-operate in tactfully concealing their exclusiveness from some non-members while advertising it snobbishly to others. There is, however, a meaningful contrast between the concepts team and clique. In large social establishments, individuals within a given status level are thrown together by virtue of the fact that they must co-operate in maintaining a definition of the situation toward those above and below them. Thus a set of individuals who might be dissimilar in important respects, and hence desirous of maintaining social distance from one another, find they are in a relation of enforced familiarity characteristic of teammates engaged in staging a show. Often it seems that small cliques form not to further the interests of those with whom the individual stages a show but rather to protect him from an unwanted identification with them. Cliques, then, often function to protect the individual not from persons of other ranks but from persons of his own rank. Thus, while all the members of one's clique may be of the same status level, it may be crucial that not all persons of one's status level be allowed into the clique.[8]

A final comment must be added on what a team is not. Individuals may be bound together formally or informally into an action group in order to further like or collective ends by any means available to them. In so far as they co-operate in maintaining a given impression, using this device as a means of achieving their ends, they constitute what has here been called a team. But it should be made

[8] There are, of course, many bases of clique formation. Edward Gross, *Informal Relations and the Social Organization of Work in an Industrial Office* (unpublished Ph.D. dissertation, Department of Sociology, University of Chicago, 1949), suggests that cliques may cross ordinary age and ethnic lines in order to bring together individuals whose work activity is not seen as a competitive reflection upon one another.

quite clear that there are many means by which an action group can achieve ends other than by dramaturgical cooperation. Other means to ends, such as force or bargaining power, may be increased or decreased by strategic manipulation of impressions, but the exercise of force or bargaining power gives to a set of individuals a source of group formation unconnected with the fact that on certain occasions the group thus formed is likely to act, dramaturgically speaking, as a team. (Similarly, an individual who is in a position of power or leadership may increase or decrease his strength by the degree to which his appearance and manner are appropriate and convincing, but it is not claimed that the dramaturgical qualities of his action necessarily or even commonly constitute the fundamental basis of his position.)

If we are to employ the concept of team as a fundamental point of reference, it will be convenient to retrace earlier steps and redefine our framework of terms in order to adjust for the use of team, rather than individual performer, as the basic unit.

It has been suggested that the object of a performer is to sustain a particular definition of the situation, this representing, as it were, his claim as to what reality is. As a one-man team, with no teammates to inform of his decision, he can quickly decide which of the available stands on a matter to take and then wholeheartedly act as if his choice were the only one he could possibly have taken. And his choice of position may be nicely adjusted to his own particular situation and interests.

When we turn from a one-man team to a larger one, the character of the reality that is espoused by the team changes. Instead of a rich definition of the situation, reality may become reduced to a thin party line, for one may expect the line to be unequally congenial to the members of the team. We may expect ironic remarks by which a teammate jokingly rejects the line while seriously accepting it. On the other hand, there will be the new factor of loyalty to one's team and one's teammates to provide support for the team's line.

It seems to be generally felt that public disagreement among the members of the team not only incapacitates them for united action but also embarrasses the reality sponsored by the team. To protect this impression of reality, members of the team may be required to postpone taking public stands until the position of the team has been settled; and once the team's stand has been taken, all members may be obliged to follow it. (The question of the amount of "Soviet self-criticism" that is allowed, and from whom it is allowed, before the team's position is announced, is not here at issue.) An illustration may be taken from the civil service:

> At such committees [Cabinet Committee meetings] civil servants share in the discussions and express their views freely, subject to one qualification: they will not directly oppose their own Minister. The possibility of such open disagreement very rarely arises, and ought never to arise: in nine cases out of ten, the Minister and the civil servant who attends the committee with him have agreed beforehand what line is to be taken, and in the tenth the civil servant who disagrees with his Minister's view on a particular point will stay away from the meeting where it is to be discussed.[9]

Another illustration may be cited from a recent study of the power structure of a small city:

> If one has been engaged in community work on any scale at all, he is impressed over and over with what might be termed the "principle of unanimity." When policy is finally formulated by the leaders in the community, there is an immediate demand on their part for strict conformity of opinion. Decisions are not usually arrived at hurriedly. There is ample time, particularly among the top leaders, for discussion of most projects before a state of action is set. This is true for community projects. When the time for discussion is past and the

9 Dale, *op. cit.*, p. 141.

line is set, then unanimity is called for. Pressures are put upon dissenters, and the project is under way.[10]

Open disagreement in front of the audience creates, as we say, a false note. It may be suggested that literal false notes are avoided for quite the same reasons that figurative false notes are avoided; in both cases it is a matter of sustaining a definition of the situation. This may be illustrated from a brief book on the work problems of the professional concert-artist accompanist:

> The nearest that the singer and pianist can get to an ideal performance is to do exactly what the composer wants, yet sometimes the singer will require his partner to do something which is in flat contradiction to the composer's markings. He will want an accent where there should be none, he will make a *firmata* where it is not needed, he will make a *rallentundo* when it should be *a tempo:* he will be *forte* when he should be *piano:* he may sentimentalize when the mood should be *nobilmente.*
>
> The list is by no means exhausted. The singer will swear with his hand on his heart and tears in his eyes that he does and always aims to do exactly what the composer has written. It is very awkward. If he sings it one way and the pianist plays it another way the result is chaotic. Discussion may be of no avail. But what is an accompanist to do?
>
> At the performance he must *be with the singer,* but afterwards let him erase the memory of it from his mind . . .[11]

However, unanimity is often not the sole requirement of the team's projection. There seems to be a general feeling that the most real and solid things in life are ones whose description individuals independently agree upon. We tend to feel that if two participants in an event decide to be as

[10] Floyd Hunter, *Community Power Structure* (Chapel Hill: University of North Carolina Press, 1953), p. 181. See also p. 118 and p. 212.

[11] Gerald Moore, *The Unashamed Accompanist* (New York: Macmillan, 1944), p. 60.

honest as they can in recounting it, then the stands they take will be acceptably similar even though they do not consult one another prior to their presentation. Intention to tell the truth presumably makes such prior consultation unnecessary. And we also tend to feel that if the two individuals wish to tell a lie or to slant the version of the event which they offer, then not only will it be necessary for them to consult with one another in order, as we say, "to get their story straight," but it will also be necessary to conceal the fact that an opportunity for such prior consultation was available to them. In other words, in staging a definition of the situation, it may be necessary for the several members of the team to be unanimous in the positions they take and secretive about the fact that these positions were not independently arrived at. (Incidentally, if the members of the team are also engaged in maintaining a show of self-respect before one another, it may be necessary for the members of the team to learn what the line is to be, and take it, without admitting to themselves and to one another the extent to which their position is not independently arrived at, but such problems carry us somewhat beyond the team-performance as the basic point of reference.)

It should be noted that just as a teammate ought to wait for the official word before taking his stand, so the official word ought to be made available to him so that he can play his part on the team and feel a part of it. For example, in commenting on how some Chinese merchants set the price of their goods according to the appearance of the customer, one writer goes on to say:

> One particular result of this study of a customer is seen in the fact that if a person enters a store in China, and, after examining several articles, asks the price of any one of them, unless it is positively known that he has spoken to but one clerk, no answer will be made by him to whom the question is put until every other clerk has been asked if he has named a price for the article in question to the gentleman. If, as very rarely happens, this im-

portant precaution is neglected, the sum named by different clerks will almost invariably be unlike, thus showing that they fail to agree in their estimates of the customer.[12]

To withhold from a teammate information about the stand his team is taking is in fact to withhold his character from him, for without knowing what stand he will be taking he may not be able to assert a self to the audience. Thus, if a surgeon is to operate on a patient referred to him by another doctor, common courtesy may oblige the surgeon to tell the referring doctor when the operation will be and, if the referring doctor does not appear at the operation, to telephone him the result of the operation. By thus being "filled in," the referring doctor can, more effectively than otherwise, present himself to the patient's kinfolk as someone who is participating in the medical action.[13]

I would like to add a further general fact about maintaining the line during a performance. When a member of the team makes a mistake in the presence of the audience, the other team members often must suppress their immediate desire to punish and instruct the offender until, that is, the audience is no longer present. After all, immediate corrective sanctioning would often only disturb the interaction further and, as previously suggested, make the audience privy to a view that ought to be reserved for teammates. Thus, in authoritarian organizations, where a team of superordinates maintains a show of being right every time and of possessing a united front, there is often a strict rule that one superordinate must not show hostility or disrespect toward any other superordinate while in the presence of a member of the subordinate team. Army officers show consensus when before enlisted men, parents when before children,[14] managers when before workers,

[12] Chester Holcombe, *The Real Chinaman* (New York: Dodd, Mead, 1895), p. 293.

[13] Solomon, *op. cit.*, p. 75.

[14] An interesting dramaturgical difficulty in the family is that sex and lineal solidarity, which crosscut conjugal solidarity, make it difficult for husband and wife to "back each other up"

nurses when before patients,[15] and the like. Of course,
when the subordinates are absent, open, violent criticism
may and does occur. For example in a recent study of the
teaching profession, it was found that teachers felt that
if they are to sustain an impression of professional competence and institutional authority, they must make sure that
when angry parents come to the school with complaints,
the principal will support the position of his staff, at least
until the parents have left.[16] Similarly, teachers feel
strongly that their fellow teachers ought not to disagree
with or contradict them in front of students. "Just let another teacher raise her eyebrow funny, just so they [the
children] know, and they don't miss a thing and their
respect for you goes right away."[17] Similarly, we learn
that the medical profession has a strict code of etiquette
whereby a consultant in the presence of the patient and his
doctor is careful never to say anything which would embarrass the impression of competence that the patient's
doctor is attempting to maintain. As Hughes suggests. "The
[professional] etiquette is a body of ritual which grows up
informally to preserve, before the clients, the common front
of the profession."[18] And, of course this kind of solidarity
in the presence of subordinates also occurs when performers
are in the presence of superordinates. For example in a
recent study of the police we learn that a patrolling team
of two policemen, who witness each other's illegal and semi-
illegal acts and who are in an excellent position to discredit
each other's show of legality before the judge, possess

in a show of authority before children or a show of either distance or familiarity with extended kin. As previously suggested,
such crosscutting lines of affiliation prevent the widening of
structural cleavages.

[15] Taxel op. cit., pp. 53–54.
[16] Howard S. Becker, "The Teacher in the Authority System
of the Public School," *Journal of Educational Sociology*, XXVII,
p. 134.
[17] *Ibid.*, from an interview, p. 139.
[18] E. C Hughes, "Institutions," *New Outline of the Principles
of Sociology*, ed. Alfred M. Lee (New York: Barnes and Noble,
1946), p. 273.

heroic solidarity and will stick by each other's story no matter what atrocity it covers up or how little chance there is of anyone believing it.[19]

It is apparent that if performers are concerned with maintaining a line they will select as teammates those who can be trusted to perform properly. Thus children of the house are often excluded from performances given for guests of a domestic establishment because often children cannot be trusted to "behave" themselves, i.e., to refrain from acting in a way inconsistent with the impression that is being fostered.[20] Similarly, those who are known to become intoxicated when drink is available and who become verbose or "difficult" when this occurs constitute a performance risk, as do those who are sober but foolishly indiscreet, and those who refuse to "enter into the spirit" of the occasion and help sustain the impression that guests tacitly unite in maintaining to the host.

I have suggested that in many interaction settings some of the participants co-operate together as a team or are in a position where they are dependent upon this co-operation in order to maintain a particular definition of the situation. Now when we study concrete social establishments we often find that there will be a significant sense in which all the remaining participants, in their several performances of response to the team-show put on before them, will themselves constitute a team. Since each team will be playing through its routine for the other, one may speak of dramatic interaction, not dramatic action, and we can see this interaction not as a medley of as many voices as there are participants but rather as a kind of dialogue and interplay between two teams. I do not know of any general reason why interaction in natural settings usually takes the form

[19] William Westley, "The Police" (unpublished Ph.D. dissertation, Department of Sociology, University of Chicago, 1952), pp. 187–96.

[20] In so far as children are defined as "non-persons" they have some license to commit gauche acts without requiring the audience to take the expressive implications of these acts too seriously. However, whether treated as non-persons or not, children are in a position to disclose crucial secrets.

of two-team interplay, or is resolvable into this form, instead of involving a larger number, but empirically this seems to be the case. Thus, in large social establishments, where several different status grades prevail, we find that for the duration of any particular interaction, participants of many different statuses are typically expected to align themselves temporarily into two team groupings. For example, a lieutenant at an Army post will find himself aligned with all the officers and opposed to all enlisted men in one situation; at other times he will find himself aligned with junior officers, presenting with them a show for the benefit of senior officers present. There are, of course, aspects of certain interactions for which a two-team model is apparently not suitable. Important elements, for example, of arbitration hearings seem to fit a three-team model, and aspects of some competitive and "social" situations suggest a multi-team model. It should also be made clear that whatever the number of teams, there will be a sense in which the interaction can be analyzed in terms of the co-operative effort of all participants to maintain a working consensus.

If we treat an interaction as a dialogue between two teams, it will sometimes be convenient to call one team the performers and to call the other team the audience or the observers, neglecting momentarily that the audience, too, will be presenting a team-performance. In some cases, as when two one-person teams interact in a public institution or in the home of a mutual friend, it may be an arbitrary choice as to which team to call the performer and which to call the audience. In many important social situations, however, the social setting in which the interaction occurs is assembled and managed by one of the teams only, and contributes in a more intimate way to the show this team puts on than to the show put on in response by the other team. A customer in a shop, a client in an office, a group of guests in the home of their hosts—these persons put on a performance and maintain a front, but the setting in which they do this is outside of their immediate control, being an integral part of the presentation made by those into whose presence they have come. In such cases, it will often be convenient to call the team which controls the setting the performing team, and to call the other team the audience. So, too, it will sometimes be convenient to label as performer the team which contributes the more activity to the interaction, or plays the more dramatically prominent part in it, or sets the pace and direction which both teams will follow in their interactive dialogue.

The obvious point must be stated that if the team is to sustain the impression that it is fostering, then there must be some assurance that no individual will be allowed to join both team and audience. Thus, for example, if the proprietor of a small ladies' ready-to-wear is to put a dress on sale and tell his customer that it is marked down because of soilage, or end of the season, or last of a line, etc., and conceal from her that it is really marked down because it won't sell, or is a bad color or style, and if he is to impress her by talking about a buying office in New York which he does not have or an adjustment manager who is really a salesgirl, then he must make sure that if he finds it necessary to hire an extra girl for part-time work on Saturday he does not hire one from the neighborhood who has been a customer and who will soon be one again.[21]

It is often felt that control of the setting is an advantage during interaction. In a narrow sense, this control allows a team to introduce strategic devices for determining the information the audience is able to acquire. Thus, if doctors are to prevent cancer patients from learning the identity of their disease, it will be useful to be able to scatter the cancer patients throughout the hospital so that they will not be able to learn from the identity of their ward the identity of their disorder. (The hospital staff, incidentally, may be forced to spend more time walking corridors and moving equipment because of this staging strategy than would otherwise be necessary.) Similarly, the master barber who regulates the flow of appointments by means of a

[21] These illustrations are taken from George Rosenbaum, "An Analysis of Personalization in Neighborhood Apparel Retailing" (unpublished M.A. thesis, Department of Sociology, University of Chicago, 1953), pp. 86–87.

scheduling book open to his public is in a position to protect his coffee break by filling a properly timed appointment with a dummy code name. A prospective customer can then see for himself that it will not be possible for him to have an appointment at that time. Another interesting use of setting and props is reported in an article on American sororities, where a description is given of how the sorority sisters, who give a tea for prospective members, are able to sort out good prospects from bad without giving the impression that guests of the house are being treated differentially:

> "Even with recommends, it's hard to remember 967 girls by just meeting them for a few minutes in a receiving line " admitted Carol. "So we've worked out this gimmick to separate the good ones from the dull characters. We have three trays for the rushees' calling cards—one for golden girls, one for look-agains, one for pots.
> "The active who is talking with the rushee at the party is supposed to escort her subtly to the appropriate tray when she's ready to leave her card," Carol continued. "The rushees never figure out what we're doing!"[22]

Another illustration may be cited from the arts of hotel management. If any member of a hotel staff is suspicious of the intentions or character of a guest couple, a secret signal can be given to the bellboy to "throw the latch."

> This is simply a device which makes it easier for employees to keep an eye on suspected parties.
> After rooming the couple, the bellman, in closing the door behind him, pushes a tiny button on the inside of the knob handle. This turns a little tumbler inside the lock and makes a black stripe show against the circular center of the latch on the outside. It's inconspicuous enough so as not to be noticed by the guest, but maids, patrols, waiters and bellmen are all trained to watch for

[22] Joan Beck, "What's Wrong with Sorority Rushing?" *Chicago Tribune Magazine,* January 10, 1954, pp. 20–21.

them . . . and to report any loud conversations or unusual occurrences which take place behind them.[23]

More broadly, control of the setting may give the controlling team a sense of security. As one student suggests concerning the pharmacist-doctor relation:

> The store is another factor. The doctor often comes to the pharmacist's store for medicine, for bits of information, for conversation. In these conversations the man behind the counter has approximately the same advantage that a standing speaker has over a sitting audience.[24]

> One thing that contributes to this feeling of the independence of the pharmacist's medical practice is his store. The store is, in a sense, a part of the pharmacist. Just as Neptune is pictured as rising from the sea, while at the same time being the sea; so in the pharmaceutical ethos there is a vision of a dignified pharmacist towering above shelves and counters of bottles and equipment, while at the same time being part of their essence.[25]

A nice literary illustration of the effects of being robbed of control over one's setting is given by Franz Kafka, in *The Trial*, where K.'s meeting with the authorities in his own boardinghouse is described:

> When he was fully dressed he had to walk, with Willem treading on his heels, through the next room, which was now empty, into the adjoining one, whose double doors were flung open. This room, as K. knew quite well, had recently been taken by a Fraulein Bürstner, a typist, who went very early to work, came home late, and with whom he had exchanged little more than few words in passing. Now the night-table beside her bed had been pushed into the middle of the floor to serve as desk, and the inspector was sitting behind it. He

---

[23] Dev Collans, with Stewart Sterling, *I Was a House Detective* (New York: Dutton, 1954), p. 56. Ellipsis dots the authors'.
[24] Weinlein, *op. cit.*, p. 105.
[25] *Ibid.*, pp. 105–6.

had crossed his legs, and one arm was resting on the back of the chair.

. . . "Joseph K.?" asked the inspector, perhaps merely to draw K.'s distracted glance upon himself. K. nodded. "You are presumably very surprised at the events of this morning?" asked the inspector, with both hands re-arranging the few things that lay on the night-table, a candle and a matchbox, a book and a pincushion, as if they were objects which he required for his interrogation. "Certainly," said K., and he was filled with pleasure at having encountered a sensible man at last, with whom he could discuss the matter. "Certainly, I am surprised, but I am by no means very surprised." "Not very surprised?" asked the inspector, setting the candle in the middle of the table and then grouping the other things around it. "Perhaps you misunderstand me," K. hastened to add. "I mean"—here K. stopped and looked round him for a chair. "I suppose I may sit down?" he asked. "It's not usual," answered the inspector.[26]

A price must, of course, be paid for the privilege of giving a performance on one's home ground; one has the opportunity of conveying information about oneself through scenic means but no opportunity of concealing the kinds of facts that are conveyed by scenery. It is to be expected then that a potential performer may have to avoid his own stage and its controls in order to prevent an unflattering performance, and that this can involve more than the postponement of a social party because the new furniture has not yet arrived. Thus, of a slum area in London we learn that:

. . . mothers in this area, more than mothers elsewhere, prefer their children to be born in hospital. The main reason for this preference seems to be the expense of an at-home birth since proper equipment must be bought, towels for instance, and bathing basins, so that every-

[26] Franz Kafka, *The Trial* (New York: Knopf, 1948), pp. 14–15.

thing measures up to the standards required by the midwife. It also means the presence in the home of a strange woman, which in turn means a special cleaning out.[27]

When one examines a team-performance, one often finds that someone is given the right to direct and control the progress of the dramatic action. The equerry in court establishments is an example. Sometimes the individual who dominates the show in this way and is, in a sense, the director of it, plays an actual part in the performance he directs. This is illustrated for us by a novelist's view of the ministerial functions at a wedding ceremony:

> The minister left the door ajar, so that they [Robert, the groom, and Lionel, the best-man] might hear their cue and enter without delay. They stood at the door like eavesdroppers. Lionel touched his pocket, felt the round outline of the ring, then put his hand on Robert's elbow. As the cue word approached, Lionel opened the door and, on cue, propelled Robert forward.
>
> The ceremony moved without a hitch under the firm and experienced hand of the minister, who came down hard on the cues and used his eyebrows to menace the performers. The guests did not notice that Robert had a hard time getting the ring on the bride's finger; they did, however, notice that the bride's father cried overmuch and the mother not at all. But these were small things soon forgotten.[28]

In general, the members of the team will differ in the ways and the degree to which they are allowed to direct the performance. It may be noted, incidentally, that the structural similarities of apparently diverse routines are nicely reflected in the like-mindedness that arises in directors everywhere. Whether it is a funeral, a wedding, a bridge party, a one-day sale, a hanging, or a picnic, the director may tend to see the performance in terms of whether or

[27] B. M. Spinley, *The Deprived and the Privileged* (London: Routledge and Kegan Paul, 1953), p. 45.

[28] Warren Miller, *The Sleep of Reason* (Boston: Little, Brown and Company, 1958), p. 254.

not it went "smoothly," "effectively," and "without a hitch," and whether or not all possible disruptive contingencies were prepared for in advance.

In many performances two important functions must be fulfilled, and if the team has a director he will often be given the special duty of fulfilling these functions.

First, the director may be given the special duty of bringing back into line any member of the team whose performance becomes unsuitable. Soothing and sanctioning are the corrective processes ordinarily involved. The role of the baseball umpire in sustaining a particular kind of reality for the fans may be taken as an illustration.

All umpires insist that players keep themselves under control, and refrain from gestures that reflect contempt for their decisions.[29]

I certainly had blown off my share of steam as a player, and I knew there had to be a safety valve for release of the terrific tension. As an umpire I could sympathize with the players. But as an umpire I had to decide how far I could let a player go without delaying the game and without permitting him to insult, assault, or ridicule me and belittle the game. Handling trouble and men on the field was as important as calling them right—and more difficult.

It is easy for any umpire to thumb a man out of the game. It is often a much more difficult job to keep him in the game—to understand and anticipate his complaint so that a nasty rhubarb cannot develop.[30]

I do not tolerate clowning on the field, and neither will any other umpire. Comedians belong on the stage or on television, not in baseball. A travesty or burlesque of the game can only cheapen it, and also hold the umpire up to scorn for allowing such a sketch to take place. That's why you will see the funnymen and wise guys chased as soon as they begin their routine.[31]

[29] Pinelli, *op. cit.*, p. 141.
[30] *Ibid.*, p. 131.
[31] *Ibid.*, p. 139.

Often, of course, the director will not so much have to smother improper affect as he will have to stimulate a show of proper affective involvement; "sparking the show" is the phrase sometimes employed for this task in Rotarian circles.

Secondly, the director may be given the special duty of allocating the parts in the performance and the personal front that is employed in each part, for each establishment may be seen as a place with a number of characters to dispose of to prospective performers and as an assemblage of sign-equipment or ceremonial paraphernalia to be allocated.

It is apparent that if the director corrects for improper appearances and allocates major and minor prerogatives, then other members of the team (who are likely to be concerned with the show they can put on for one another as well as with the show they can collectively stage for the audience) will have an attitude toward the director that they do not have toward their other teammates. Further, if the audience appreciates that the performance has a director, they are likely to hold him more responsible than other performers for the success of the performance. The director is likely to respond to this responsibility by making dramaturgical demands on the performance that they might not make upon themselves. This may add to the estrangement they may already feel from him. A director, hence starting as a member of the team, may find himself slowly edged into a marginal role between audience and performers, half in and half out of both camps, a kind of go-between without the protection that go-betweens usually have. The factory foreman has been a recently discussed example.[32]

When we study a routine which requires a team of sev-

---

[32] See, for example, Donald E. Wray, "Marginal Men of Industry: The Foreman," *American Journal of Sociology*, LIV, pp. 298–301, and Fritz Roethlisberger, "The Foreman: Master and Victim of Double Talk," *Harvard Business Review*, XXIII, pp. 285–94. The role of go-between is considered later.

eral performers for its presentation, we sometimes find that
one member of the team is made the star, lead, or center of
attention. We may see an extreme example of this in traditional court life, where a room full of court attendants will
be arranged in the manner of a living tableau, so that the
eye, starting from any point in the room will be led to the
royal center of attention. The royal star of the performance
may also be dressed more spectacularly and seated higher
than anyone else present. An even more spectacular center-
ing of attention may be found in the dance arrangements
of large musical comedies, in which forty or fifty dancers
are made to prostrate themselves around the heroine.

The extravagance of the performances found at royal
appearances should not blind us to the utility of the concept
of a court: courts in fact are commonly found outside of
palaces, one instance being the commissaries of Hollywood
production studios. While it seems abstractly true that individuals are convivially endogamous, tending to restrict informal ties to those of their own social status, still, when a
social class is examined closely, one may find it to be made
up of separated social sets, each set containing one and only
one complement of differently placed performers. And frequently the set will form around one dominant figure who
is constantly maintained as the center of attention in the
center of the stage. Evelyn Waugh suggests this theme in
a discussion of the British upper class:

> Look back twenty-five years to the time when there
> was still a fairly firm aristocratic structure and the coun-
> try was still divided into spheres of influence among
> hereditary magnates. My memory is that the grandees
> avoided one another unless they were closely related.
> They met on state occasions and on the racecourse. They
> did not frequent one another's houses. You might find
> almost anyone in a ducal castle—convalescent, penurious
> cousins, advisory experts, sycophants, gigolos and plain
> blackmailers. The one thing you could be sure of not
> finding was a concourse of other dukes. English society,
> it seemed to me, was a complex of tribes, each with its

chief and elders and witch-doctors and braves, each with its own dialect and deity, each strongly xenophobic.[33]

The informal social life conducted by the staffs of our universities and other intellectual bureaucracies seems to break up in something of the same way: the cliques and factions which form the smaller parties of administrative politics form the courts of convivial life, and it is here that local heroes can safely sustain the eminence of their wit, their competence and their profundity.

In general, then, one finds that those who help present a team-performance differ in the degree of dramatic dominance given each of them and that one team-routine differs from another in the extent to which differentials in dominance are given its members.

The conceptions of dramatic and directive dominance, as contrasting types of power in a performance, can be applied, *mutatis mutandis*, to an interaction as a whole, where it will be possible to point out which of the two teams has more of which of the two types of power and which performers, taking the participants of both teams all together, lead in these two regards.

Frequently, of course, the performer or team which has one kind of dominance will have the other, but this is by no means always the case. For example, during the showing of the body at a funeral home, usually the social setting and all participants, including both the bereaved team and the establishment's team, will be arranged so as to express their feelings for the deceased and their ties to him; he will be the center of the show and the dramatically dominant participant in it. However, since the bereaved are inexperienced and grief-laden, and since the star of the show must stay in character as someone who is in a deep sleep, the undertaker himself will direct the show, although he may all the while be self-effacing in the presence of the corpse or be in another room of the establishment getting ready for another showing.

[33] Evelyn Waugh, "An Open Letter," in Nancy Mitford, editor, *Noblesse Oblige* (London: Hamish Hamilton, 1956), p. 78.

It should be made clear that dramatic and directive dominance are dramaturgical terms and that performers who enjoy such dominance may not have other types of power and authority. It is common knowledge that performers who have positions of visible leadership are often merely figureheads, selected as a compromise, or as a way of neutralizing a potentially threatening position, or as a way of strategically concealing the power behind the front and hence the power behind the power behind the front. So also, whenever inexperienced or temporary incumbents are given formal authority over experienced subordinates, we often find that the formally empowered person is bribed with a part that has dramatic dominance while the subordinates tend to direct the show.[34] Thus it has often been said about the British infantry in World War I that experienced working-class sergeants managed the delicate task of covertly teaching their new lieutenants to take a dramatically expressive role at the head of the platoon and to die quickly in a prominent dramatic position, as befits public-school men. The sergeants themselves took their modest place at the rear of the platoon and tended to live to train still other lieutenants.

Dramatic and directive dominance have been mentioned as two dimensions along which each place on a team can vary. By changing the point of reference a little, we can discern a third mode of variation.

In general, those who participate in the activity that occurs in a social establishment become members of a team when they co-operate together to present their activity in a particular light. However, in taking on the role of a performer, the individual need not cease to devote some of his effort to non-dramaturgical concerns, that is, to the activity itself of which the performance offers an acceptable dramatization. We may expect, then, that the individuals who perform on a particular team will differ among themselves in the way they apportion their time between mere activity

[34] See David Riesman, in collaboration with Reuel Denny and Nathan Glazer, *The Lonely Crowd* (New Haven: Yale University Press, 1950), "The Avocational Counselors," pp. 363-67.

and mere performance. At one extreme there will be individuals who rarely appear before the audience and are little concerned with appearances. At the other extreme are what are sometimes called "purely ceremonial roles," whose performers will be concerned with the appearance that they make, and concerned with little else. For example, both the president and the research director of a national union may spend time in the main office of the union headquarters appearing suitably dressed and suitably spoken in order to give the union a front of respectability. However one may find that the president also engages in making many important decisions whereas the research director may have little to do except be present in body as part of the president's retinue. Union officials conceive of such purely ceremonial roles as part of "window dressing."[35] The same division of labor can be found in domestic establishments, where something more general than task-qualities must be exhibited. The familiar theme of conspicuous consumption describes how husbands in modern society have the job of acquiring socio-economic status, and wives the job of displaying this acquisition. During somewhat earlier times, the footman provided an even more clear instance of this specialization:

But the chief value of the footman lay in one of these [domestic] services directly. It was the efficiency with which he advertised the extent of his master's wealth. All domestics served that end, since their presence in an establishment demonstrated their master's ability to pay and maintain them in return for little or no productive work. But all were not equally effective in this respect. Those whose uncommon skills and specialized training commanded a high remuneration reflected more credit upon their employers than those who were paid at lower rates; those whose duties brought them obtrusively into

[35] See Harold L. Wilensky, "The Staff 'Expert:' A Study of the Intelligence Function in American Trade Unions" (unpublished Ph.D. dissertation, Department of Sociology, University of Chicago, 1953), chap. iv. In addition to his thesis material, I am indebted to Mr. Wilensky for many suggestions.

view more effectively suggested their master's wealth than those whose work kept them constantly out of sight. Livery servants, from the coachman down to the footboy, were among the most effective of the lot. Their routines endowed them with the highest visibility. Moreover, the livery itself emphasized their remoteness from productive labor. Their effectiveness achieved its maximum in the footman, for his routine exposed him to view more consistently than did that of any of the others. He was, in consequence, one of the most vital parts of his master's display.[36]

It may be remarked that an individual with a purely ceremonial role need not have a dramatically dominant one.

A team, then, may be defined as a set of individuals whose intimate co-operation is required if a given projected definition of the situation is to be maintained. A team is a grouping, but it is a grouping not in relation to a social structure or social organization but rather in relation to an interaction or series of interactions in which the relevant definition of the situation is maintained.

We have seen, and will see further, that if a performance is to be effective it will be likely that the extent and character of the co-operation that makes this possible will be concealed and kept secret. A team, then, has something of the character of a secret society. The audience may appreciate, of course, that all the members of the team are held together by a bond no member of the audience shares. Thus, for example, when customers enter a service establishment, they clearly appreciate that all employees are different from customers by virtue of this official role. However, the individuals who are on the staff of an establishment are not members of a team by virtue of staff status, but only by virtue of the co-operation which they maintain in order to sustain a given definition of the situation. No

[36] J. J. Hecht, *The Domestic Servant Class in Eighteenth-Century England* (London: Routledge, Kegan Paul, 1956), pp. 53-54.

effort may be made in many cases to conceal who is on the staff; but they form a secret society, a team, in so far as a secret is kept as to how they are co-operating together to maintain a particular definition of the situation. Teams may be created by individuals to aid the group they are members of, but in aiding themselves and their group in this dramaturgical way, they are acting as a team, not a group. Thus a team, as used herein, is the kind of secret society whose members may be known by non-members to constitute a society, even an exclusive one, but the society these individuals are known to constitute is not the one they constitute by virtue of acting as a team.

Since we all participate on teams we must all carry within ourselves something of the sweet guilt of conspirators. And since each team is engaged in maintaining the stability of some definitions of the situation, concealing or playing down certain facts in order to do this, we can expect the performer to live out his conspiratorial career in some furtiveness.

Chapter III

REGIONS AND REGION BEHAVIOR

A region may be defined as any place that is bounded to some degree by barriers to perception. Regions vary, of course, in the degree to which they are bounded and according to the media of communication in which the barriers to perception occur. Thus thick glass panels, such as are found in broadcasting control rooms, can isolate a region aurally but not visually, while an office bounded by beaverboard partitions is closed off in the opposite way.

In our Anglo-American society—a relatively indoor one—when a performance is given it is usually given in a highly bounded region, to which boundaries with respect to time are often added. The impression and understanding fostered by the performance will tend to saturate the region and time span, so that any individual located in this space-time manifold will be in a position to observe the performance and be guided by the definition of the situation which the performance fosters.[1]

Often a performance will involve only one focus of visual attention on the part of performer and audience, as, for example, when a political speech is presented in a hall or when a patient is talking to a doctor in the latter's consulting room. However, many performances involve, as constituent

[1] Under the term "behavioral setting," Wright and Barker, in a research methodology report, give a very clear statement of the senses in which expectations regarding conduct come to be associated with particular places. See Herbert F. Wright and Roger G. Barker, *Methods in Psychological Ecology* (Topeka, Kansas: Ray's Printing Service, 1950).

parts, separate knots or clusters of verbal interaction. Thus a cocktail party typically involves several conversational subgroups which constantly shift in size and membership. Similarly, the show maintained on the floor of a shop typically involves several foci of verbal interaction, each composed of attendant-customer pairs.

Given a particular performance as a point of reference, it will sometimes be convenient to use the term "front region" to refer to the place where the performance is given. The fixed sign-equipment in such a place has already been referred to as that part of front called "setting." We will have to see that some aspects of a performance seem to be played not to the audience but to the front region.

The performance of an individual in a front region may be seen as an effort to give the appearance that his activity in the region maintains and embodies certain standards. These standards seem to fall into two broad groupings. One grouping has to do with the way in which the performer treats the audience while engaged in talk with them or in gestural interchanges that are a substitute for talk. These standards are sometimes referred to as matters of politeness. The other group of standards has to do with the way in which the performer comports himself while in visual or aural range of the audience but not necessarily engaged in talk with them. I shall use the term "decorum" to refer to this second group of standards, although some excuses and some qualifications will have to be added to justify the usage.

When we look at the requirements of decorum in a region, requirements of the kind not related to the handling of others in conversation, we tend to divide these again into two subgroupings, moral and instrumental. Moral requirements are ends in themselves and presumably refer to rules regarding non-interference and non-molestation of others, rules regarding sexual propriety, rules regarding respect for sacred places, etc. Instrumental requirements are not ends in themselves and presumably refer to duties such as an employer might demand of his employees—care of property, maintenance of work levels, etc. It may be felt that the

term decorum ought to cover only the moral standards and
that another term should be used to cover the instrumental
ones. When we examine the order that is maintained in a
given region, however, we find that these two kinds of demands, moral and instrumental, seem to affect in much the
same way the individual who must answer to them, and
that both moral and instrumental grounds or rationalizations are put forth as justifications for most standards that
must be maintained. Providing the standard is maintained
by sanctions and by a sanctioner of some kind, it will often
be of small moment to the performer whether the standard
is justified chiefly on instrumental grounds or moral ones,
and whether or not he is asked to incorporate the standard.

It may be noted that the part of personal front I have
called "manner" will be important in regard to politeness
and that the part called appearance" will be important
in regard to decorum. It may also be noted that while
decorous behavior may take the form of showing respect
for the region and setting one finds oneself in, this show of
respect may, of course, be motivated by a desire to impress
the audience favorably, or avoid sanctions, etc. Finally, it
should be noted that the requirements of decorum are
more pervasive ecologically than are the requirements of
politeness. An audience can subject an entire front region
to a continuous inspection as regards decorum, but while
the audience is so engaged, none or only a few of the performers may be obliged to talk to the audience and hence
to demonstrate politeness. Performers can stop giving expressions but cannot stop giving them off.

In the study of social establishments it is important to
describe the prevailing standards of decorum; it is difficult
to do so because informants and students tend to take many
of these standards for granted, not realizing they have done
so until an accident, or crisis, or peculiar circumstance
occurs. It is known, for example, that different business
offices have different standards as regards informal chatter
among clerks, but it is only when we happen to study an
office that has a sizable number of foreign refugee employees that we suddenly appreciate that permission to

engage in informal talk may not constitute permission to engage in informal talk in a foreign language.[2]

We are accustomed to assuming that the rules of decorum that prevail in sacred establishments, such as churches, will be much different from the ones that prevail in everyday places of work. We ought not to assume from this that the standards in sacred places are more numerous and more strict than those we find in work establishments. While in church, a woman may be permitted to sit, daydream, and even doze. However, as a saleswoman on the floor of a dress shop, she may be required to stand, keep alert, refrain from chewing gum, keep a fixed smile on her face even when not talking to anyone, and wear clothes she can ill afford.

One form of decorum that has been studied in social establishments is what is called "make-work." It is understood in many establishments that not only will workers be required to produce a certain amount after a certain length of time but also that they will be ready, when called upon, to give the impression that they are working hard at the moment. Of a shipyard we learn the following:

> It was amusing to watch the sudden transformation whenever word got round that the foreman was on the hull or in the shop or that a front-office superintendent was coming by. Quartermen and leadermen would rush to their groups of workers and stir them to obvious activity. "Don't let him catch you sitting down," was the universal admonition, and where no work existed a pipe was busily bent and threaded, or a bolt which was already firmly in place was subjected to further and unnecessary tightening. This was the formal tribute invariably attending a visitation by the boss, and its conventions were as familiar to both sides as those surrounding a five-star general's inspection. To have neglected any detail of the false and empty show would have been interpreted as a mark of singular disrespect.[3]

[2] See Gross, *op. cit.*, p. 186.

[3] Katherine Archibald, *Wartime Shipyard* (Berkeley and Los Angeles: University of California Press, 1947), p. 159.

Similarly, of a hospital ward we learn:

> The observer was told very explicitly by other attendants
> on his first day of work on the wards not to "get caught"
> striking a patient, to appear busy when the supervisor
> makes her rounds, and not to speak to her unless first
> spoken to. It was noted that some attendants watch for
> her approach and warn the other attendants so that no
> one will get caught doing undesirable acts. Some attend-
> ants will save work for when the supervisor is present so
> they will be busy and will not be given additional tasks.
> In most attendants the change is not so obvious, depend-
> ing largely on the individual attendant, the supervisor,
> and the ward situation. However, with nearly all attend-
> ants there is some change in behavior when an official,
> such as a supervisor, is present. There is no open flouting
> of the rules and regulations, . . .[4]

From a consideration of make-work it is only a step to
consideration of other standards of work activity for which
appearances must be maintained, such as pace, personal
interest economy, accuracy, etc.[5] And from a consideration
of work standards in general it is only a step to consideration of other major aspects of decorum, instrumental and
moral, in work places, such as: mode of dress; permissible
sound levels, proscribed diversions, indulgences, and affective expressions.

Make-work, along with other aspects of decorum in work
places, is usually seen as the particular burden of those of
low estate. A dramaturgical approach, however, requires
us to consider together with make-work the problem of
staging its opposite, make-no-work. Thus, in a memoir
written about life in the early nineteenth century among
the barely genteel, we learn that:

> People were extremely punctilious on the subject of
> calls—one remembers the call in the *Mill on the Floss.*

[4] Willoughby, *op. cit.,* p. 43.

[5] An analysis of some major work standards may be found in
Gross, *op. cit.,* from which the above examples of such standards
are taken.

The call was due at regular intervals, so that even the
day should almost be known in which it was paid or
returned. It was a ceremonial which contained a great
deal of ceremony and make-believe. No one, for instance,
was to be surprised in doing any kind of work. There was
a fiction in genteel families that the ladies of the house
never did anything serious or serviceable after dinner;
the afternoon was supposed to be devoted either to walking, or to making calls, or to elegant trifling at home.
Therefore if the girls were at the moment engaged upon
any useful work—they crammed it under the sofa, and
pretended to be reading a book, or painting, or knitting,
or to be engaged in easy and fashionable conversation.
Why they went through this elaborate pretense I have
not the least idea, because everybody knew that every
girl in the place was always making, mending, cutting
out, basting, gusseting, trimming, turning and contriving.
How do you suppose that the solicitor's daughters made
so brave a show on Sunday if they were not clever enough
to make up things for themselves? Everybody, of course,
knew it, and why the girls would not own up at once
one cannot now understand. Perhaps it was a sort of
suspicion, or a faint hope, or a wild dream, that a reputation for ladylike uselessness might enable them to cross
the line at the county Ball, and mingle with the Country
people.[6]

It should be plain that while persons who are obliged to
make-work and make-no-work are likely to be on the opposite sides of the track, they must yet adapt themselves to
the same side of the footlights.

It was suggested earlier that when one's activity occurs
in the presence of other persons, some aspects of the activity
are expressively accentuated and other aspects, which
might discredit the fostered impression, are suppressed. It
is clear that accentuated facts make their appearance in
what I have called a front region; it should be just as clear

6 Sir Walter Besant, "Fifty Years Ago," *The Graphic Jubilee
Number,* 1887, quoted in James Laver, *Victorian Vista* (Boston:
Houghton Mifflin, 1955), p. 147.

that there may be another region—a "back region" or "back-stage"—where the suppressed facts make an appearance.

A back region or backstage may be defined as a place, relative to a given performance, where the impression fostered by the performance is knowingly contradicted as a matter of course. There are, of course, many characteristic functions of such places. It is here that the capacity of a performance to express something beyond itself may be painstakingly fabricated; it is here that illusions and impressions are openly constructed. Here stage props and items of personal front can be stored in a kind of compact collapsing of whole repertoires of actions and characters.[7] Here grades of ceremonial equipment, such as different types of liquor or clothes, can be hidden so that the audience will not be able to see the treatment accorded them in comparison with the treatment that could have been accorded them. Here devices such as the telephone are sequestered so that they can be used "privately." Here costumes and other parts of personal front may be adjusted and scrutinized for flaws. Here the team can run through its performance, checking for offending expressions when no audience is present to be affronted by them; here poor members of the team, who are expressively inept, can be schooled or dropped from the performance. Here the performer can relax; he can drop his front, forgo speaking his lines, and step out of character. Simone de Beauvoir provides a rather vivid picture of this backstage activity in describing situations from which the male audience is absent.

What gives value to such relations among women is the truthfulness they imply. Confronting man woman is

---

[7] As Métraux (*op. cit.*, p. 24) suggests, even the practice of voodoo cults will require such facilities:

Every case of possession has its theatrical side, as shown in the matter of disguises. The rooms of the sanctuary are not unlike the wings of a theater where the possessed find the necessary accessories. Unlike the hysteric, who reveals his anguish and his desires through symptoms—a personal means of expression—the ritual of possession must conform to the classic image of a mythical personage.

always play-acting; she lies when she makes believe that she accepts her status as the inessential other, she lies when she presents to him an imaginary personage through mimicry, costumery, studied phrases. These histrionics require a constant tension: when with her husband, or with her lover, every woman is more or less conscious of the thought: "I am not being myself:" the male world is harsh, sharp edged, its voices are too resounding, the lights are too crude, the contacts rough. With other women, a woman is behind the scenes; she is polishing her equipment, but not in battle; she is getting her costume together, preparing her make-up, laying out her tactics; she is lingering in dressing-gown and slippers in the wings before making her entrance on the stage; she likes this warm, easy, relaxed atmosphere. . . .

For some women this warm and frivolous intimacy is dearer than the serious pomp of relations with men.[8]

Very commonly the back region of a performance is located at one end of the place where the performance is presented, being cut off from it by a partition and guarded passageway. By having the front and back regions adjacent in this way, a performer out in front can receive backstage assistance while the performance is in progress and can interrupt his performance momentarily for brief periods of relaxation. In general, of course, the back region will be the place where the performer can reliably expect that no member of the audience will intrude.

Since the vital secrets of a show are visible backstage and since performers behave out of character while there, it is natural to expect that the passage from the front region to the back region will be kept closed to members of the audience or that the entire back region will be kept hidden from them. This is a widely practiced technique of impression management, and requires further discussion.

[8] De Beauvoir, *op. cit.*, p. 543.

Obviously, control of backstage plays a significant role in the process of "work control" whereby individuals attempt to buffer themselves from the deterministic demands that surround them. If a factory worker is to succeed in giving the appearance of working hard all day, then he must have a safe place to hide the jig that enables him to turn out a day's work with less than a full day's effort.[9] If the bereaved are to be given the illusion that the dead one is really in a deep and tranquil sleep, then the undertaker must be able to keep the bereaved from the workroom where the corpses are drained, stuffed, and painted in preparation for their final performance.[10] If a mental hospital staff is to give a good impression of the hospital to those who come to visit their committed kinfolk, then it will be important to be able to bar visitors from the wards, especially the chronic wards, restricting the outsiders to special visiting rooms where it will be practicable to have relatively nice furnishings and to ensure that all patients present are well dressed, well washed, well handled and relatively well behaved. So, too, in many service trades, the customer is asked to leave the thing that needs service and to go away so that the tradesman can work in private. When the customer returns for his automobile—or watch, or trousers, or radio—it is presented to him in good working order, an order that incidentally conceals the amount and kind of work that had to be done, the number of mistakes that were first made before getting it fixed, and other details the client would have to

[9] See Orvis Collins, Melville Dalton, and Donald Roy, "Restriction of Output and Social Cleavage in Industry," *Applied Anthropology* (now *Human Organization*), IV, pp. 1–14, esp. p. 9.

[10] Mr. Habenstein has suggested in seminar that in some states the undertaker has a legal right to prevent relatives of the deceased from entering the workroom where the corpse is in preparation. Presumably the sight of what has to be done to the dead to make them look attractive would be too great a shock for non-professionals and especially for kinfolk of the deceased. Mr. Habenstein also suggests that kinfolk may want to be kept from the undertaker's workroom because of their own fear of their own morbid curiosity.

know before being able to judge the reasonableness of the fee that is asked of him.

Service personnel so commonly take for granted the right to keep the audience away from the back region that attention is drawn more to cases where this common strategy cannot be applied than to cases where it can. For example, the American filling station manager has numerous troubles in this regard.[11] If a repair is needed, customers often refuse to leave their automobile overnight or all day, in trust of the establishment, as they would do had they taken their automobile to a garage. Further, when the mechanic makes repairs and adjustments, customers often feel they have the right to watch him as he does his work. If an illusionary service is to be rendered and charged for, it must, therefore, be rendered before the very person who is to be taken in by it. Customers, in fact, not only disregard the right of the station personnel to their own back region but often also define the whole station as a kind of open city for males, a place where an individual runs the risk of getting his clothes dirty and therefore has the right to demand full backstage privileges. Male motorists will saunter in, tip back their hats, spit, swear, and ask for free service or free travel advice. They will barge in to make familiar use of the toilet, the station's tools, the office telephone, or to search in the stockroom for their own supplies.[12] In order

[11] The statements which follow are taken from a study by Social Research, Inc., of two hundred small-business managers.

[12] At a sports car garage the following scene was reported to me by the manager regarding a customer who went into the storeroom himself to obtain a gasket, presenting it to the manager from behind the storeroom counter:

Customer: "How much?"
Manager: "Sir, where did you get in and what would happen if you went behind the counter in a bank and got a roll of nickels and brought them to the teller?"
Customer: "But this ain't a bank."
Manager: "Well, those are my nickels. Now, what did you want, sir?"
Customer: "If that's the way you feel about it, OK. That's your privilege. I want a gasket for a '51 Anglia."

to avoid traffic lights, motorists will cut right across the station driveway, oblivious to the manager's proprietary rights.

Shetland Hotel provides another example of the problems workers face when they have insufficient control of their backstage. Within the hotel kitchen, where the guests' food was prepared and where the staff ate and spent their day, crofters' culture tended to prevail. It will be useful to suggest some of the details of this culture here.

In the kitchen, crofter employer-employee relations prevailed. Reciprocal first-naming was employed, although the scullery boy was fourteen and the male owner over thirty. The owning couple and employees ate together, participating with relative equality in mealtime small talk and gossip. When the owners held informal kitchen parties for friends and extended kin, the hotel workers participated. This pattern of intimacy and equality between management and employees was inconsistent with the appearance both elements of the staff gave when guests were present, as it was inconsistent with the guests' notions of the social distance which ought to obtain between the official with whom they corresponded when arranging for their stay, and the porters and maids who carried luggage upstairs, polished the guests' shoes each night, and emptied their chamber pots.

Similarly, in the hotel kitchen, island eating patterns were employed. Meat, when available, tended to be boiled. Fish, often eaten, tended to be boiled or salted. Potatoes, an inevitable item in the day's one big meal, were almost always boiled in their jackets and eaten in the island manner: each eater selects a potato by hand from the central bowl, then pierces it with his fork and skins it with his knife, keeping the peels in a neat pile alongside his place, to be scooped in with his knife after the meal is finished. Oilcloth was used as a cover for the table. Almost every meal was

---

Manager: "That's for a '54."
While the manager's anecdote may not be a faithful reproduction of the words and actions that were actually interchanged, it does tell us something faithful about his situation and his feelings in it.

preceded by a bowl of soup, and soup bowls, instead of plates, tended to be used for the courses that came after. (Since most of the food was boiled anyway, this was a practical usage.) Forks and knives were sometimes grasped fist-like, and tea was served in cups without saucers. While the island diet in many ways seemed to be adequate, and while island table manners could be executed with great delicacy and circumspection—and often were—the whole eating complex was well understood by islanders to be not only different from the British middle-class pattern, but somehow a violation of it. Perhaps this difference in pattern was most evident on occasions when food given to guests was also eaten in the kitchen. (This was not uncommon and was not more common because the staff often preferred island food to what the guests were given.) At such times the kitchen portion of the food was prepared and served in the island manner, with little stress on individual pieces and cuts, and more stress on a common source of servings. Often the remains of a joint of meat or the broken remains of a batch of tarts would be served—the same food as appeared in the guest dining hall but in a slightly different condition, yet one not offensive by island kitchen standards. And if a pudding made from stale bread and cake did not pass the test of what was good enough for guests, it was eaten in the kitchen.

Crofter clothing and postural patterns also tended to appear in the hotel kitchen. Thus, the manager would sometimes follow local custom and leave his cap on; the scullery boys would use the coal bucket as a target for the well-aimed expulsion of mucus; and the women on the staff would rest sitting with their legs up in unladylike positions.

In addition to these differences due to culture, there were other sources of discrepancy between kitchen ways and parlor ways in the hotel, for some of the standards of hotel service that were shown or implied in the guests' regions were not fully adhered to in the kitchen. In the scullery wing of the kitchen region, mold would sometimes form on soup yet to be used. Over the kitchen stove, wet socks would be dried on the steaming kettle—a standard practice on the island. Tea, when guests had asked for it newly infused, would be brewed in a pot encrusted at the bottom with tea leaves that were weeks old. Fresh herrings would be cleaned by splitting them and then scraping out the innards with newspaper. Pats of butter, softened, misshapen, and partly used during their sojourn in the dining hall, would be rerolled to look fresh, and sent out to do duty again. Rich puddings, too good for kitchen consumption, would be sampled aggressively by the finger-full before distribution to the guests. During the mealtime rush hour, once-used drinking glasses would sometimes be merely emptied and wiped instead of being rewashed, thus allowing them to be put back into circulation quickly.[13]

Given, then, the various ways in which activity in the kitchen contradicted the impression fostered in the guests' region of the hotel, one can appreciate why the doors leading from the kitchen to the other parts of the hotel were a constant sore spot in the organization of work. The maids wanted to keep the doors open to make it easier to carry food trays back and forth, to gather information about whether guests were ready or not for the service which was to be performed for them, and to retain as much contact as possible with the persons they had come to work to learn about. Since the maids played a servant role before the guests, they felt they did not have too much to lose by being observed in their own milieu by guests who glanced into the kitchen when passing the open doors. The managers, on the other hand, wanted to keep the door closed so that the middle-class role imputed to them by the guests would not be discredited by a disclosure of their kitchen habits. Hardly a day passed when these doors were not angrily banged shut and angrily pushed open. A kick-door

[13] These illustrations of the discrepancy between the reality and appearances of standards should not be considered extreme. Close observation of the backstage of any middle-class home in Western cities would be likely to disclose discrepancies between reality and appearance that were equally as great. And wherever there is some degree of commercialization, discrepancies no doubt are often greater.

of the kind modern restaurants use would have provided a partial solution for this staging problem. A small glass window in the doors that could act as a peephole—a stage device used by many small places of business—would also have been helpful.

Another interesting example of backstage difficulties is found in radio and television broadcasting work. In these situations, back region tends to be defined as all places where the camera is not focused at the moment or all places out of range of "live" microphones. Thus an announcer may hold the sponsor's product up at arm's length in front of the camera while he holds his nose with his other hand, his face being out of the picture, as a way of joking with his teammates. Professionals, of course, tell many exemplary tales of how persons who thought they were backstage were in fact on the air and how this backstage conduct discredited the definition of the situation being maintained on the air. For technical reasons, then, the walls that broadcasters have to hide behind can be very treacherous, tending to fall at the flick of a switch or a turn of the camera. Broadcasting artists must live with this staging contingency.

A somewhat related instance of special backstage difficulty is to be found in the architecture of some current housing projects. For walls that are really thin partitions can separate domestic establishments visually, but allow the backstage and frontstage activity of one unit to sound through into the neighboring establishment. Thus, British researchers employ the term "party wall," and describe its consequences in this way:

Residents are aware of many "vicinal" noises, extending from the usual clamor of birthday celebrations to the sound of the daily routine. Informants mention the wireless, the baby crying at night, coughing, shoes dropped at bedtime, children running up and down the stairs or on the bedroom floors, strumming at the piano, and laughing or loud talk. In the connubial bedroom, the intimations from the neighbor may be shocking: "You can even hear them use the pot; that's how bad it is. It's terrible"; or disturbing: "I heard them having a row in bed. One wanted to read, and the other one wanted to go to sleep. It's embarrassing to hear noises in bed, so I turned my bed the other way round" . . . "I like to read in bed and I'm light of hearing, so it disturbs me to hear them talk"; or a little inhibiting: "You sometimes hear them say rather private things, as, for example, a man telling his wife that her feet are cold. It makes you feel that *you* must say private things in a whisper"; and, "It does make you feel a bit restrained, as if you ought to walk on tiptoe into our bedroom at night.[14]

Here neighbors who may know each other very little find themselves in the embarrassing position of knowing that each knows about the other too well.

A final example of backstage difficulties may be cited from the contingencies of being an exalted person. Persons may become so sacred that the only fitting appearance they can make is in the center of a retinue and ceremony; it may be thought improper for them to appear before others in any other context, as such informal appearances may be thought to discredit the magical attributes imputed to them. Therefore members of the audience must be prohibited from all the places the exalted one is likely to relax in, and if the place for relaxation is large, as in the case of the Chinese emperor in the nineteenth century, or if there is uncertainty about where the exalted one will be, problems of trespass become considerable. Thus Queen Victoria enforced the rule that anyone seeing her approach when she was driving in her pony-cart on the palace grounds should turn his head or walk in another direction; therefore great statesmen sometimes were required to sacrifice their own dignity and jump behind the shrubbery when the queen unexpectedly approached.[15]

[14] Leo Kuper, "Blueprint for Living Together," in Leo Kuper and others, *Living in Towns* (London: The Cresset Press, 1953), pp. 14–15.

[15] Ponsonby, *op. cit.*, p. 32.

While some of these examples of back region difficulty are extreme, it would seem that no social establishment can be studied where some problems associated with backstage control do not occur.

Work and recreation regions represent two areas for backstage control. Another area is suggested by the very widespread tendency in our society to give performers control over the place in which they attend to what are called biological needs. In our society, defecation involves an individual in activity which is defined as inconsistent with the cleanliness and purity standards expressed in many of our performances. Such activity also causes the individual to disarrange his clothing and to "go out of play," that is, to drop from his face the expressive mask that he employs in face-to-face interaction. At the same time it becomes difficult for him to reassemble his personal front should the need to enter into interaction suddenly occur. Perhaps that is a reason why toilet doors in our society have locks on them. When asleep in bed the individual is also immobilized, expressively speaking, and may not be able to bring himself into an appropriate position for interaction or bring a sociable expression to his face until some moments after being wakened, thus providing one explanation of the tendency to remove the bedroom from the active part of the house. The utility of such seclusion is reinforced by the fact that sexual activity is likely to occur in bedrooms, a form of interaction which also renders its performers incapable of immediately entering into another interaction.

One of the most interesting times to observe impression management is the moment when a performer leaves the back region and enters the place where the audience is to be found, or when he returns therefrom, for at these moments one can detect a wonderful putting on and taking off of character. Orwell, speaking of waiters, and speaking from the backstage point of view of dishwashers, provides us with an example:

It is an instructive sight to see a waiter going into a hotel dining-room. As he passes the door a sudden change comes over him. The set of his shoulders alters; all the dirt and hurry and irritation have dropped off in an instant. He glides over the carpet, with a solemn priest-like air. I remember our assistant *maître d'hôtel,* a fiery Italian, pausing at the dining-room door to address his apprentice who had broken a bottle of wine. Shaking his fist above his head he yelled (luckily the door was more or less soundproof).

"Tu me fais— Do you call yourself a waiter, you young bastard? You a waiter! You're not fit to scrub floors in the brothel your mother came from. *Maquereau!"*

Words failing him, he turned to the door; and as he opened it he delivered a final insult in the same manner as Squire Western in *Tom Jones.*

Then he entered the dining-room and sailed across it dish in hand, graceful as a swan. Ten seconds later he was bowing reverently to a customer. And you could not help thinking, as you saw him bow and smile, with that benign smile of the trained waiter, that the customer was put to shame by having such an aristocrat to serve him.[16]

Another illustration is provided by another English downwardly-participating observer:

The said maid—her name was Addie, I discovered—and the two waitresses were behaving like people acting in a play. They would sweep into the kitchen as if coming off stage into the wings, with trays held high and a tense expression of hauteur still on their faces; relax for a moment in the frenzy of getting the new dishes loaded, and glide off again with faces prepared to make their next entrance. The cook and I were left like stagehands among the debris, as if having seen a glimpse of another world, we almost listened for the applause of the unseen audience.[17]

[16] George Orwell, *Down and Out in Paris and London* (London: Secker and Warburg, 1951), pp. 68–69.
[17] Monica Dickens, *One Pair of Hands* (London: Michael Joseph, Mermaid Books, 1952), p. 13.

The decline of domestic service has forced quick changes of the kind mentioned by Orwell upon the middle-class housewife. In serving a dinner for friends she must manage the kitchen dirty work in such a way as to enable her to switch back and forth between the roles of domestic and hostess, altering her activity, her manner, and her temper, as she passes in and out of the dining room. Etiquette books provide helpful directions for facilitating such changes, suggesting that if the hostess must withdraw to a back region for an extended period of time, as when making up the beds, then it will protect appearances if the host takes the guests for a little walk in the garden.

The line dividing front and back regions is illustrated everywhere in our society. As suggested, the bathroom and bedroom, in all but lower-class homes, are places from which the downstairs audience can be excluded. Bodies that are cleansed, clothed, and made up in these rooms can be presented to friends in others. In the kitchen, of course, there is done to food what in the bathroom and bedroom is done to the human body. It is, in fact, the presence of these staging devices that distinguishes middle-class living from lower-class living. But in all classes in our society there is a tendency to make a division between the front and back parts of residential exteriors. The front tends to be relatively well decorated, well repaired, and tidy; the rear tends to be relatively unprepossessing. Correspondingly, social adults enter through the front, and often the socially incomplete—domestics, delivery men, and children—enter through the rear.

While we are familiar with the stage arrangements in and around a dwelling place, we tend to be less aware of other stage arrangements. In American residential neighborhoods, boys of eight to fourteen and other profane persons appreciate that entrances to back lanes and alleys lead somewhere and are to be used; they see these openings in a vivid way that will be lost to them when they become older. Similarly, janitors and scrubwomen have a clear perception of the small doors that lead to the back regions of business buildings and are intimately familiar with the profane transportation system for secretly transporting dirty cleaning equipment, large stage props, and themselves. There is a similar arrangement in stores, where places "behind the counter" and the storeroom serve as back regions.

Given the values of a particular society, it is apparent that the backstage character of certain places is built into them in a material way, and that relative to adjacent areas these places are inescapably back regions. In our society the decorator's art often does this for us, apportioning dark colors and open brickwork to the service parts of buildings and white plaster to the front regions. Pieces of fixed equipment add permanency to this division. Employers complete the harmony by hiring persons with undesirable visual attributes for back region work, placing persons who "make a good impression" in the front regions. Reserves of unimpressive-looking labor can be used not only for activity that must be concealed from the audience, but also for activity that can be concealed but need not. As Everett Hughes has suggested,[18] Negro employees can more easily than otherwise be given staff status in American factories if, as in the case of chemists, they can be sequestered from the main areas of factory operation. (All of this involves a kind of ecological sorting that is well known but little studied.) And often it is expected that those who work backstage will achieve technical standards while those who work in the front region will achieve expressive ones.

The decorations and permanent fixtures in a place where a particular performance is usually given, as well as the performers and performance usually found there, tend to fix a kind of spell over it; even when the customary performance is not being given in it, the place tends to retain some of its front region character. Thus a cathedral and a schoolroom retain something of their tone even when only repairmen are present, and while these men may not behave reverently while doing their work, their irreverence tends to be of a structured kind, specifically oriented to what in some sense they ought to be feeling but are not. So, too, a given

[18] In seminar, University of Chicago.

place may become so identified as a hide-out where certain
standards need not be maintained that it becomes fixed
with an identity as a back region. Hunting lodges and
locker rooms in athletic social establishments may serve
as illustrations. Summer resorts, too, seem to fix permissive-
ness regarding front, allowing otherwise conventional people to appear in public streets in costumes they would not
ordinarily wear in the presence of strangers. So, too, criminal hangouts and even criminal neighborhoods are to be
found, where the act of being "legit" need not be maintained. An interesting example of this is said to have existed
in Paris:

> In the seventeenth century, therefore, in order to be-
> come a thorough Argotier, it was necessary not only to
> solicit alms like any mere beggar, but also to possess the
> dexterity of the cut-purse and the thief. These arts were
> to be learned in the places which served as the habitual
> rendezvous of the very dregs of society, and which were
> generally known as the *Cours des Miracles*. These houses,
> or rather resorts, had been so called, if we are to believe
> a writer of the early part of the seventeenth century,
> "Because rogues . . . and others, who have all day been
> cripples, maimed, dropsical, and beset with every sort
> of bodily ailment, come home at night, carrying under
> their arms a sirloin of beef, a joint of veal, or a leg of
> mutton, not forgetting to hang a bottle of wine to their
> belts, and, on entering the court, they throw aside their
> crutches, resume their healthy and lusty appearance,
> and, in imitation of the ancient Bacchanalian revelries,
> dance all kinds of dances with their trophies in their
> hands, whilst the host is preparing their suppers. Can
> there be a greater *miracle* than is to be seen in this court,
> where the maimed walk upright?"[19]

In back regions such as these, the very fact that an important effect is not striven for tends to set the tone for

[19] Paul LaCroix, *Manners, Custom, and Dress during the Middle Ages and during the Renaissance Period* (London: Chapman
and Hall, 1876), p. 471.

interaction, leading those who find themselves there to act as if they were on familiar terms with one another in all matters.

However, while there is a tendency for a region to become identified as the front region or back region of a performance with which it is regularly associated, still there are many regions which function at one time and in one sense as a front region and at another time and in another sense as a back region. Thus the private office of an executive is certainly the front region where his status in the organization is intensively expressed by means of the quality of his office furnishings. And yet it is here that he can take his jacket off, loosen his tie, keep a bottle of liquor handy, and act in a chummy and even boisterous way with fellow executives of his own rank.[20] So, too, a business organization that employs a presentable fancy bond letterhead paper for correspondence with persons outside the firm may follow this advice:

> Paper for interoffice correspondence is bound by economics more than by etiquette. Cheap paper, colored paper, mimeographed or printed paper—anything goes when "it's all in the family."[21]

And yet the same source of advice will suggest some limits to this backstage definition of the situation:

> Personalized memo paper, usually intended for scribbled notes within the office, can also be practical and uninhibited. One caution: juniors should not order such

[20] The fact that a small private office can be transformed into a back region by the manageable method of being the only one in it provides one reason why stenographers sometimes prefer to work in a private office as opposed to a large office floor. On a large open floor someone is always likely to be present before whom an impression of industriousness must be maintained; in a small office all pretense of work and decorous behavior can be dropped when the boss is out. See Richard Rencke, "The Status Characteristics of Jobs in a Factory" (unpublished Master's thesis, Department of Sociology, University of Chicago, 1953), p. 53.

[21] *Esquire Etiquette*, p. 65.

memo pads, however convenient, on their own. Like a rug on the floor and a name on the door, the personalized memo pad is a status symbol in some offices.[22]

Similarly, of a Sunday morning, a whole household can use the wall around its domestic establishment to conceal a relaxing slovenliness in dress and civil endeavor, extending to all rooms the informality that is usually restricted to the kitchen and bedrooms. So, too, in American middle-class neighborhoods, on afternoons the line between the children's playground and home may be defined as backstage by mothers, who pass along it wearing jeans, loafers and a minimum of make-up, a cigarette dangling from their lips as they push their baby carriages and openly talk shop with their colleagues. So also, in working-class *quartiers* in Paris in the early morning, women feel they have a right to extend the backstage to their circle of neighboring shops, and they patter down for milk and fresh bread, wearing bedroom slippers, bathrobe, hair net, and no make-up. One finds in the chief American cities that models, wearing the dress that they will be photographed in, may carefully hurry through the most formal streets, partly oblivious to those around them; hatbox in hand, net protecting their coiffure, they may carry themselves not to create an effect but to avoid disarranging themselves while in transit to the building-backdrop before which their real, photographed performance will begin. And, of course, a region that is thoroughly established as a front region for the regular performance of a particular routine often functions as a back region before and after each performance, for at these times the permanent fixtures may undergo repair, restoration, and rearrangement, or the performers may hold dress rehearsals. To see this we need only glance into a restaurant, or store, or home, a few minutes before these establishments are opened to us for the day. In general, then, it must be kept in mind that in speaking of front and back regions we speak from the reference point of a particular performance, and we speak of the function that

[22] *Ibid.*, p. 65.

the place happens to serve at that time for the given performance.

It was suggested that persons who co-operate in staging the same team-performance tend to be in a familiar relation to one another. This familiarity tends to be expressed only when the audience is not present, for it conveys an impression of self and teammate which is ordinarily inconsistent with the impression of self and teammate one wants to sustain before the audience. Since back regions are typically out of bounds to members of the audience, it is here that we may expect reciprocal familiarity to determine the tone of social intercourse. Similarly, it is in the front region that we may expect a tone of formality to prevail.

Throughout Western society there tends to be one informal or backstage language of behavior, and another language of behavior for occasions when a performance is being presented. The backstage language consists of reciprocal first-naming, co-operative decision-making, profanity, open sexual remarks, elaborate griping, smoking, rough informal dress, "sloppy" sitting and standing posture, use of dialect or sub-standard speech, mumbling and shouting, playful aggressivity and "kidding," inconsiderateness for the other in minor but potentially symbolic acts, minor physical self-involvements such as humming, whistling, chewing, nibbling, belching, and flatulence. The frontstage behavior language can be taken as the absence (and in some sense the opposite) of this. In general, then, backstage conduct is one which allows minor acts which might easily be taken as symbolic of intimacy and disrespect for others present and for the region, while front region conduct is one which disallows such potentially offensive behavior. It may be noted here that backstage behavior has what psychologists might call a "regressive" character. The question, of course, is whether a backstage gives individuals an opportunity to regress or whether regression, in the clinical sense, is backstage conduct invoked on inappropriate occasions for motives that are not socially approved.

By invoking a backstage style, individuals can transform

any region into a backstage. Thus we find that in many social establishments the performers will appropriate a section of the front region and by acting there in a familiar fashion symbolically cut it off from the rest of the region. For instance, in some restaurants in America, especially those called "one-arm joints," the staff will hold court in the booth farthest from the door or closest to the kitchen, and there conduct themselves, at least in some respects, as if they were backstage. Similarly, on uncrowded evening airline flights, after their initial duties have been performed, stewardesses may settle down in the rearmost seat, change from regulation pumps into loafers, light up a cigarette, and there create a muted circle of non-service relaxation, even at times extending this to include the one or two closest passengers.

More important, one ought not to expect that concrete situations will provide pure examples of informal conduct or formal conduct, although there is usually a tendency to move the definition of the situation in one of these two directions. We will not find these pure cases because teammates in regard to one show will be to some degree performers and audience for another show, and performers and audience for one show will to some extent, however slight, be teammates with respect to another show. Thus in a concrete situation we may expect a predominance of one style or the other, with some feelings of guilt or doubt concerning the actual combination or balance that is achieved between the two styles.

I would like to emphasize the fact that activity in a concrete situation is always a compromise between the formal and informal styles. Three common limitations on backstage informality are therefore cited. First, when the audience is not present, each member of the team is likely to want to sustain the impression that he can be trusted with the secrets of the team and that he is not likely to play his part badly when the audience is present. While each team member will want the audience to think of him as a worthy character, he is likely to want his teammates to think of him as a loyal, well-disciplined performer. Secondly, there are often moments backstage when the performers will have to sustain one another's morale and maintain the impression that the show that is about to be presented will go over well or that the show that has just been presented did not really go over so badly. Thirdly, if the team contains representatives of fundamental social divisions, such as different age-grades, different ethnic groups, etc., then some discretionary limits will prevail on freedom of backstage activity. Here, no doubt, the most important division is the sexual one, for there seems to be no society in which members of the two sexes, however closely related, do not sustain some appearances before each other. In America, for instance, we learn the following about West Coast shipyards:

> In their ordinary relationships with women workers most of the men were courteous and even gallant. As the women infiltrated the hulls and the remoter shacks of the yard, the men amiably removed their galleries of nudes and pornography from the walls and retired them to the gloom of the tool box. In deference to the presence of "ladies," manners were improved, faces were shaved more often, and language was toned down. The taboo against improprieties of speech within earshot of women was so extreme as to be amusing, particularly since the women themselves frequently gave audible proof that the forbidden words were neither unfamiliar nor disturbing to them. Yet I have often seen men who wanted to use strong language, and with good excuse for it, flush with sudden embarrassment and drop their voices to a mutter on becoming conscious of a feminine audience. In the lunchtime companionship of men and women workers and in the casual chat at any leisure moment, in all that pertained to familiar social contacts, even amid the unfamiliar surroundings of the shipyards, the men preserved almost intact the pattern of behavior which they practiced at home: the respect for the decent wife and the good mother, the circumspect friendliness with the sister,

and even the protective affection for the inexperienced daughter of the family.[23]

Chesterfield makes a similar suggestion about another society:

> In mixed companies with your equals (for in mixed companies all people are to a certain degree equal) greater ease and liberty are allowed; but they too have their bounds within *bienseance*. There is a social respect necessary; you may start your own subject of conversation with modesty, taking great care, however, *de ne jamais parler de cordes dans la maison d'un pendu*. Your words, gestures, and attitudes, have a greater degree of latitude, though by no means an unbounded one. You may have your hands in your pockets, take snuff, sit, stand, or occasionally walk, as you like; but I believe you would not think it very *bienseant* to whistle, put your hat on, loosen your garters or your buckles, lie down upon a couch, or go to bed and welter in an easy chair. These are negligences and freedoms which one can only take when quite alone; they are injurious to superiors, shocking and offensive to equals, brutal and insulting to inferiors.[24]

Kinsey's data on the extent of the nudity taboo between husband and wife, especially in the older generation of the American working class, documents the same point.[25] Modesty, of course, is not the sole force operating here. Thus, two female informants in Shetland Isle claimed they would always wear a nightgown to bed after their impending marriages—not because of mere modesty but because their figures departed too far from what they considered to be the modern urban ideal. They could point to one or two of their girl friends whom they claimed had no need for

[23] Archibald, *op. cit.*, pp. 16–17.

[24] *Letters of Lord Chesterfield to His Son* (Everyman's ed.; New York: Dutton, 1929), p. 239.

[25] Alfred C. Kinsey, Wardell B. Pomeroy, and Clyde E. Martin, *Sexual Behavior in the Human Male* (Philadelphia: Saunders, 1948), p. 366–67.

this delicacy; presumably a sudden loss of weight might diminish their own modesty too.

In saying that performers act in a relatively informal, familiar, relaxed way while backstage and are on their guard when giving a performance, it should not be assumed that the pleasant interpersonal things of life—courtesy, warmth, generosity, and pleasure in the company of others —are always reserved for those backstage and that suspiciousness, snobbishness, and a show of authority are reserved for front region activity. Often it seems that whatever enthusiasm and lively interest we have at our disposal we reserve for those before whom we are putting on a show and that the surest sign of backstage solidarity is to feel that it is safe to lapse into an asociable mood of sullen, silent irritability.

It is interesting to note that while each team will be in a position to appreciate the unsavory "unperformed" aspects of its own backstage behavior, it is not likely to be in a position to come to a similar conclusion about the teams with which it interacts. When pupils leave the schoolroom and go outside for a recess of familiarity and misconduct, they often fail to appreciate that their teachers have retired to a "common room" to swear and smoke in a similar recess of backstage behavior. We know, of course, that a team with only one member can take a very dark view of itself and that not a few psychotherapists find employment in alleviating this guilt, making their living by telling individuals the facts of other people's lives. Behind these realizations about oneself and illusions about others is one of the important dynamics and disappointments of social mobility, be it mobility upward, downward, or sideways. In attempting to escape from a two-faced world of front region and back region behavior, individuals may feel that in the new position they are attempting to acquire they will be the character projected by individuals in that position and not at the same time a performer. When they arrive, of course, they find their new situation has unanticipated similarities with their old one; both involve a presentation of front to an audience and both involve the presenter in the grubby, gossipy business of staging a show.

It is sometimes thought that coarse familiarity is merely a cultural thing, a characteristic, say, of the working classes, and that those of high estate do not conduct themselves in this way. The point, of course, is that persons of high rank tend to operate in small teams and tend to spend much of their day engaged in spoken performances, whereas working-class men tend to be members of large teams and tend to spend much of their day backstage or in unspoken performances. Thus the higher one's place in the status pyramid, the smaller the number of persons with whom one can be familiar, the less time one spends backstage, and the more likely it is that one will be required to be polite as well as decorous. However, when the time and company are right, quite sacred performers will act, and be required to act, in a quite vulgar fashion. For numerical and strategic reasons, however, we are likely to learn that laborers use a backstage manner and unlikely to learn that lords use it too. An interesting limiting case of this situation is found in connection with heads of state, who have no teammates. Sometimes these individuals may make use of a set of cronies to whom they give a courtesy rank of teammate when moments of relaxing recreation are called for, this constituting an instance of the "side-kick" function previously considered. Court equerries often fill this office, as Ponsonby illustrates in his description of King Edward's visit in 1904 to the Danish Court:

> Dinner consisted of several courses and many wines, and usually lasted one and a half hours. We then all filed out arm in arm to the drawing-room, where again the King of Denmark and all the Danish Royal Family circled round the room. At eight we retired to our rooms to smoke, but as the Danish suite accompanied us the conversation was limited to polite enquiries into the customs of the two countries. At nine we returned to the drawing-room where we played round games, generally Loo, without stakes.

At ten we were mercifully released and allowed to go to our rooms. These evenings were a high trial to everyone, but the King behaved like an angel, playing whist, which was then quite out of date, for very low points. After a week of this, however, he determined to play bridge, but only after the King of Denmark had retired to bed. We went through the usual routine till ten o'clock, and then Prince Demidoff of the Russian Legation came to the King's rooms and played bridge with the King, Seymour Fortescue, and myself, for fairly high points. We continued thus till the end of the visit, and it was a pleasure to relax ourselves from the stiffness of the Danish Court.[26]

A final point must be suggested about backstage relationships. When we say that persons who co-operate in presenting a performance may express familiarity with one another when not in the presence of the audience, it must be allowed that one can become so habituated to one's front region activity (and front region character) that it may be necessary to handle one's relaxation from it as a performance. One may feel obliged, when backstage, to act out of character in a familiar fashion and this can come to be more of a pose than the performance for which it was meant to provide a relaxation.

In this chapter I have spoken of the utility of control over backstage and of the dramaturgical trouble that arises when this control cannot be exerted. I would like now to consider the problem of controlling access to the front region, but in order to do so it will be necessary to extend a little the original frame of reference.

Two kinds of bounded regions have been considered: front regions where a particular performance is or may be in progress, and back regions where action occurs that is related to the performance but inconsistent with the appearance fostered by the performance. It would seem reasonable to add a third region, a residual one, namely, all places other than the two already identified. Such a region could

[26] Ponsonby, op. cit., p. 269.

be called "the outside." The notion of an outside region that is neither front nor back with respect to a particular performance conforms to our common-sense notion of social establishments, for when we look at most buildings we find within them rooms that are regularly or temporarily used as back regions and front regions, and we find that the outer walls of the building cut both types of rooms off from the outside world. Those individuals who are on the outside of the establishment we may call "outsiders."

While the notion of outside is obvious, unless handled with care it can mislead and confuse us, for when we shift our consideration from the front or back region to the outside we tend also to shift our point of reference from one performance to another. Given a particular ongoing performance as a point of reference, those who are outside will be persons for whom the performers actually or potentially put on a show, but a show (as we shall see) different from, or all too similar to, the one in progress. When outsiders unexpectedly enter the front or the back region of a particular performance-in-progress, the consequence of their inopportune presence can often best be studied not in terms of its effects upon the performance-in-progress but rather in terms of its effects upon a different performance, namely, the one which the performers or the audience would ordinarily present before the outsiders at a time and place when the outsiders would be the anticipated audience.

Other kinds of conceptual care are also required. The wall that cuts the front and back regions off from the outside obviously has a function to play in the performance staged and presented in these regions, but the outside decorations of the building must in part be seen as an aspect of another show; and sometimes the latter contribution may be the more important one. Thus, of houses in an English village we learn:

> The type of curtain material to be found on the windows of most village houses varied directly in proportion to the general visibility of each window. The "best" curtains were to be found where they could be most clearly seen,

and were far superior to those on windows which were hidden from the public. Furthermore, it was common for that kind of material which has a design printed on one side only to be used in such a way that the design faced outwards. This use of the most "fashionable" and most expensive material so that it can be seen to the best advantage is a typical device for gaining prestige.[27]

In Chapter One of this report it was suggested that performers tend to give the impression, or tend not to contradict the impression, that the role they are playing at the time is their most important role and that the attributes claimed by or imputed to them are their most essential and characteristic attributes. When individuals witness a show that was not meant for them, they may, then, become disillusioned about this show as well as about the show that was meant for them. The performer, too, may become confused, as Kenneth Burke suggests:

> We are all, in our compartmentalized responses, like the man who is a tyrant in his office and a weakling among his family, or like the musician who is assertive in his art and self-effacing in his personal relationships. Such dissociation becomes a difficulty when we attempt to unite these compartments (as, were the man who is a tyrant in his office and a weakling in his home suddenly to employ his wife or children, he would find his dissociative devices inadequate, and might become bewildered and tormented).[28]

These problems can become especially acute when one of the individual's shows depends upon an elaborate stage setting. Hence the implied disillusionment in Herman Melville's discussion of how the captain of his ship did not "see" him whenever they met on board but was affable to him when, after Melville's period of service, they chanced to meet socially at a Washington party:

[27] W. M. Williams, *The Sociology of an English Village* (London: Routledge and Kegan Paul, 1956), p. 112.
[28] Kenneth Burke, *Permanence and Change* (New York: New Republic, Inc., 1953), fn. p. 309.

And though, while on board the frigate, the commodore never in any manner personally addressed me—nor did I him—yet, at the Minister's social entertainment, we *there* became exceedingly chatty; nor did I fail to observe, among that crowd of foreign dignitaries and magnates from all parts of America, that my worthy friend did not appear so exalted as when leaning, in solitary state, against the brass railing of the Neversink's quarterdeck. Like many other gentlemen, he appeared to the best advantage, and was treated with the most deference in the bosom of his home, the frigate.[29]

The answer to this problem is for the performer to segregate his audiences so that the individuals who witness him in one of his roles will not be the individuals who witness him in another of his roles. Thus some French Canadian priests do not want to lead so strict a life that they cannot go swimming at the beach with friends, but they tend to feel that it is best to swim with persons who are not their parishioners, since the familiarity required at the beach is incompatible with the distance and respect required in the parish. Front region control is one measure of audience segregation. Incapacity to maintain this control leaves the performer in a position of not knowing what character he will have to project from one moment to the next, making it difficult for him to effect a dramaturgical success in any one of them. It is not difficult to sympathize with the pharmacist who acts like a salesman or like a begrimed stockman to a customer who proves to have a prescription in her hand, while at the next moment he projects his dignified, disinterested, medical, professionally-spotless pose to someone who happens to want a three-cent stamp or a chocolate fudge sundae.[30]

It should be clear that just as it is useful for the performer to exclude persons from the audience who see him in another and inconsistent presentation, so also is it useful for

[29] Herman Melville, *White Jacket* (New York: Grove Press, n.d.), p. 277.

[30] See Weinlein, *op. cit.*, pp. 147–48.

the performer to exclude from the audience those before whom he performed in the past a show inconsistent with the current one. Persons who are strongly upward or downward mobile accomplish this in a grand manner by making sure to leave the place of their origins. And just as it is convenient to play one's different routines before different persons, so also is it convenient to separate the different audiences one has for the same routine, since that is the only way in which each audience can feel that while there may be other audiences for the same routine, none is getting so desirable a presentation of it. Here again front region control is important.

By proper scheduling of one's performances, it is possible not only to keep one's audiences separated from each other (by appearing before them in different front regions or sequentially in the same region) but also to allow a few moments in between performances so as to extricate oneself psychologically and physically from one personal front, while taking on another. Problems sometimes arise, however, in those social establishments where the same or different members of the team must handle different audiences at the same time. If the different audiences come within hearing distance of each other, it will be difficult to sustain the impression that each is receiving special and unique services. Thus, if a hostess wishes to give each of her guests a warm special greeting or farewell—a special performance, in fact—then she will have to arrange to do this in an anteroom that is separated from the room containing the other guests. Similarly, in cases where a firm of undertakers is required to conduct two services on the same day, it will be necessary to route the two audiences through the establishment in such a way that their paths will not cross, lest the feeling that the funeral home is a home away from home be destroyed. So, too, in furniture salesrooms, a clerk who is "switching" a customer from one suite of furniture to another of higher price must be careful to keep his audience out of earshot of another clerk who may be switching another customer from a still cheaper suite to the one from which the first clerk is trying to switch his customer, for at such times the suite that one clerk is disparaging will be the suite that the other clerk is praising.[31] Of course, if walls separate the two audiences, the performer can sustain the impressions he is fostering by darting rapidly from one region to another. This staging device, possible with two examining rooms, is increasingly popular among American dentists and doctors.

When audience segregation fails and an outsider happens upon a performance that was not meant for him, difficult problems in impression management arise. Two accommodative techniques for dealing with these problems may be mentioned. First, all those already in the audience may be suddenly accorded, and accept, temporary backstage status and collusively join the performer in abruptly shifting to an act that is a fitting one for the intruder to observe. Thus a husband and wife in the midst of their daily bickering, when suddenly faced with a guest of brief acquaintance, will put aside their intimate quarrels and play out between themselves a relationship that is almost as distant and friendly as the one played out for the sudden arrival. Relationships, as well as types of conversation, which cannot be shared among the three will be laid aside. In general, then, if the newcomer is to be treated in the manner to which he has become accustomed, the performer must switch rapidly from the performance he was giving to one that the newcomer will feel is proper. Rarely can this be done smoothly enough to preserve the newcomer's illusion that the show suddenly put on is the performer's natural show. And even if this is managed, the audience already present is likely to feel that what they had been taking for the performer's essential self was not so essential.

It has been suggested that an intrusion may be handled by having those present switch to a definition of the situation into which the intruder can be incorporated. A second way of handling the problem is to accord the intruder a clear-cut welcome as someone who should have been in the region all along. The same show, more or less, is thus carried

31 See Louise Conant, "The Borax House," *The American Mercury*, XVII, p. 172.

on, but it is made to include the newcomer. Thus when an individual pays an unexpected visit to his friends and finds them giving a party, he is usually welcomed loudly and coaxed into staying. If the welcome were not enthusiastically extended, his discovery that he has been excluded might discredit the front of friendliness and affection that obtains between the intruder and his hosts on other occasions.

Ordinarily, however, neither of these techniques seems to be very effective. Usually when intruders enter the front region, the performers tend to get ready to begin the performance they stage for the intruders at another time or place, and this sudden readiness to act in a particular way brings at least momentary confusion to the line of action the performers are already engaged in. The performers will find themselves temporarily torn between two possible realities, and until signals can be given and received members of the team may have no guide as to what line they are to follow. Embarrassment is almost certain to result. Under such circumstances it is understandable that the intruder may be accorded neither of the accommodative treatments mentioned but rather treated as if he were not there at all or quite unceremoniously asked to stay out.

Chapter IV

DISCREPANT ROLES

One over-all objective of any team is to sustain the definition of the situation that its performance fosters. This will involve the over-communication of some facts and the under-communication of others. Given the fragility and the required expressive coherence of the reality that is dramatized by a performance, there are usually facts which, if attention is drawn to them during the performance, would discredit, disrupt, or make useless the impression that the performance fosters. These facts may be said to provide "destructive information." A basic problem for many performances, then, is that of information control; the audience must not acquire destructive information about the situation that is being defined for them. In other words, a team must be able to keep its secrets and have its secrets kept.

Before proceeding it will be convenient to add some suggestions about types of secrets, because disclosure of different types of secrets can threaten a performance in different ways. The suggested types will be based upon the function the secret performs and the relation of the secret to the conception others have about the possessor; I will assume that any particular secret can represent more than one such type.

First, there are what are sometimes called "dark" secrets. These consist of facts about a team which it knows and conceals and which are incompatible with the image of self that the team attempts to maintain before its audience. Dark secrets are, of course, double secrets: one is the crucial fact that is hidden and another is the fact that crucial facts have not been openly admitted. Dark secrets were considered in Chapter One in the section on misrepresentation.

Secondly, there are what might be called "strategic" secrets. These pertain to intentions and capacities of a team which it conceals from its audience in order to prevent them from adapting effectively to the state of affairs the team is planning to bring about. Strategic secrets are the ones that businesses and armies employ in designing future actions against the opposition. So long as a team makes no pretense of being the sort of team that does not have strategic secrets, its strategic secrets need not be dark ones. Yet it is to be noted that even when the strategic secrets of a team are not dark ones, still the disclosure or discovery of such secrets disrupts the team's performance, for suddenly and unexpectedly the team finds it useless and foolish to maintain the care, reticence, and studied ambiguity of action that was required prior to loss of its secrets. It may be added that secrets that are merely strategic tend to be ones which the team eventually discloses, perforce, when action based upon secret preparations is consummated, whereas an effort may be made to keep dark secrets secret forever. It may also be added that information is often held back not because of its known strategic importance but because it is felt that it may someday acquire such importance.

Thirdly, there are what might be called "inside" secrets. These are ones whose possession marks an individual as being a member of a group and helps the group feel separate and different from those individuals who are not "in the know."[1] Inside secrets give objective intellectual content to subjectively felt social distance. Almost all information in a social establishment has something of this exclusion function and may be seen as none of somebody's business.

Inside secrets may have little strategic importance and may not be very dark. When this is the case, such secrets may be discovered or accidentally disclosed without radically disrupting the team performance; the performers need

[1] Cf. Riesman's discussion of the "inside dopester," *op. cit.*, pp. 199–209.

only shift their secret delight to another matter. Of course, secrets that are strategic and/or dark serve extremely well as inside secrets and we find, in fact, that the strategic and dark character of secrets is often exaggerated for this reason. Interestingly enough, the leaders of a social group are sometimes faced with a dilemma regarding important strategic secrets. Those in the group who are not brought in on the secret will feel excluded and affronted when the secret finally comes to light; on the other hand, the greater the number of persons who are brought in on the secret, the greater the likelihood of intentional or unintentional disclosure.

The knowledge that one team can have of another's secrets provides us with two other types of secrets. First, there are what might be called "entrusted" secrets. This is the kind which the possessor is obliged to keep because of his relation to the team to which the secret refers. If an individual who is entrusted with a secret is to be the person he claims he is, he must keep the secret, even though it is not a secret about himself. Thus, for example, when a lawyer discloses the improprieties of his clients, two quite different performances are threatened: the client's show of innocence to the court, and the lawyer's show of trustworthiness to his client. It may also be noted that a team's strategic secrets, whether dark or not, are likely to be the entrusted secrets of the individual members of the team, for each member of the team is likely to present himself to his teammates as someone who is loyal to the team.

The second type of information about another's secrets may be called "free." A free secret is somebody else's secret known to oneself that one could disclose without discrediting the image one was presenting of oneself. A person may acquire free secrets by discovery, involuntary disclosure, indiscreet admissions, retransmission, etc. In general we must see that the free or entrusted secrets of one team may be the dark or strategic secrets of another team, and so a team whose vital secrets are possessed by others will try to oblige the possessors to treat these secrets as secrets that are entrusted and not free.

This chapter is concerned with the kinds of persons who

learn about the secrets of a team and with the bases and the threats of their privileged position. Before proceeding, however, it should be made clear that all destructive information is not found in secrets, and that information control involves more than keeping secrets. For example, there seem to be facts about almost every performance which are incompatible with the impression fostered by the performance but which have not been collected and organized into a usable form by anyone. Thus, a union newspaper may have so few readers that the editor, concerned about his job, may refuse to allow a professional survey to be made of readership, thereby ensuring that neither he nor anyone else will have proof of the suspected ineffectiveness of his work.[2] These are latent secrets, and the problems of keeping secrets are quite different from the problems of keeping latent secrets latent. Another example of destructive information not embodied in secrets is found in such events as unmeant gestures, previously referred to. These events introduce information—a definition of the situation—which is incompatible with the projected claims of the performers, but these untoward events do not constitute secrets. Avoidance of such expressively inappropriate events is also a kind of information control but will not be considered in this chapter.

Given a particular performance as the point of reference, we have distinguished three crucial roles on the basis of function: those who perform; those performed to; and outsiders who neither perform in the show nor observe it. We may also distinguish these crucial roles on the basis of information ordinarily available to those who play them. Performers are aware of the impression they foster and ordinarily also possess destructive information about the show. The audience know what they have been allowed to perceive, qualified by what they can glean unofficially by close observation. In the main, they know the definition of the situation that the performance fosters but do not have destructive information about it. Outsiders know neither the secrets of the performance nor the appearance of reality

[2] Reported in Wilensky, *op. cit.*, Ch. VII.

fostered by it. Finally, the three crucial roles mentioned could be described on the basis of the regions to which the role-player has access: performers appear in the front and back regions: the audience appears only in the front region; and the outsiders are excluded from both regions. It is to be noted then that during the performance we may expect to find correlation among function, information available, and regions of access, so that, for example, if we knew the regions into which an individual had access we would know the role he played and the information he possessed about the performance.

In actual fact, however, the congruence among function, information possessed, and accessible regions is seldom complete. Additional points of vantage relative to the performance develop which complicate the simple relation among function. information, and place. Some of these peculiar vantage points are so often taken and their significance for the performance comes to be so clearly understood that we can refer to them as roles, although, relative to the three crucial ones, they might best be called discrepant roles. Some of the more obvious ones will be considered here.

Perhaps the most spectacularly discrepant roles are those which bring a person into a social establishment in a false guise. Some varieties may be mentioned.

First there is the role of "informer." The informer is someone who pretends to the performers to be a member of their team, is allowed to come backstage and to acquire destructive information, and then openly or secretly sells out the show to the audience. The political, military, industrial and criminal variants of this role are famous. If it appears that the individual first joined the team in a sincere way and not with the premeditated plan of disclosing its secrets we sometimes call him a traitor, turncoat, or quitter, especially if he is the sort of person who ought to have made a decent teammate. The individual who all along has meant to inform on the team, and originally joins only for this purpose, is sometimes called a spy. It has frequently been noted, of course, that informers, whether traitors or spies, are often in an excellent position to play a double game, selling out the secrets of those who buy secrets from them. Informers can, of course, be classified in other ways: as Hans Speier suggests, some are professionally trained for their work, others are amateurs; some are of high estate and some of low; some work for money and others work from conviction.[3]

Secondly, there is the role of "shill." A shill is someone who acts as though he were an ordinary member of the audience but is in fact in league with the performers. Typically, the shill either provides a visible model for the audience of the kind of response the performers are seeking or provides the kind of audience response that is necessary at the moment for the development of the performance. The designations "shill" and "claque," employed in the entertainment business, have come into common use. Our appreciation of this role no doubt stems from fairgrounds, the following definitions suggesting the origins of the concept:

Stick, n. An individual—sometimes a local rube—hired by the operator of a *set-joint* [a "fixed" gambling booth] to win flashy prizes so that the crowd will be induced to gamble. When the "live ones" [natives] have been started, the *sticks* are removed and deliver their winnings to a man outside who has no apparent connection with the joint.[4]

Shillaber, n. An employee of the circus who rushes up to the kid show ticket box at the psychological moment when the barker concludes his spiel. He and his fellow *shillabers* purchase tickets and pass inside and the crowd of towners in front of the bally stand are not slow in doing likewise.[5]

We must not take the view that shills are found only in non-respectable performances (even though it is only the non-respectable shills, perhaps, who play their role system-

[3] Hans Speier, *Social Order and the Risks of War* (Glencoe: The Free Press, 1952), p. 264.

[4] David Maurer, "Carnival Cant," *American Speech*, VI, p. 336.

[5] P. W. White, "A Circus List," *American Speech*, I, p. 283.

atically and without personal illusion). For example, at informal conversational gatherings, it is common for a wife to look interested when her husband tells an anecdote and to feed him appropriate leads and cues, although in fact she has heard the anecdote many times and knows that the show her husband is making of telling something for the first time is only a show. A shill, then, is someone who appears to be just another unsophisticated member of the audience and who uses his unapparent sophistication in the interests of the performing team.

We consider now another impostor in the audience, but this time one who uses his unapparent sophistication in the interests of the audience, not the performers. This type can be illustrated by the person who is hired to check up on the standards that performers maintain in order to ensure that in certain respects fostered appearances will not be too far from reality. He acts, officially or unofficially, as a protective agent for the unsuspecting public, playing the role of audience with more perception and ethical strictness than ordinary observers are likely to employ.

Sometimes these agents play their hand in an open way, giving the performers preliminary warning that the next performance is about to be examined. Thus first-night performers and arrested persons have fair warning that anything they say will be held as evidence in judging them. A participant observer who admits his objectives from the beginning gives the performers whom he observes a similar opportunity.

Sometimes, however, the agent goes underground and by acting as an ordinary gullible member of the audience gives the performers rope with which to hang themselves. In the everyday trades, agents who give no warning are sometimes called "spotters," as they will be here, and are understandably disliked. A salesperson may find that she has been short-tempered and impolite to a customer who is really a company agent checking up on the treatment *bona fide* customers receive. A grocer may find that he has sold goods at illegal prices to customers who are experts on prices and have authority concerning them. Railroaders have had the same problem:

> Once a train conductor could demand respect from passengers; now a "spotter" may "turn him in" if he fails to remove his cap as he enters a car where women are seated or does not exude that oily subservience which increasing class consciousness, diffusion of pattern from the European and the hotel world, and the competition with other forms of transportation have forced upon him.[6]

Similarly, a woman of the streets may find that on occasion the audience encouragement she receives in the initial phases of her routine comes from a *trick* who is really a *bull*,[7] and that this ever present possibility makes her just a little wary with a strange audience, partly spoiling her act.

Incidentally, we must be careful to distinguish real spotters from self-appointed ones, often called "knockers" or "wiseguys," who do not possess the knowledge of backstage operations that they claim to possess and who are not empowered by law or custom to represent the audience.

Today we are accustomed to think of agents who check up on the standards of a performance and on the performers (whether this is done openly or without warning) as part of the service structure, and especially as part of the social control that government organizations exert on behalf of the consumer and taxpayer. Frequently, however, this kind of work has been done in a wider social field. Offices of heraldry and offices of protocol provide familiar examples, these agencies serving to keep the nobility and high government officers, and those who falsely claim these statuses, in their proper relative places.

There is yet another peculiar fellow in the audience. He is the one who takes an unremarked, modest place in the audience and leaves the region when they do, but when he leaves he goes to his employer, a competitor of the team

[6] W. Fred Cottrell, *The Railroader* (Stanford: Stanford University Press, 1940), p. 87.

[7] J. M. Murtagh and Sara Harris, *Cast the First Stone* (New York: Pocket Books, Cardinal Edition, 1958), p. 100; pp. 225–30.

whose performance he has witnessed, to report what he has seen. He is the professional shopper—the Gimbel's man in Macy's and the Macy's man in Gimbel's; he is the fashion spy and the foreigner at National Air Meets. The shopper is a person who has a technical right to see the show but ought to have the decency, it is sometimes felt, to stay in his own back region, for his interest in the show is from the wrong perspective, at once more lively and more bored than that of a thoroughly legitimate spectator.

Another discrepant role is one that is often called the go-between or mediator. The go-between learns the secrets of each side and gives each side the true impression that he will keep its secrets; but he tends to give each side the false impression that he is more loyal to it than to the other. Sometimes, as in the case of the arbitrator in some labor disputes, the go-between may function as a means by which two obligatorily hostile teams can come to a mutually profitable agreement. Sometimes, as in the case of the theatrical agent, the go-between may function as a means by which each side is given a slanted version of the other that is calculated to make a closer relationship between the two sides possible. Sometimes, as in the case of the marriage broker, the go-between may serve as a means of conveying tentative overtures from one side to the other which, if openly presented, might lead to an embarrassing acceptance or rejection.

When a go-between operates in the actual presence of the two teams of which he is a member, we obtain a wonderful display, not unlike a man desperately trying to play tennis with himself. Again we are forced to see that the individual is not the natural unit for our consideration but rather the team and its members. As an individual, the go-between's activity is bizarre, untenable, and undignified, vacillating as it does from one set of appearances and loyalties to another. As a constituent part of two teams, the go-between's vacillation is quite understandable. The go-between can be thought of simply as a double-shill.

One illustration of the go-between's role appears in recent studies of the function of the foreman. Not only must he accept the duties of the director, guiding the show on the factory floor on behalf of the managerial audience, but he must also translate what he knows and what the audience sees into a verbal line which his conscience and the audience will be willing to accept.[8] Another illustration of the go-between's role is found in the chairman of formally conducted meetings. As soon as he has called the group to order and introduced the guest speaker, he is likely to serve thereafter as a highly visible model for the other listeners, illustrating by exaggerated expressions the involvement and appreciation they ought to be showing, and providing them with advance cues as to whether a particular remark ought to be greeted by seriousness, laughter, or appreciative chuckles. Speakers tend to accept invitations to speak on the assumption that the chairman will "take care of them," which he does by being the very model of a listener and thoroughly confirming the notion that the speech has real significance. The chairman's performance is effective partly because the listeners have an obligation to him, an obligation to confirm any definition of the situation which he sponsors, an obligation, in short, to follow the listening-line that he takes. The dramaturgical task of ensuring that the speaker appears to be appreciated and that the listeners are enthralled is of course not easy, and often leaves the chairman in no frame of mind to give thought to what he is ostensibly listening to.

The role of go-between seems to be especially significant in informal convivial interaction, again illustrating the utility of the two-team approach. When one individual in a conversational circle engages in action or speech which receives the concerted attention of the others present, he defines the situation, and he may define it in a way that is not easily acceptable to his audience. Someone present will feel greater responsibility for and to him than the others feel, and we may expect this person closest to him to make an effort to translate the differences between speaker and listeners into a view that is more acceptable collectively than

[8] See Roethlisberger, *op. cit.*

the original projection. A moment later, when someone else takes the floor, another individual may find himself taking on the role of go-between and mediator. A spate of informal conversation can, in fact, be seen as the formation and re-formation of teams, and the creation and re-creation of go-betweens.

Some discrepant roles have been suggested: the informer, the shill, the spotter, the shopper, and the go-between. In each case we find an unexpected, unapparent relation among feigned role, information possessed, and regions of access. And in each case we deal with someone who may participate in the actual interaction between the performers and audience. A further discrepant role may be considered, that of the "non-person"; those who play this role are present during the interaction but in some respects do not take the role either of performer or of audience, nor do they (as do informers, shills, and spotters) pretend to be what they are not.[9]

Perhaps the classic type of non-person in our society is the servant. This person is expected to be present in the front region while the host is presenting a performance of hospitality to the guests of the establishment. While in some senses the servant is part of the host's team (as I have treated him previously), in certain ways he is defined by both performers and audience as someone who isn't there. Among some groups, the servant is also expected to enter freely into the back regions, on the theory that no impression need be maintained for him. Mrs. Trollope gives us some examples:

> I had, indeed, frequent opportunities of observing this habitual indifference to the presence of their slaves. They talk of them, of their condition, of their faculties, of their conduct, exactly as if they were incapable of hearing. I once saw a young lady, who, when seated at table between a male and a female, was induced by her modesty to intrude on the chair of her female neighbor to avoid

[9] For a fuller treatment of the role see Goffman, op. cit., chap. xvi.

the indelicacy of touching the elbow of *a man*. I once saw this very young lady lacing her stays with the most perfect composure before a Negro footman. A Virginian gentleman told me that ever since he had married, he had been accustomed to have a Negro girl sleep in the same chamber with himself and his wife. I asked for what purpose this nocturnal attendance was necessary? "Good Heaven!" was the reply. "If I wanted a glass of water during the night, what would become of me."[10]

This is an extreme example. While servants tend to be addressed only when a "request" is to be given them, still their presence in a region typically places some restrictions upon the behavior of those who are fully present, the more so, apparently, when the social distance between servant and served is not great. In the case of other servant-like roles in our society, such as that of elevator operator and cabdriver, there seems to be uncertainty on both sides of the relationship as to what kind of intimacies are permissible in the presence of the non-person.

In addition to those in servant-like roles, there are other standard categories of persons who are sometimes treated in their presence as if they were not there; the very young, the very old, and the sick are common examples. Further, we find today a growing body of technical personnel—recording stenographers, broadcasting technicians, photographers, secret police, etc.—who play a technical role during important ceremonies but not a scripted one.

It would seem that the role of non-person usually carries with it some subordination and disrespect, but we must not underestimate the degree to which the person who is given or who takes such a role can use it as a defense. And it must be added that situations can arise when subordinates find that the only feasible way that they can handle a superordinate is to treat him as if he were not present. Thus, in Shetland Isle, when the British public-school doctor attended patients in the homes of poor crofters, the residents

10 Mrs. Trollope, *Domestic Manners of the Americans* (2 vols.; London: Whittaker, Treacher, 1832), II, pp. 56–57.

sometimes handled the difficulty of relating themselves to the doctor by treating him, as best they could, as if he were not present. It may also be added that a team can treat an individual as if he were not present, doing this not because it is the natural thing or the only feasible thing to do, but as a pointed way of expressing hostility to an individual who has conducted himself improperly. In such situations, the important show is to show the outcast that he is being ignored, and the activity that is carried on in order to demonstrate this may itself be of secondary importance.

We have considered some types of persons who are not, in a simple sense, performers, audience, or outsiders, having access to information and regions we would not expect of them. We consider now four additional discrepant roles, involving, in the main, persons who are not present during a performance but who have unexpected information about it.

First, there is an important role that might be called "service specialist." It is filled by individuals who specialize in the construction, repair, and maintenance of the show their clients maintain before other people. Some of these workers, like architects and furniture salesmen, specialize in settings; some, such as dentists, hairdressers, and dermatologists, deal with personal front; others, such as staff economists, accountants, lawyers, and researchers, formulate the factual elements of a client's verbal display, that is, his team's argument-line or intellectual position.

On the basis of concrete research it would seem that service specialists can hardly attend to the needs of an individual performer without acquiring as much, or more destructive information about some aspects of the individual's performance as the individual himself possesses. Service specialists are like members of the team in that they learn the secrets of the show and obtain a backstage view of it. Unlike members of the team, however, the specialist does not share the risk, the guilt, and the satisfaction of presenting before an audience the show to which he has contributed. And, unlike members of the team, in learning the secrets of others, the others do not learn corresponding secrets about him. It is in this context that we can understand why professional ethics often oblige the specialist to show "discretion," i.e., not to give away a show whose secrets his duties have made him privy to. Thus, for example, psychotherapists who vicariously participate so widely in the domestic warfare of our times are pledged to remain silent about what they have learned, except to their supervisors.

When the specialist is of higher general social status than the individuals for whom he provides a service, his general social valuation of them may be confirmed by the particular things he must learn about them. In some situations this becomes a significant factor in maintaining the *status quo*. Thus in American towns upper-middle-class bankers come to see that the owners of some small businesses present a front for tax purposes that is inconsistent with their banking transactions, and that other businessmen present a confident public front of solvency while privately requesting a loan in an abject, fumbling manner. Middle-class doctors on charity duty who must treat shameful diseases in shameful surroundings are in a similar position, for they make it impossible for a lower-class person to protect himself from the intimate insight of his superordinates. Similarly, a landlord learns that all of his tenants act as if they were the sort who always paid their rent on time but that for some tenants this act is only an act. (Persons who are not service specialists are sometimes given the same disillusioning view. In many organizations, for example, an executive officer is required to observe the show of bustling competence that the personnel maintains, although he may secretly possess an accurate and low opinion of some of those who work under him.)

Sometimes we find, of course, that the general social status of the client is higher than that of the specialists who are retained to attend to his front. In such cases an interesting dilemma of status occurs, with high status and low information control on one side, and low status and high information control on the other. In such cases it is possible for the specialist to become overimpressed with the weaknesses in the show that his betters put on and to forget the weaknesses in his own. In consequence, such specialists sometimes develop a characteristic ambivalence, feeling cynical about the "better" world for the same reasons that make them vicariously intimate with it. Thus the janitor, by virtue of the service he provides, learns what kind of liquor the tenants drink, what kind of food they eat, what letters they receive, what bills they leave unpaid, and whether the lady of the apartment is menstruating behind her uncontaminated front, and how clean the tenants keep the kitchen, bathroom, and other back regions.[11] Similarly, the filling station manager is in a position to learn that a man who affects a new Cadillac may buy only a dollar's worth of gas, or buy a cut-price variety, or seek to work the station for free service. And he also knows that the show some men put on of masculine know-how about cars is false, for they can neither diagnose the trouble with their car correctly, although claiming to, nor drive up to the gasoline pumps in a competent way. So, too, persons who sell dresses learn that customers of whom they would not have expected it sometimes have dirty underwear and that customers unabashedly judge a garment by its capacity to misrepresent the facts. Those who sell men's clothing learn that the gruff show men maintain of being little concerned with how they look is sometimes merely a show and that strong, silent men will try on suit after suit, hat after hat, until they appear in the mirror exactly as they want to see themselves. So also, policemen learn from the things that reputable businessmen want them to do and not do that the pillars of society have a slight tilt.[12] Hotel maids learn that male guests who make passes at them upstairs are not quite what the seemliness of their downstairs conduct suggests.[13] And hotel security officers, or house dicks, as they are more commonly called, learn that a wastebasket may conceal two rejected drafts of a suicide note:

[11] See Ray Gold, "The Chicago Flat Janitor" (unpublished Master's thesis, Department of Sociology, University of Chicago, 1950), especially Chap. IV, "The Garbage."

[12] Westley, *op. cit.*, p. 131.

[13] Writer's study of Shetland Hotel.

Darling—

By the time you get this I will be where nothing you can do will hurt me—

By the time you read this, nothing you can do will be able to hurt[14]

showing that the final feelings of a desperately uncompromising person were somewhat rehearsed in order to strike just the right note and in any case were not final. Service specialists of questionable repute who maintain an office in the back regions of a city so that clients will not be seen seeking assistance clearly provide another example. In Mr. Hughes's words:

A common scene in fiction depicts a lady of degree seeking, veiled and alone, the address of the fortuneteller or the midwife of doubtful practice in an obscure corner of the city. The anonymity of certain sections of cities allows people to seek specialized services, legitimate but embarrassing as well as illegimate, from persons with whom they would not want to be seen by members of their own social circle.[15]

The specialist may, of course, carry his anonymity with him, as does the exterminator who advertises that he will come to the client's house in a van that wears a plain wrapper. Any guarantee of anonymity is, of course, a rather blatant claim that the client has need of it and is willing to make use of it.

It is plain that the specialist whose work requires him to take a backstage view of other people's performances will be an embarrassment to them. By changing the performance which serves as a point of reference, other consequences can be seen. We regularly find that clients may retain a specialist not in order to obtain help with a show they are putting on for others but for the very act that is provided by having a specialist attend them. Many women,

[14] Collans, *op. cit.*, p. 156.

[15] E. C. Hughes and Helen M. Hughes, *Where People Meet* (Glencoe, Ill.: The Free Press, 1952), p. 171.

it seems, go to beauty parlors to be fussed over and called madam and not merely because they need to have their hair done. It has sometimes been claimed, for example, that in Hindu India the procurement of proper service specialists for ritually significant tasks is of crucial significance in confirming one's own caste position.[16] In such cases as these, the performer may be interested in being known by the specialist who serves him and not by the show that the service allows him later to perform. And so we find that special specialists arise who fulfill needs that are too shameful for the client to take to specialists before whom he is ordinarily not shameful. Thus the performance that a client stages for his doctor sometimes forces the client to go to a pharmacist for abortives, contraceptives, and venereal disease cures.[17] Similarly, in America, an individual involved in unseemly entanglements may take his troubles to a Negro lawyer because of the shame he might feel before a white one.[18]

It is apparent that service specialists who possess entrusted secrets are in a position to exploit their knowledge in order to gain concessions from the performer whose secrets they possess. The law, professional ethics, and enlightened self-interest often put a stop to the grosser forms of blackmail, but small concessions delicately requested are frequently unchecked by these forms of social control. Perhaps the tendency to place a lawyer, accountant, economist, or other specialists in verbal fronts on a retainer, and to bring those who are on a retainer into the firm partly represents an effort to ensure discretion; once the verbal specialist becomes part of the organization, presumably new methods can be employed to ensure his trustworthiness. By bringing the specialist into one's organization and even one's team, there is also greater assurance that he will employ

[16] For this and other data on India, and for suggestions in general, I am indebted to McKim Marriott.

[17] Weinlein, op. cit., p. 106.

[18] William H. Hale, "The Career Development of the Negro Lawyer" (unpublished Ph.D. dissertation, Department of Sociology, University of Chicago, 1949), p. 72.

his skills in the interests of one's show and not in the interests of praiseworthy but irrelevant matters such as a balanced view, or the presentation of interesting theoretical data to the specialist's professional audience.[19]

A note should be added about one variety of specialist role, the role of "training specialist." Individuals who take this role have the complicated task of teaching the performer how to build up a desirable impression while at the same time taking the part of the future audience and illustrating by punishments the consequences of improprieties Parents and schoolteachers are perhaps the basic examples of this role in our society; the sergeants who drill officer cadets provide a further example.

Performers often feel uneasy in the presence of a trainer whose lessons they have long since learned and taken for granted. Trainers tend to evoke for the performer a vivid image of himself that he had repressed, a self-image of someone engaged in the clumsy and embarrassing process of becoming. The performer can make himself forget how

---

[19] The specialist in verbal fronts who is brought into the organization will be expected to assemble and present data in such a way as to lend maximum support to the claims the team is making at the time. The facts of the case will ordinarily be an incidental matter, merely one ingredient to be considered along with others such as the likely arguments of one's opponents, the predisposition of the public at large to which the team may want to appeal for support, the principles to which everyone concerned will feel obliged to give lip service, etc. Interestingly enough the individual who helps collect and formulate the array of facts used in a team's verbal show may also be employed in the distinctly different task of presenting or conveying this front in person to the audience. It is the difference between writing the ceremony for a show and performing the ceremony in the show. Here there is a potential dilemma. The more the specialist can be made to set aside his professional standards and consider only the interests of the team which employs him, the more useful may be the arguments he formulates for them; but the more he has a reputation for being an independent professional, interested only in the balanced facts of the case, the more effective he is likely to be when he appears before the audience and presents his findings. A very rich source of data on these matters is to be found in Wilensky, *op. cit.*

foolish he once was, but he cannot make the trainer forget. As Riezler suggests about any shameful fact, "if others know, the fact is established and his image of himself is put beyond his own power of remembering and forgetting."[20] Perhaps there is no consistent easy stand that we can take to persons who have seen behind our current front—persons who "knew us when"—if at the same time they are persons who must symbolize the audience's response to us and cannot, therefore, be accepted as old teammates might be.

The service specialist has been mentioned as one type of person who is not a performer yet has access to back regions and destructive information. A second type is the person who plays the role of "confidant." Confidants are persons to whom the performer confesses his sins, freely detailing the sense in which the impression given during a performance was merely an impression. Typically, confidants are located outside and participate only vicariously in back and front region activity. It is to a person of this kind, for instance, that a husband brings home a daily tale of how he fared in office stratagems, intrigues, unspoken feelings, and bluffs; and when he writes a letter requesting, resigning from, or accepting a job it is this person who will check through the draft to make sure the letter strikes exactly the right note. And when ex-diplomats and ex-boxers write their memoirs, the reading public is taken behind the scenes and becomes a watered-down confidant of one of the great shows, albeit one that is by then quite over.

A person in whom another confides, unlike the service specialist, does not make a business of receiving such confidances; he accepts the information without accepting a fee, as an expression of the friendship, trust, and regard the informant feels for him. We find, however, that clients often attempt to transform their service specialists into confidants (perhaps as a means of ensuring discretion), especially when the work of the specialist is merely to listen and talk, as is the case with priests and psychotherapists.

A third role remains to be considered. Like the role of

specialist and confidant, the role of colleague affords those who play it some information about a performance they do not attend.

Colleagues may be defined as persons who present the same routine to the same kind of audience but who do not participate together, as teammates do, at the same time and place before the same particular audience. Colleagues as it is said, share a community of fate. In having to put on the same kind of performance, they come to know each other's difficulties and points of view; whatever their tongues, they come to speak the same social language. And while colleagues who compete for audiences may keep some strategic secrets from one another, they cannot very well hide from one another certain things that they hide from the audience. The front that is maintained before others need not be maintained among themselves; relaxation becomes possible. Hughes has recently provided a statement of the complexities of this kind of solidarity.

> Part of the working code of a position is discretion; it allows the colleagues to exchange confidences concerning their relations to other people. Among these confidences one finds expressions of cynicism concerning their mission, their competence, and the foibles of their superiors. themselves their clients, their subordinates, and the public at large. Such expressions take the burden from one's shoulders and serve as a defense as well. The unspoken mutual confidence necessary to them rests on two assumptions concerning one's fellows. The first is that the colleague will not misunderstand; the second is that he will not repeat to uninitiated ears. To be sure that a new fellow will not misunderstand requires a sparring match of social gestures. The zealot who turns the sparring match into a real battle, who takes a friendly initiation too seriously, is not likely to be trusted with the lighter sort of comment on one's work or with doubts and misgivings: nor can he learn those parts of the working code which are communicated only by hint and gesture. He is not to be trusted, for, though he is not fit for stratagems,

he is suspected of being prone to treason. In order that men may communicate freely and confidentially they must be able to take a good deal of each other's sentiments for granted. They must feel easy about their silences as well as about their utterances.[21]

A good statement of some other aspects of collegial solidarity is given by Simone de Beauvoir; her intention is to describe the peculiar situation of women, her effect is to tell us about all collegial groups:

> The female friendships that she succeeds in keeping or forming are precious to a woman, but they are very different in kind from relations between men. The latter communicate as individuals through ideas and projects of personal interest, while women are confined within their general feminine lot and bound together by a kind of immanent complicity. And what they look for first of all among themselves is the affirmation of the universe they have in common. They do not discuss opinions and general ideas, but exchange confidences and recipes; they are in league to create a kind of counter-universe, the values of which will outweigh masculine values. Collectively they find strength to shake off their chains; they negate the sexual domination of the males by admitting their frigidity to one another, while deriding the men's desires or their clumsiness; and they question ironically the moral and intellectual superiority of their husbands, and of men in general.
>
> They compare experiences: pregnancies, births, their own and their children's illnesses, and household cares become the essential events of the human story. Their work is not a technique: by passing on recipes for cooking and the like, they endow it with the dignity of a secret science founded on oral tradition.[22]

It should be apparent, then, why the terms used to designate one's colleagues, like the terms used to designate one's

[21] Hughes and Hughes, *op. cit.*, pp. 168–69.
[22] De Beauvoir, *op. cit.*, p. 542.

teammates, come to be in-group terms, and why terms used to designate audiences tend to be loaded with out-group sentiment.

It is interesting to note that when teammates come in contact with a stranger who is their colleague, a sort of ceremonial or honorific team membership may be temporarily accorded the newcomer. There is a visiting-fireman complex whereby teammates treat their visitor as if he had suddenly come into very intimate and long-standing relationships with them. Whatever their associational prerogatives, he tends to be given club rights. These courtesies are especially given when the visitor and the hosts happen to have received their training in the same establishment or from the same trainers, or both. Graduates of the same household, the same professional school, the same penitentiary, the same public school, or the same small town provide clear examples. When "old boys" meet, it may be difficult to sustain backstage horseplay and the dropping of one's customary pose may become an obligation and a pose in itself, but it may be more difficult to do anything else.

An interesting implication of these suggestions is that a team which constantly performs its routines to the same audience may yet be socially more distant from this audience than from a colleague who momentarily comes into contact with the team. Thus the gentry in Shetland Isle knew their crofter neighbors very well, having played out the gentry role to them since childhood. Yet a gentry visitor to the island, properly sponsored and introduced, could become more intimate with the island gentry in the course of an afternoon tea than could a crofter during a lifetime of contact with his gentry neighbors. For afternoon tea among the gentry was backstage to gentry-crofter relations. Here crofters were made fun of, and the restrained manner ordinarily employed in their presence gave way to the gentry's version of convivial horseplay. Here the gentry faced up to the fact that they were similar to the crofters in crucial ways and dissimilar to them in some undesirable ways, all with a secret playfulness that many crofters did not suspect them of.[23]

It may be suggested that the good will one colleague ceremonially extends to another is perhaps a kind of peace offering: "You don't tell on us and we won't tell on you." This partly explains why doctors and shopkeepers often give professional courtesies or reductions in price to those who are in some way connected with the trade. We have here a kind of bribery of those who are well enough informed to become spotters.

The nature of colleagueship allows us to understand something about the important social process of endogamy, whereby a family of one class, caste, occupation, religion, or ethnicity tends to restrict its marriage ties to families of the same status. Persons who are brought together by affinal ties are brought to a position from which they can see behind each other's front; this is always embarrassing but it is less embarrassing if the newcomers backstage have themselves been maintaining the same kind of show and have been privy to the same destructive information. A misalliance is something that brings backstage and into the team someone who should be kept outside or at least in the audience.

It is to be noted that persons who are colleagues in one capacity, and hence on terms of some reciprocal familiarity, may not be colleagues in other respects. It is sometimes felt that a colleague who is in other respects a man of lesser power or status may overextend his claims of familiarity and threaten the social distance that ought to be maintained on the basis of these other statuses. In American society, middle-class persons of low minority-group status are often threatened this way by the presumption of their lower-

---

[23] Island gentry sometimes discussed how it could hardly work to socialize with the natives, since there would be no common interest. While the gentry thus showed good insight into what would happen if a crofter came to tea, they seemed less aware of how dependent the teatime *esprit* was on there being crofters available to not have to tea.

class brethren. As Hughes suggests in regard to interracial colleague relations:

> The dilemma arises from the fact that, while it is bad for the profession to let laymen see rifts in their ranks, it may be bad for the individual to be associated in the eyes of his actual or potential patients with persons, even colleagues, of so despised a group as the Negro. The favored way of avoiding the dilemma is to shun contacts with the Negro professional.[24]

Similarly, employers who patently have lower-class status, as do some American filling station managers, often find that their employees expect that the whole operation will be conducted in a backstage manner and that commands and directions will be issued only in a pleading or joking fashion. Of course, this kind of threat is increased by the fact that non-colleagues may similarly simplify the situation and judge the individual too much by the collegial company he keeps. But here again we deal with issues that cannot be fully explored unless we change the point of reference from one performance to another.

Just as some persons are thought to cause difficulty by making too much of their colleagueship, so others cause trouble by not making enough of it. It is always possible for a disaffected colleague to turn renegade and sell out to the audience the secrets of the act that his onetime brethren are still performing. Every role has its defrocked priests to tell us what goes on in the monastery, and the press has always shown a lively interest in these confessions and exposés. Thus a doctor will describe in print how his colleagues split fees, steal each other's patients, and specialize in unnecessary operations that require the kind of apparatus which gives the patient a dramatic medical show for his money.[25] In Burke's term, we are thereby supplied with information about the "rhetoric of medicine:"

---

[24] Hughes and Hughes, op. cit., p. 172.
[25] Lewis G. Arrowsmith, "The Young Doctor in New York," The American Mercury, XXII, pp. 1–10.

Applying this statement to our purposes, we could observe that even the medical equipment of a doctor's office
is not to be judged purely for its diagnostic usefulness,
but also has a function in the *rhetoric* of medicine. Whatever it is as apparatus, it also appeals as imagery; and if
a man has been treated to a fulsome series of tappings,
scrutinizings, and listenings, with the aid of various
scopes, meters, and gauges, he may feel content to have
participated as a patient in such histrionic action, though
absolutely no material thing has been done for him,
whereas he might count himself cheated if he were given
a real cure, but without the pageantry.[26]

Of course, in a very limited sense, whenever any non-
colleague is allowed to become a confidant, someone will
have had to be a renegade.

Renegades often take a moral stand, saying that it is
better to be true to the ideals of the role than to the performers who falsely present themselves in it. A different
mode of disaffection occurs when a colleague "goes native"
or becomes a backslider, making no attempt to maintain the
kind of front which his authorized status makes or leads his
colleagues and the audience to expect of him. Such deviants
are said to "let down the side." Thus in Shetland Isle the
inhabitants, in an effort to present themselves as progressive
farmers to visitors from the outside world, felt somewhat
hostile to the few crofters who apparently didn't care and
who refused to shave or wash, or construct a front yard, or
to supplant the thatched roof of their cottage with something less symbolic of traditional peasant status. Similarly,
in Chicago there has been an organization of blind war
veterans who, militant in their desire not to accept a pitiable
role, tour the city in order to check up on fellow blind men
who let down the side by appealing for alms on street
corners.

A final note must be added about colleagueship. There
are some colleague groupings whose members are rarely

[26] Kenneth Burke, *A Rhetoric of Motives* (New York: Prentice-Hall, 1953), p. 171.

held responsible for each other's good conduct. Thus mothers are in some respects a colleague grouping, and yet ordinarily the misdeeds of one, or her confessions, do not seem to affect closely the respect that is accorded the other members. On the other hand, there are colleague groupings of a more corporate character, whose members are so closely identified in the eyes of other people that the good reputation of one practitioner depends on the good conduct of the others. If one member is exposed and causes a scandal, then all lose some public repute. As cause and effect of such identification we often find that the members of the grouping are formally organized into a single collectivity which is allowed to represent the professional interests of the grouping and allowed to discipline any member who threatens to discredit the definition of the situation fostered by the other members. Obviously, colleagues of this kind constitute a kind of team, a team that differs from ordinary teams in that the members of its audience are not in immediate face-to-face contact with one another and must communicate their responses to one another at a time when the shows they have seen are no longer before them. Similarly, the collegial renegade is a kind of traitor or turncoat.

The implications of these facts about colleague groupings force us to modify a little the original framework of definitions. We must include a marginal type of "weak" audience whose members are not in face-to-face contact with one another during a performance, but who come eventually to pool their responses to the performance they have independently seen. Colleague groupings are not, of course, the only sets of performers who find an audience of this kind. For example, a department of state or foreign office may lay down the current official line to diplomats who are scattered throughout the world. In their strict maintenance of this line, and in the intimate co-ordination of the character and timing of their actions, these diplomats obviously function, or are meant to function, as a single team putting on a single world-wide performance. But of course, in such cases, the several members of the audience are not in immediate face-to-face contact with one another.

Chapter V

COMMUNICATION OUT OF CHARACTER

When two teams present themselves to each other for purposes of interaction, the members of each team tend to
maintain the line that they are what they claim to be; they
tend to stay in character. Backstage familiarity is suppressed
lest the interplay of poses collapse and all the participants
find themselves on the same team, as it were, with no one
left to play to. Each participant in the interaction ordinarily
endeavors to know and keep his place, maintaining whatever balance of formality and informality has been established for the interaction, even to the point of extending this
treatment to his own teammates. At the same time, each
team tends to suppress its candid view of itself and of the
other team, projecting a conception of self and a conception
of other that is relatively acceptable to the other. And to
ensure that communication will follow established, narrow
channels, each team is prepared to assist the other team,
tacitly and tactfully, in maintaining the impression it is attempting to foster.

Of course, at moments of great crisis, a new set of motives
may suddenly become effective and the established social
distance between the teams may sharply increase or decrease. An example may be cited from a study of a hospital
ward on which experimental treatment was given to volun
teers suffering from metabolic disorders about which little
was known and for which little could be done.[1] In face of

[1] Renee Claire Fox, "A Sociological Study of Stress: Physician
and Patient on a Research Ward" (unpublished Ph.D. dissertation, Department of Social Relations, Radcliffe College, 1953).

the research demands made upon the patients and the general feeling of hopelessness about prognosis, the usual sharp line between doctor and patient was blunted. Doctors respectfully consulted with their patients at length about symptoms, and patients came to think of themselves in part as research associates. However, in general, when the crisis is past, the previous working consensus is likely to be reestablished, albeit bashfully. Similarly, during sudden disruptions of a performance, and especially at times when a misidentification is discovered, a portrayed character can momentarily crumble while the performer behind the character "forgets himself" and blurts out a relatively unperformed exclamation. Thus, the wife of an American general recounts an incident occurring when she and her husband, informally attired, took a summer evening's drive together in an open army jeep:

The next sound we heard was the screeching brakes, as a Military Police jeep pulled us over to the side of the road. The MPs alighted and walked over to our jeep.

"You've got a government vehicle and a dame in it," the toughest of the soldiers snapped. "Let's see your trip ticket."

In the army, of course, nobody is supposed to drive a military vehicle without a trip ticket that says who gave the authority for the use of the jeep. The soldier was being very thorough and went on to ask for Wayne's driver's permit—another military paper Wayne should have had.

He had neither permit nor trip ticket, of course. But he did have his four-star overseas cap on the seat beside him. He popped it on his head quietly, but fast, while the MPs were digging in their jeep for the forms on which they planned to charge Wayne with every violation in the book. They got the forms, turned back to us, and stopped dead in their tracks, openmouthed.

Four stars!

Before he could think, the first soldier, who had done all the talking, blurted out, "Good Lord!" and then, really frightened, slapped his hand over his mouth. He made a valiant effort to recover what he could from a bad situation by saying, "I didn't recognize you, sir."[2]

In our Anglo-American society, it may be noted, "Good Lord!", "My God!", or their facial equivalents often serve as a performer's admission that he has momentarily placed himself in a position in which it is patent that no performed character can be sustained. These expressions represent an extreme form of communication out of character, and yet have become so conventionalized as almost to constitute a performed plea for forgiveness on the grounds that we are all poor fellow performers.

These crises are exceptional, however; a working consensus and a public keeping of place is the rule. But underneath this typical gentleman's agreement there are more usual but less apparent currents of communication. If these currents were not undercurrents, if these conceptions were officially communicated instead of communicated in a surreptitious way, they would contradict and discredit the definition of the situation officially projected by the participants. When a social establishment is studied, these discrepant sentiments are almost always found. They demonstrate that while a performer may act as if his response in a situation were immediate, unthinking, and spontaneous, and while he himself may think this to be the case, still it will always be possible for situations to arise in which he will convey to one or two persons present the understanding that the show he is maintaining is only and merely a show. The presence, then, of communication out of character provides one argument for the propriety of studying performances in terms of teams and in terms of potential interaction disruptions. It may be repeated that no claim is made that surreptitious communications are any more a reflection of the real reality than are the official communications with which they are inconsistent; the point is that the performer is typically involved in both, and this dual involvement must be carefully managed lest official projec-

2 Mrs. Mark Clark (Maurine Clark), *Captain's Bride, General's Lady* (New York: McGraw-Hill, 1956), pp. 128–29.

tions be discredited. Of the many types of communication in which the performer engages and which convey information incompatible with the impression officially maintained during interaction, four types will be considered: treatment of the absent, staging talk, team collusion, and re-aligning actions.

Treatment of the Absent

When the members of a team go backstage where the audience cannot see or hear them, they very regularly derogate the audience in a way that is inconsistent with the face-to-face treatment that is given to the audience. In service trades, for example, customers who are treated respectfully during the performance are often ridiculed, gossiped about, caricatured, cursed, and criticized when the performers are backstage; here, too, plans may be worked out for "selling" them, or employing "angles" against them, or pacifying them.[1] Thus, in the Shetland Hotel kitchen, guests would be referred to by belittling code-names; their speech, tone and mannerisms would be imitated accurately as a source of fun and a means of criticism; their foibles, weaknesses and social status would be discussed with scholarly and clinical care; their requests for minor services would be met by grotesque facial gestures and cursing, once out of sight and hearing. This equation of abuse was amply balanced by the guests when in their own circles, at which time the staff would be described as slothful pigs, as vegetable-like primitive types, as money-hungry animals. Yet when speaking directly to one another, staff and guests showed mutual regard and some sweetness of temper. Similarly, there are very few friendship relationships in which there is not some occasion when attitudes expressed about the friend behind his back are grossly incompatible with the ones expressed about him to his face.

Sometimes, of course, the opposite of derogation occurs,

[1] See, for example, the case report on "Central Haberdashery" in Robert Dubin, ed., *Human Relations in Administration* (New York: Prentice-Hall, 1951), pp. 560–63.

and performers praise their audience in a way that would be impermissible for them to do in the actual presence of the audience. But secret derogation seems to be much more common than secret praise, perhaps because such derogation serves to maintain the solidarity of the team, demonstrating mutual regard at the expense of those absent and compensating, perhaps, for the loss of self-respect that may occur when the audience must be accorded accommodative face-to-face treatment.

Two common techniques of derogating the absent audience may be suggested. First, when performers are in the region in which they will appear before the audience, and when the audience has left or has not yet arrived, the performers will sometimes play out a satire on their interaction with the audience, and with some members of the team taking the role of the audience. Frances Donovan, for example, in describing the sources of fun available to salesgirls, suggests the following:

> But unless they are busy the girls do not remain long apart. An irresistible attraction draws them together again. At every opportunity they play the game of "customer," a game which they have invented and of which they never seem to tire—a game which for caricature and comedy, I have never seen surpassed on any stage. One girl takes the part of the saleswoman, another that of the customer in search of a dress, and together they put on an act that would delight the heart of a vaudeville audience.[2]

A similar situation is described by Dennis Kincaid in his discussion of the kind of social contact that natives arranged for the British during the early part of British rule in India:

> If the young factors found little pleasure at these entertainments, their hosts, for all the satisfaction they would at other times have derived from Raji's grace and

[2] Frances Donovan, *The Saleslady* (Chicago: University of Chicago Press, 1929), p. 39. Specific examples are given on pp. 39–40.

Kaliani's wit, were too uneasy to enjoy their own party till the guests had gone. Then followed an entertainment of which few English guests were aware. The doors would be shut, and the dancing girls, excellent mimics like all Indians, would give an imitation of the bored guests who had just left, and the uncomfortable tension of the last hour would be dispelled in bursts of happy laughter. And while the English phaetons clattered home Raji and Kaliani would be dressed up to caricature English costume and be executing with indecent exaggeration an Orientalized version of English dances, those minuets and country dances which seemed so innocent and natural to English eyes, so different from the provocative posturing of Indian nautch-girls, but which to Indians appeared utterly scandalous.[8]

Among other things, this activity seems to provide a kind of ritual profanation of the front region as well as of the audience.[4]

Secondly, a consistent difference between terms of reference and terms of address often appears. In the presence of the audience, the performers tend to use a favorable form of address to them. This involves, in American society, a politely formal term, such as "sir" or "Mr.—," or a warmly familiar term, such as first name or nickname, the formality or informality being determined by the wishes of the person addressed. In the absence of the audience, the audience tends to be referred to by bare surname, first name where this is not permissible to their faces, nickname, or slighting pronunciation of full name. Sometimes members of the au-

[8] Dennis Kincaid, *British Social Life in India, 1608–1937* (London: Routledge, 1938), pp. 106–7.

[4] A related tendency may be mentioned. In some offices that are divided into ranked regions, the lunchtime break will find the topmost level leaving the social establishment and everyone else in it moving up a region for lunch or for a few moments of after-lunch talk. Momentary possession of the work-place of one's superordinates seems to offer, among other things, an opportunity to profanize it in some ways.

dience are referred to not even by a slighting name but by a code title which assimilates them fully to an abstract category. Thus doctors in the absence of a patient may refer to him as "the cardiac" or "the strep"; barbers privately refer to their customers as "heads of hair." So, too, the audience may be referred to in their absence by a collective term combining distance and derogation, suggesting an in-group—out-group split. Thus musicians will call customers squares; native American office girls may secretly refer to their foreign colleagues as "G. R.'s";[5] American soldiers may secretly refer to English soldiers with whom they work as "Limeys";[6] pitchmen in carnivals present their spiel before persons whom they refer to in private, as rubes, natives, or towners; and Jews act out the routines of the parent society for an audience called *goyim,* while Negroes, when among themselves, will sometimes refer to whites by such terms as "ofay." In an excellent study of pickpocket mobs, a similar point is made:

> The mark's pockets are important to the pickpocket only because they contain money. In fact, the pockets have become so symbolic of both the mark and his money that a mark is very often—perhaps predominantly—referred to by pockets, as a *left britch,* a *kick out,* or an *insider* which was taken at a particular time or place. In fact, the mark is thought of in terms of the pocket for

[5] "German Refugees." See Gross, *op. cit.,* p. 186.

[6] See Daniel Glaser, "A Study of Relations between British and American Enlisted Men at 'SHAEF' " (unpublished Master's thesis, Department of Sociology, University of Chicago, 1947). Mr. Glaser says, p. 16:

"The term 'limey,' as used by the Americans in place of 'British,' was generally employed with derogatory implications. They would refrain from using it in the presence of the British though the latter usually either didn't know what it meant or didn't give it a derogatory significance. Indeed, the Americans' care in this respect was much like that of Northern whites who use the term 'nigger' but refrain from using it in front of a Negro. This nickname phenomenon is, of course, a common feature of ethnic relations in which categoric contacts prevail."

which he was robbed, and the whole mob shares this imagery.[7]

Perhaps the cruelest term of all is found in situations where an individual asks to be called by a familiar term to his face, and this is tolerantly done, but in his absence he is referred to by a formal term. Thus in Shetland Isle a visitor who asked the local crofters to call him by his first name was sometimes obliged to his face, but in the absence of the visitor a formal term of reference would push him back into what was felt to be his proper place.

I have suggested two standard ways in which performers derogate their audiences—mock role-playing and uncomplimentary terms of reference. There are other standard ways. When no member of the audience is present, the members of the team may refer to aspects of their routine in a cynical or purely technical way, giving forceful evidence to themselves that they do not take the same view of their activity as the view they maintain for their audience. When teammates are warned that the audience is approaching, the teammates may hold off their performance, purposely, until the very last minute, until the audience almost catches a glimpse of backstage activity. Similarly, the team may race into backstage relaxation the moment the audience has departed. By means of this purposely rapid switch into or out of their act, the team in a sense can contaminate and profanize the audience by backstage conduct, or rebel against the obligation of maintaining a show before the audience, or make extremely clear the difference between team and audience, and do all of these things without quite being caught out by the audience. Still another standard aggression against those absent occurs in the kidding and ribbing a member of the team receives when he is about to leave (or merely desires to leave) his teammates and rise or fall or move laterally into the ranks of the audience. At such times the teammate who is ready to move can be treated as if he had already moved, and abuse or familiarity can be

[7] David W. Maurer, *Whiz Mob* (Gainesville, Florida: American Dialect Society, 1955), p. 113.

heaped upon him with impunity, and, by implication, upon the audience. And a final instance of aggression is found when someone from the audience is officially brought into the team. Again, he may be jokingly mistreated and "given a hard time," for much the same reason that he was abused when he departed from the team he has just left.[8]

The techniques of derogation which have been considered point out the fact that, verbally, individuals are treated relatively well to their faces and relatively badly behind their backs. This seems to be one of the basic generalizations that can be made about interaction, but we should not seek in our all-too-human nature an explanation of it. As previously suggested, backstage derogation of the audience serves to maintain the morale of the team. And when the audience is present, considerate treatment of them is necessary, not for their sake, or for their sake merely, but so that continuance of peaceful and orderly interaction will be assured. The "actual" feelings of the performers for a member of the audience (whether positive or negative) seem to have little to do with the question, either as a determinant of how this member of the audience is treated to his face or as a determinant of how he is treated behind his back. It may be true that backstage activity often takes the form of a council of war; but when two teams meet on the field of interaction it seems that they generally do not meet for peace or for war. They meet under a temporary truce, a working consensus, in order to get their business done.

Staging Talk

When teammates are out of the presence of the audience, discussion often turns to problems of staging. Questions are raised about the condition of sign-equipment; stands, lines, and positions are tentatively brought forth and "cleared" by the assembled membership; the merits and demerits of

[8] Cf. Kenneth Burke, A *Rhetoric of Motives*, p. 234 ff., who gives a social analysis of the individual being initiated, using as a key word "hazing."

available front regions are analyzed; the size and character of possible audiences for the performance are considered; past performance disruptions and likely disruptions are talked about; news about the teams of one's colleagues is transmitted; the reception given one's last performance is mulled over in what are sometimes called "post mortems"; wounds are licked and morale is strengthened for the next performance.

Staging talk, when called by other names such as gossip, "shop talk," etc., is a well-worn notion. I have stressed it here because it helps point up the fact that individuals with widely different social roles live in the same climate of dramaturgical experience. The talks that comedians and scholars give are quite different, but their talk about their talk is quite similar. To a surprising degree, before the talk, talkers talk to their friends about what will and will not hold the audience, what will and will not give offense; after the talk, all talkers talk to their friends about the kind of hall they spoke in, the kind of audience they drew, and the kind of reception they obtained. Staging talk has already been referred to in the discussion of backstage activity and collegial solidarity and will not be further discussed here.

Team Collusion

When a participant conveys something during interaction, we expect him to communicate only through the lips of the character he has chosen to project, openly addressing all of his remarks to the whole interaction so that all persons present are given equal status as recipients of communication. Thus whispering, for example, is often considered improper and prohibited, for it can destroy the impression that the performer is only what he appears to be and that things are as he has claimed them to be.[1]

---

[1] In recreational games, whispered huddles may be defined as acceptable, as they may before audiences such as children or foreigners to whom little consideration need be given. In social arrangements in which knots or clusters of persons hold separate conversations in each other's visible presence, an effort is often

In spite of the expectation that everything said by the performer will be in keeping with the definition of the situation fostered by him, he may convey a great deal during an interaction that is out of character and convey it in such a way as to prevent the audience as a whole from realizing that anything out of keeping with the definition of the situation has been conveyed. Persons who are admitted to this secret communication are placed in a collusive relationship to one another vis-à-vis the remainder of the participants. By acknowledging to one another that they are keeping relevant secrets from the others present, they acknowledge to one another that the show of candor they maintain, a show of being only the characters they officially project, is merely a show. By means of such byplay, performers can affirm a backstage solidarity even while engaged in a performance expressing with impunity unacceptable things about the audience as well as things about themselves that the audience would find unacceptable. I shall call "team collusion" any collusive communication which is carefully conveyed in such a way as to cause no threat to the illusion that is being fostered for the audience.

One important kind of team collusion is found in the system of secret signals through which performers can surreptitiously receive or transmit pertinent information, requests for assistance, and other matters of a kind relevant to the successful presentation of a performance. Typically, these staging cues come from, or to, the director of the performance, and it greatly simplifies his task of managing impressions to have such a subterranean language available. Staging cues often relate those engaged in presenting a performance to those who are offering assistance or direction backstage. Thus, by means of a foot-buzzer, a hostess can give directions to her kitchen staff while acting as if she is fully involved in the mealtime conversation. Similarly, during radio and television productions a vocabulary of signs is employed by those in the control room to guide

---

made by the participants in each cluster to act as if what they are saying *could be* said in the other clusters even though it is not.

performers, especially as regards their timing, without allowing the audience to become aware that a system of control communication is in operation in addition to the communication in which performers and audience are officially participating. So also, in business offices, executives who want to terminate interviews both rapidly and tactfully will train their secretaries to interrupt interviews at the proper time with the proper excuse. Another example may be taken from the kind of social establishment in America in which shoes are commonly sold. Sometimes a customer who wants a shoe of larger size than the one that is available or the one that fits may be handled as follows:

> To impress the customer as to the effectiveness of his stretching the shoe, the salesman may tell the customer that he is going to stretch the shoes on the *thirty-four last*. This phrase tells the wrapper not to stretch the shoes, but to wrap them up as they are and hold them under the counter for a short while.[2]

Staging cues are, of course, employed between performers and a shill or confederate in the audience, as in the case of "Cross fire" between a pitchman and his plant among the suckers. More commonly we find these cues employed among teammates while engaged in a performance, these cues in fact providing us with one reason for employing the concept of team instead of analyzing interaction in terms of a pattern of individual performances. This kind of teammate collusion, for example, plays an important role in impression management in American shops. Clerks in a given store commonly develop their own cues for handling the performance presented to the customer, although certain terms in the vocabulary seem to be relatively standardized and occur in the same form in many shops across the country. When clerks are members of a foreign language group, as is sometimes the case, they may employ this language for secret communication—a practice also employed by parents who spell out words in front of young children and by mem-

[2] David Geller, "Lingo of the Shoe Salesman," *American Speech*, IX, p. 285.

bers of our better classes who talk to each other in French about things they do not want their children, their domestics, or their tradesmen to hear. However, this tactic, like whispering, is considered crude and impolite; secrets can be kept in this way but not the fact that secrets are being kept. Under such circumstances, teammates can hardly maintain their front of sincere solicitude for the customer (or frankness to the children, etc.). Harmless-sounding phrases which the customer thinks he understands are more useful to· salespersons. For example, if a customer in a shoe store deeply desires, say, a B width, the salesman can convince the customer that that is what she is getting:

> . . . the salesman will call to another salesman down the aisle and say, *"Benny,* what size is this shoe?" By calling the salesman, *"Benny"* he implies that the answer should be that the width is B.[8]

An engaging illustration of this kind of collusion is given in a paper on the Borax furniture house:

> Now that the customer is in the store, suppose she can't be sold? The price is too high; she must consult her husband; she is only shopping. To let her walk (i.e., escape without buying) is treason in a Borax House. So an SOS is sent out by the salesman through one of the numerous foot-pushes in the store. In a flash the "manager" is on the scene, preoccupied with a suite and wholly oblivious of the Aladdin who sent for him.
>
> "Pardon me, Mr. Dixon," says the salesman, simulating reluctance in disturbing such a busy personage. "I wonder if you could do something for my customer. She thinks the price of this suite is too high. Madam, this is our manager, Mr. Dixon."
>
> Mr. Dixon clears his throat impressively. He is all of six feet, has iron-gray hair and wears a Masonic pin on the lapel of his coat. Nobody would suspect from his appearance that he is only a T.O. man, a special salesman to whom difficult customers are turned over.

[8] David Geller, *op. cit.,* p. 284.

"Yes," says Mr. Dixon, stroking his well-shaven chin, "I see. You go on, Bennett. I'll take care of madam myself. I'm not so busy at the moment anyhow."

The salesman slips away, valet-like, though he'll give Dixon hell if he muffs that sale.[4]

The practice described here of "T.O.-ing" a customer to another salesman who takes the role of the manager is apparently common in many retail establishments. Other illustrations may be taken from a report on the language of furniture salesmen:

"Give me the number of this article," is a question concerning the price of the article. The forthcoming response is in code. The code is universal throughout the United States and is conveyed by simply doubling the cost, the salesman knowing what percentage of profit to add on to that.[5]

Verlier is used as a command . . . , meaning "lose yourself." It is employed when a salesman wants to let another salesman know that the latter's presence is interfering with a sale.[6]

In the semi-illegal and high-pressure fringes of our commercial life, it is common to find that teammates use an explicitly learned vocabulary through which information crucial to the show can be secretly conveyed. Presumably this kind of code is not commonly found in thoroughly respectable circles.[7] We find, however, that teammates

[4] Conant, op. cit., p. 174.
[5] Charles Miller, "Furniture Lingo," American Speech, VI, p. 128.
[6] Ibid., p. 126.
[7] An exception, of course, is found in the boss-secretary relation in respectable establishments. Esquire Etiquette, for example, approves the following; p. 24.
"If you share your office with your secretary, you will do well to arrange a signal which means you'd like her to get out while you talk to a visitor in private. 'Will you leave us alone for a

everywhere employ an informally and often unconsciously learned vocabulary of gestures and looks by which collusive staging cues can be conveyed.

Sometimes these informal cues or "high signs" will initiate a phase in a performance. Thus, when "in company," a husband may convey to his wife, by subtle shadings in his tone of voice, or a change in his posture, that the two of them will definitely now start making their farewells. The conjugal team can then maintain an appearance of unity in action which looks spontaneous but often presupposes a strict discipline. Sometimes cues are available by which one performer can warn another that the other is beginning to act out of line. The kick under the table and the narrowed eyes have become humorous examples. A piano accompanist suggests a way by which deviating concert singers can be brought back into tune:

> He [the accompanist] does this by getting more sharpness into his tone, so that his tone will penetrate to the singer's ears, over or rather through his voice. Perhaps one of the notes in the pianoforte harmony is the very note that the singer should be singing, and so he makes this note predominate. When this actual note is not written in the pianoforte part, he must add it in the treble clef, where it will pipe loud and clear for the singer to hear. If the latter is singing a quarter of a tone sharp, or a quarter of a tone flat, it will be an extraordinary feat on his part to continue to sing out of tune, especially if the accompanist plays the vocal line with him for the whole phrase. Once having seen the danger signal the accompanist will continue to be on the *qui vive* and will sound the singer's note from time to time.[8]

The same writer goes on to say something that applies to many kinds of performances:

---

while, Miss Smith?' embarrasses everybody; it's easier all around if you can convey the same idea, by prearrangement, with something like. 'Will you see if you can settle that business with the merchandising department, Miss Smith?' "

[8] Moore, *op. cit.*, pp. 56–57.

A sensitive singer will need only the most delicate of cues from his partner. Indeed they can be so delicate that even the singer himself while profiting by them will not be consciously aware of them. The less sensitive the singer, the more pointed and therefore the more obvious these cues will have to be.[9]

Another example may be cited from Dale's discussion of how civil servants during a meeting can cue their minister that he is on treacherous ground:

But in the course of conversation new and unforeseen points may well arise. If a civil servant at the committee then sees his Minister taking a line which he thinks wrong, he will not say so flatly; he will either scribble a note to the Minister or he will delicately put forward some fact or suggestion as a minor modification of his Minister's view. An experienced Minister will perceive the red light at once and gently withdraw, or at least postpone discussion. It will be clear that the mixture of Ministers and civil servants in a Committee requires on occasion some exercise of tact and some quickness of perception on both sides.[10]

Very frequently informal staging cues will warn teammates that the audience has suddenly come into their presence. Thus, in Shetland Hotel, when a guest was forward enough to step into the kitchen uninvited, the first person to see this would call out in a special tone of voice either the name of the other staff person present or a collective name, such as "bairns," if more than one other were present. On this signal, males would remove caps from head, feet from chairs, the females would bring their limbs into more proper array, and all present would visibly stiffen in preparation for a forced performance. A well-known performance warning that is formally learned is the visual signal employed in broadcasting studios. These literally or sym-

9 *Ibid.*, p. 57.
10 Dale, *op. cit.*, p. 141.

bolically read: "You are on the air." An equally broad cue is reported by Ponsonby:

> The Queen [Victoria] often went to sleep during these hot drives, and in order that she should not be seen like this by a crowd in a village, I used to dig my spurs into the horse whenever I saw a large crowd ahead and make the astonished animal jump about and make a noise. Princess Beatrice always knew that this meant a crowd, and if the Queen didn't wake with the noise I made, she woke her herself.[11]

Many other kinds of persons have stood watch, of course, over the relaxation of many other kinds of performers, as may be illustrated from Katherine Archibald's study of work in a shipyard:

> At times when work was especially slack I have myself stood guard at the door of a tool shack, ready to warn of the approach of a superintendent or a front-office boss, while for day after day nine or ten lesser bosses and workmen played poker with passionate absorption.[12]

So, too, there are typical staging cues which tell the performers that the coast is now clear and that relaxation of front is possible. Other warning signs tell the performers that while it may seem all right to drop their guard of discretion there are in fact members of the audience present, making it inadvisable to do so. In the criminal world, in fact the warning that "legit" ears are listening or legit eyes are watching is so important that it has a special name, called "giving the office." Such signs, of course, can also tell the team that an innocent-looking member of the audience is really a spotter or shopper or someone who is in other ways more or less than he seems.

It would be difficult for any team—a family, for example—to manage the impressions it fosters without such a set of warning signals. A memoir concerning a mother and daugh-

[11] Ponsonby, *op. cit.*, p. 102.
[12] Archibald, *op. cit.*, p. 194.

ter who lived in one room in London provides the following example:

> On the way past Gennaro's I became filled with apprehension about our lunch, wondering how my mother would take to Scotty [a manicurist-colleague she was bringing home to lunch for the first time] and what Scotty would think of my mother, and we were no sooner on the staircase than I started to talk in a loud voice to warn her that I was not alone. Indeed, this was quite a signal between us, for when two people live in a single room there is no telling what sort of untidiness can meet the unexpected visitor's eye. There was nearly always a cooking-pan or a dirty plate where it should not be, or stockings or a petticoat drying above the stove. My mother, warned by the raised voice of her ebullient daughter, would rush round like a circus dancer hiding the pan or the plate or the stockings, and then turn herself into a pillar of frozen dignity, very calm, all ready for the visitor. If she had cleared things up too quickly, and forgotten something very obvious, I would see her vigilant eye fixed upon it and I would be expected to do something about it without exciting the visitor's attention.[13]

It may be noted, finally, that the more unconsciously these cues are learned and employed, the easier it will be for the members of a team to conceal even from themselves that they do in fact function as a team. As previously suggested, even to its own members, a team may be a secret society.

Closely associated with staging cues, we find that teams work out ways of conveying extended verbal messages to one another in such a way as to protect a projected impression that might be disrupted were the audience to appreciate that information of this kind was being conveyed. Again we may cite an illustration from the British civil service:

[13] Mrs. Robert Henrey, *Madeleine Grown Up* (New York: Dutton, 1953), pp. 46–47.

It is a very different matter when a civil servant is called on to watch over a Bill in its passage through Parliament, or to go down to either House for a debate. He cannot speak in his own person; he can only supply the Minister with material and suggestions, and hope that he will make good use of them. It need hardly be said that the Minister is carefully "briefed" beforehand for any set speech, as on the second or third reading of an important Bill, or the introduction of the Department's annual estimates: for such an occasion the Minister is supplied with full notes on every point likely to be raised, even with anecdotes and "light relief" of a decorous official nature. He himself, his Private Secretary, and the Permanent Secretary probably spend a good deal of time and labor in selecting from these notes the most effective points to emphasize, arranging them in the best order and devising an impressive peroration. All this is easy both for the Minister and his officials; it is done in quiet and at leisure. But the crux is the reply at the end of a debate. There the Minister must mainly depend on himself. It is true that the civil servants sitting with patient endurance in the little gallery on the Speaker's right or at the entrance to the House of Lords, have noted down inaccuracies and distortions of fact, false inferences, misunderstandings of the Government proposals and similar weaknesses, in the case presented by Opposition speakers: but it is often difficult to get this ammunition up to the firing-line. Sometimes the Minister's Parliamentary Private Secretary will rise from his seat just behind his chief, stroll carelessly along to the official gallery and hold a whispered conversation with the civil servants: sometimes a note will be passed along to the Minister: very rarely he himself will come for a moment and ask a question. All these little communications must go on under the eyes of the House, and no Minister cares to seem like an actor who does not know his part and requires to be prompted.[14]

[14] Dale, *op. cit.*, pp. 148–49.

Business etiquette, perhaps more concerned with strategic secrets than with moral ones, offers the following suggestions:

> . . . Guard your end of a phone conversation if an outsider is within earshot. If you are taking a message from someone else, and you want to be sure you've got it straight, don't repeat the message in the usual fashion; instead, ask the caller to repeat it, so your clarion tones won't announce a possibly private message to all bystanders.
>
> . . . Cover your papers before an outside caller arrives, or make a habit of keeping them in folders or under a covering blank sheet.
>
> . . . If you must speak to someone else in your organization when he is with an outsider, or with anyone who is not concerned with your message, do it in such a way that the third person doesn't pick up any information. You might use the interoffice telephone rather than the intercom, say, or write your message on a note you can hand over instead of speaking your piece in public.[15]

A visitor who is expected should be announced immediately. If you are closeted with another person your secretary interrupts you to say something like, "Your three o'clock appointment is here. I thought you'd like to know." (She doesn't mention the visitor's name in the hearing of an outsider. If you are not likely to remember who your "three o'clock appointment" is, she writes the name on a slip of paper and hands it to you, or uses your private phone instead of the loudspeaker system.)[16]

Staging cues have been suggested as one main type of team collusion; another type involves communications which function chiefly to confirm for the performer the fact that he does not really hold with the working consensus, that the show he puts on is only a show, thereby providing himself with at least a private defense against the claims

---

[15] *Esquire Etiquette, op. cit.*, p. 7. Ellipsis dots the authors'.
[16] *Esquire Etiquette, op. cit.*, pp. 22–23.

made by the audience. We may label this activity "derisive collusion"; it typically involves a secret derogation of the audience although sometimes conceptions of the audience may be conveyed that are too complimentary to fit within the working consensus. We have here a furtive public counterpart of what was described in the section called "Treatment of the Absent."

Derisive collusion occurs most frequently, perhaps, between a performer and himself. School children provide examples of this when they cross their fingers while telling a lie or stick out their tongues when the teacher momentarily moves to a position where she cannot see the tribute. So, too, employees will often grimace at their boss, or gesticulate a silent curse, performing these acts of contempt or insubordination at an angle such that those to whom these acts are directed cannot see them. Perhaps the most timid form of this kind of collusion is found in the practice of "doodling" or of "going away" to imaginary pleasant places, while still maintaining some show of performing the part of listener.

Derisive collusion also occurs between members of a team when they are presenting a performance. Thus, while a secret code of verbal insults may perhaps be employed only on the lunatic fringe of our commercial life, there is no commercial establishment so reputable that its clerks do not cast each other knowing looks when in the presence of an undesirable client or a desirable client who conducts himself in an undesirable way. Similarly, in our society it is very difficult for a husband and wife, or two close friends, to spend an evening in convivial interaction with a third person without at some time looking at each other in such a way as to contradict secretly the attitude they are officially maintaining toward the third person.

A more damaging form of this kind of aggression against the audience is found in situations where the performer is forced to take a line which is deeply contrary to his inward feelings. An example may be cited from a report outlining some of the defensive actions taken by prisoners of war in Chinese indoctrination camps:

It should be pointed out, however, that the prisoners found numerous ways to obey the letter but not the spirit of the Chinese demands. For example, during public self-criticism sessions they would often emphasize the wrong words in the sentence, thus making the whole ritual ridiculous: "I am sorry I called Comrade Wong *a no-good son-of-a-bitch.*" Another favorite device was to promise never to "get caught" committing a certain crime in the future. Such devices were effective because even those Chinese who knew English were not sufficiently acquainted with idiom and slang to detect subtle ridicule.[17]

A similar form of communication out of character occurs where one member of a team performs his part for the special and secret amusement of his teammates; for example, he may throw himself into his part with an affective enthusiasm that is at once exaggerated and precise, but so close to what the audience expects that they do not quite realize, or are not sure, that fun is being made of them. Thus, jazz musicians obliged to play "corny" music will sometimes play a little more corny than necessary, the slight exaggeration serving as a means by which the musicians can convey to each other their contempt for the audience and their own loyalty to higher things.[18] A somewhat similar form of collusion occurs when one team member attempts to tease another while both are engaged in a performance. The immediate object here will be to make one's teammate almost burst out laughing, or almost trip, or almost lose his poise in other ways. For example, in Shetland Hotel, the cook would sometimes stand at the kitchen entrance to the front regions of the hotel and solemnly answer with dignity and in standard English the questions put to him by hotel guests, while from within the kitchen the maids, straight-faced, would secretly but persistently goose him. By mocking the audience or teasing a teammate, the performer can show not only that he is not bound by the

---

[17] E. H. Schein, "The Chinese Indoctrination Program for Prisoners of War," *Psychiatry,* 19, pp. 159–60.
[18] Personal communication by Howard S. Becker.

official interaction but also that he has this interaction so much under control that he can toy with it at will.

A final form of derisive byplay may be mentioned. Often when an individual is interacting with a second individual who is offensive in some way, he will try to catch the eye of a third individual—one who is defined as an outsider to the interaction—and in this way confirm that he is not to be held responsible for the character or behavior of the second individual. It may be noted in conclusion that all of these forms of derisive collusion tend to arise almost involuntarily, through cues that are conveyed before they can be checked.

Given these many ways in which members of a team communicate to one another out of character, we might well expect that performers might develop an attachment to this kind of activity even at times when there is no practical need for it, and thus welcome partners for their solo performances. It is understandable then that one specialized team-role that seems to develop is that of the "side-kick," namely, the person who can be brought into a performance at the pleasure of another person, for the purpose of ensuring the latter the comforts of a teammate. One can expect to find this special way of being made a convenience of wherever there are marked differences in power and no taboo against social intercourse between the empowered and the powerless. The passing social role of companion provides an illustration, as suggested in a fictional autobiography written in the late eighteenth century:

> My business shortly was this; to be always ready at a moment's warning to join my lady in every party of pleasure or business she chuses to mix with. I attend her in the morning to all sales, auctions, exhibitions, &c. and particularly was present at the important affair of *shopping* . . . I attend my lady on all visits, unless the party was particularly select, and was present in all companies at home, where I acted as a kind of upper servant.[19]

[19] From *Lady's Magazine*, 1789, XX, p. 235, quoted in Hecht, *op. cit.*, p. 63.

This office seemed to have required the incumbent to attend the master at his will, not for menial purposes, or not for these purposes alone, but so that the master would always have someone to be aligned with over against the others present.

Realigning Actions

It has been suggested that when individuals come together for the purpose of interaction, each adheres to the part that has been cast for him within his team's routine, and each joins with his teammates in maintaining the appropriate mixture of formality and informality, of distance and intimacy, toward the members of the other team. This does not mean that teammates will openly treat one another in the same way as they openly treat the audience, but it does usually mean that teammates will treat one another differ-ently from the way that would be most "natural" for them. Collusive communication has been suggested as one way in which teammates can free themselves a little from the restrictive requirements of interaction between teams; it is a kind of deviation from type which the audience is meant to remain unaware of, and it tends, therefore, to leave the *status quo* intact. However, performers rarely seem content with safe channels for expressing discontent with the work-ing consensus. They often attempt to speak out of character in a way that will be heard by the audience but will not openly threaten either the integrity of the two teams or the social distance between them. These temporary unofficial, or controlled, realignments, often aggressive in character, provide an interesting area for study.

When two teams establish an official working consensus as a guarantee for safe social interaction, we may usually detect an unofficial line of communication which each team directs at the other. This unofficial communication may be carried on by innuendo, mimicked accents, well-placed jokes, significant pauses, veiled hints, purposeful kidding, expressive overtones, and many other sign practices. Rules regarding this laxity are quite strict. The communicator has the right to deny that he "meant anything" by his action, should his recipients accuse him to his face of having conveyed something unacceptable, and the recipients have the right to act as if nothing, or only something innocuous, has been conveyed.

Perhaps the most common drift of undercurrent communication is for each team subtly to put itself in a favorable light and subtly to put the other team in an unfavorable one, often under the cover of verbal courtesies and compliments which point in the other direction.[1] Teams, then, will often strain at the leash that holds them in check in a working consensus. Interestingly enough, it is these covert forces of self-elevation and other-derogation that often introduce a dreary compulsive rigidity to sociable encounters, and not the more bookish kinds of social ritual.

In many kinds of social interaction, unofficial communication provides a way in which one team can extend a definite but non-compromising invitation to the other, requesting that social distance and formality be increased or decreased, or that both teams shift the interaction to one involving the performance of a new set of roles. This is sometimes known as "putting out feelers" and involves guarded disclosures and hinted demands. By means of statements that are carefully ambiguous or that have a secret meaning to the initiate, a performer is able to discover, without dropping his defensive stand, whether or not it is safe to dispense with the current definition of the situation. For example, since it is not necessary to retain social distance or be on guard before those who are one's colleagues in occupation, ideology, ethnicity, class, etc., it is common for colleagues to develop secret signs which seem innocuous to non-colleagues while at the same time they convey to the initiate that he

[1] Potter's term for this phenomenon is "one upmanship." It is considered under the phrase "making points," in E. Goffman, "On Face-Work," *Psychiatry*, 18, 221–22; "status forcing," in A. Strauss, *Essay on Identity* (forthcoming). In some American circles, the phrase "putting a person down," is used precisely in this connection. An excellent application to one type of social intercourse is given by Jay Haley, "The Art of Psychoanalysis," *ETC*, XV, pp. 189–200.

is among his own and can relax the pose he maintains toward the public. Thus the murderous Thugs of nineteenth-century India, who hid their annual depredations behind a nine-month show of civic-minded actions, possessed a code for recognizing one another. As one writer suggests:

> When Thugs meet, though strangers, there is something in their manner which soon discovers itself to each other, and to assure the surmise thus excited, one exclaims "Alee Khan!" which, on being repeated by the other party, a recognition of each other's habit takes place . . .[2]

Similarly, men of the British working class can be found who still ask a stranger "how far East" is he; fellow Freemasons know how to answer this password and know that after they do answer it those present can relax into intolerance for Catholics and the effete classes. (In Anglo-American society the surname and the appearance of persons to whom one is introduced serve a similar function, telling one which of the segments of the population it will be impolitic to cast aspersions against.) So, too, some patrons in delicatessen restaurants will make a point of asking that their sandwiches be made with rye bread and no butter, thus giving staff a cue to the ethnicity that the patron is ready to accept for himself.[8]

The guarded disclosure by which two members of an intimate society make themselves known to each other is perhaps the least subtle version of disclosive communication. In everyday life, where individuals have no secret society to disclose their membership in, a more delicate process is involved When individuals are unfamiliar with each other's opinions and statuses. a feeling-out process occurs whereby one individual admits his views or statuses to another a little at a time. After dropping his guard just a little he waits for the other to show reason why it is safe for him to do this, and after this reassurance he can safely drop his

---

[2] Col. J. L. Sleeman, *Thugs or a Million Murders* (London: Sampson Low, n.d.), p. 79.

[8] "Team Work and Performance in a Jewish Delicatessen," unpublished paper by Louis Hirsch.

guard a little bit more. By phrasing each step in the admission in an ambiguous way, the individual is in a position to halt the procedure of dropping his front at the point where he gets no confirmation from the other, and at this point he can act as if his last disclosure were not an overture at all. Thus when two persons in conversation are attempting to discover how careful they are going to have to be about stating their true political opinions, one of them can halt his gradual disclosure of how far left or how far right he is just at the point where the other has come to the furthest extreme of his actual beliefs. In such cases, the person with the more extreme views will tactfully act as if his views are no more extreme than the other's.

This process of gradual guarded disclosure is also illustrated by some of the mythology and a few of the facts associated with heterosexual life in our society. The sexual relation is defined as one of intimacy with the initiative allocated to the male. In fact, courting practices involve a concerted aggression against the alignment between the sexes on the part of the male, as he attempts to maneuver someone for whom he must at first show respect into a position of subordinate intimacy.[4] However, an even more aggressive action against the alignment between the sexes is found in situations where the working consensus is defined in terms of superordination and distance on the part of a performer who happens to be a woman and subordination on the part of a performer who happens to be a man. The possibility arises that the male performer will redefine the situation to emphasize his sexual superordination as opposed to his socio-economic subordination.[5] In our proletarian lit-

---

[4] Protective disclosive routines in the homosexual world have a double function: the disclosing of membership in a secret society, and overtures of relationship between particular members of this society. A well-formulated literary illustration may be found in Gore Vidal's short story, "Three Stratagems," in his *A Thirsty Evil* (New York: Signet Pocket Books, 1958), esp. pp. 7-17.

[5] Perhaps because of respect for the Freudian ethic, some sociologists seem to act as if it would be in bad taste, impious, or self-revelatory to define sexual intercourse as part of the cere-

erature, for example, it is the poor man who introduces this redefinition in regard to a rich woman; *Lady Chatterley's Lover,* as has often been remarked, is a clear-cut example. And when we study service occupations, especially lowly ones, inevitably we find that practitioners have anecdotes to tell about the time they or one of their colleagues redefined the service relation into a sexual one (or had it redefined for them). Tales of such aggressive redefinitions are a significant part of the mythology not only of particular occupations but also of the male subculture generally.

Temporary realignments through which direction of the interaction may be seized in an unofficial way by a subordinate, or unofficially extended by a superordinate, attain some kind of stability and institutionalization in what is sometimes called "double-talk."[6] By this communication technique two individuals may convey information to one another in a manner or on a matter that is inconsistent with their official relationship. Double-talk involves the kind of innuendo that can be conveyed by both sides and carried on for a sustained period of time. It is a kind of collusive communication different from other types of collusion in that the characters against whom the collusion is sustained are projected by the very persons who enter into the collusion. Typically double-talk occurs during interaction between a subordinate and a superordinate concerning matters which are officially outside the competence and jurisdiction of the subordinate but which actually depend on him. By employing double-talk the subordinate can initiate lines of

---

monial system, a reciprocal ritual performed to confirm symbolically an exclusive social relationship. This chapter draws heavily on Kenneth Burke, who clearly takes the sociological view in defining courtship as a principle of rhetoric through which social estrangements are transcended. See Burke, *A Rhetoric of Motives,* p. 208 ff. and pp. 267–68.

[6] In everyday speech the term "double-talk" is also used in two other senses: it is used to refer to sentences in which sounds have been injected which seem as if they might be meaningful but really are not; it is used to refer to protectively ambiguous answers to questions for which the asker desired a clear-cut reply.

action without giving open recognition to the expressive implication of such initiation and without putting into jeopardy the status difference between himself and his superordinate. Barracks and jails apparently abound in double-talk. It is also commonly found in situations where the subordinate has had long experience with the job whereas the superordinate has not, as in the split which occurs in government offices between a "permanent" deputy minister and a politically appointed minister, and in those cases where the subordinate speaks the language of a group of employees but his superordinate does not. We may also find double-talk in situations where two persons engage in illicit agreements with each other, for by this technique communication may occur and yet neither participant need place himself in the hands of the other. A similar form of collusion is sometimes found between two teams that must maintain the impression of being relatively hostile or relatively distant toward each other and yet find it mutually profitable to come to an agreement on certain matters, providing this does not embarrass the oppositional stand they are obliged to be ready to maintain toward each other.[7] In other words, deals can be made without creating the mutual-solidarity relationship which dealing usually leads to. More important, perhaps, double-talk regularly occurs in intimate domestic and work situations, as a safe means of making and refusing requests and commands that could not be openly made or openly refused without altering the relationship.

I have considered some common realigning actions—movements around, or over, or away from the line between the teams. Processes such as unofficial grumbling, guarded disclosures, and double-talk were given as instances. I would like to add a few more types to the picture.

When the working consensus established between two teams is one involving avowed opposition, we find that the division of labor within each team may ultimately lead to

---

[7] See Dale, op. cit., pp. 182–83, for an illustration of tacit compromises between two teams officially opposed to each other. See also Melville Dalton, "Unofficial Union-Management Relations," American Sociological Review, XV, pp. 611–19.

momentary realignments of the kind that make us appreciate that not only armies have the problem of fraternization.
A specialist on one team may find that he has a great deal
in common with his opposite number on the other team and
that together they talk a language which tends to align
them together on a single team in opposition to all the remaining participants. Thus, during labor-management negotiations, opposing lawyers may find themselves exchang-
ing collusive looks when a layman on either team makes a
patent legal gaffe. When the specialists are not permanently
part of a particular team but rather hire themselves out for
the duration of negotiations, they are likely to be more loyal
in some ways to their calling and their colleagues than to
the team they happen at the time to be serving. If, then,
the impression of opposition between the teams is to be
maintained, the crosscutting loyalties of specialists will have
to be suppressed or expressed surreptitiously. Thus lawyers,
in sensing that their clients want them to be hostile to the
opposing lawyers, may wait until a backstage recess before
having a friendly collegial chat about the case in progress.
In discussing the role that civil servants play in parliamentary debates, Dale makes a similar suggestion:

> A set debate on one subject . . . as a rule takes only
> one day. If a Department is so unlucky as to have a long
> and contentious Bill in Committee of the whole House,
> the Minister and the civil servants in charge of it must be
> there from 4 p.m. till 11 p.m. (sometimes much later
> if the 11 o'clock rule is suspended), perhaps day after
> day from Monday till Thursday every week. . . . How-
> ever, the civil servants get one compensation for their
> sufferings. It is at this time that they are most likely to
> renew and extend their acquaintances in the House. The
> sense of pressure is less both among Members and among
> officials than during a set debate of one day: it is legiti-
> mate to escape from the debating chamber to the
> smoking-room or the terrace and engage in cheerful con-
> versation while a notorious bore is moving an amendment
> which everyone knows to be impossible. A certain *cama-*

raderie arises among all engaged night after night upon a Bill, Government, Opposition, and civil servants alike.[8]

Interestingly enough, in some cases even backstage fraternization may be considered too much of a threat to the show. Thus baseball players whose teams will represent opposing sides of fans are required by league ruling to refrain from convivial conversation with one another just before the game starts.

> This is a readily understandable rule. It would not be seemly to see players chinning as if they were at an afternoon tea, and then hope to support the point that they go after each other hell-bent for leather, which they do, as soon as the game begins. They have to act like opponents all the time.[9]

In all of these cases involving fraternization between opposing specialists, the point is not that the secrets of the teams will be disclosed or their interests made to suffer (although this may occur and may appear to occur) but rather that the impression of opposition that is fostered between the teams may be discredited. The contribution of the specialist must appear to be a spontaneous response to the facts of the case, independently placing him in opposition to the other team; when he fraternizes with his opposite number the technical value of his contribution may not suffer, but, dramaturgically speaking, it is shown up for what it partly is—the purchased performance of a routine task.

I do not mean to imply by this discussion that fraternization occurs only between specialists temporarily taking sides against each other. Whenever loyalties crosscut, a set of individuals may loudly form one pair of teams while quietly forming another. And whenever two teams must sustain a high pitch of mutual antagonism, or social distance, or both, a well-bounded region may come to be established as a place that is not only backstage to the performances maintained by the teams, but is also open to the members of *both* teams. In public mental hospitals, for example, one can

[8] Dale, *op. cit.*, p. 150.
[9] Pinelli, *op. cit.*, p. 169.

often find a room or a sequestered part of the grounds where patients and attendants can engage together in activity such as poker or the skilled gossip of old-timers, and where it is clearly understood that attendants will not "throw their weight around." Army camps sometimes have a similar region. A memoir of life at sea provides another illustration:

> There is an old rule that in the galley every man can speak his mind with impunity, as at Hyde Park Corner in London. An officer who held anything spoken in the galley against a man the moment he steps outside would soon find himself sabotaged off the ship or sent to Coventry.[10]

> For one thing, one is never alone with the cook. There is always somebody hanging around, listening to his gossip or tales of woe, while comfortably seated on the little bench against the warm wall opposite the stove, feet on the rail, cheeks aglow. The footrail provides the clue: the galley is the ship's village-square, and the cook and his stove the hotdog stand. It is the only place where officers and men meet on a footing of complete equality, as the young sailor will soon find out if he enters with a junior prefect's air. Short of calling him "Dear" or "Bud," the cook will put him in his place, which is beside Hank the oilman on the little bench. . . .

> Without this free exchange in the galley, the ship becomes riddled with undercurrents. Everybody agrees that, in the tropics, the tension mounts and the crews become more difficult to handle. Some attribute this to the heat, others know that it is the loss of the age-old safety valve: the galley.[11]

Often, when two teams enter social interaction, we can identify one as having the lower general prestige and the other team the higher. Ordinarily, when we think of realigning actions in such cases, we think of efforts on the

[10] Jan de Hartog, *A Sailor's Life* (New York: Harper Brothers, 1955), p. 155.

[11] *Ibid.*, pp. 154–55.

part of the lower team to alter the basis of interaction in a direction more favorable to them or to decrease the social distance and formality between themselves and the higher team. Interestingly enough, there are occasions when it serves the wider goals of the higher team to lower barriers and admit the lower team to greater intimacy and equality with it. Granting the consequences of extending backstage familiarity to one's lessers, it may be in one's long-range interest to do so momentarily. Thus, in order to prevent a strike, Mr. Barnard tells us he deliberately swore in the presence of a committee representing unemployed workers and also tells us that he was aware of the significance of this:

> In my judgment, confirmed by others whose opinion I respect, it is as a general rule exceedingly bad practice for one in a superior position to swear at or in the presence of those of subordinate or inferior status, even though the latter have no objection to oaths and even though they know the superior is accustomed to cursing. I have known very few men who could do it without adverse reactions on their influence. I suppose the reason is that whatever lowers the dignity of a superior position makes it more difficult to accept difference of position. Also, where a single organization is involved in which the superior position is symbolic of the whole organization, the prestige of the latter is thought to be injured. In the present case, an exception, the oath was deliberate and accompanied by hard pounding of the table.[12]

A similar situation is found in those mental hospitals where milieu therapy is practiced. By bringing the nurse and even attendants into what are usually sacrosanct staff conferences, these non-medical staff persons can feel that the distance between themselves and the doctors is decreasing and

---

[12] Chester I. Barnard, *Organization and Management* (Cambridge, Mass. Harvard University Press, 1949), n. pp. 73–74 This kind of conduct must be clearly distinguished from the rough language and behavior employed by a superordinate who stays within the team made up of his employees and "kids" them into work.

may show more readiness to take the doctors' point of view toward the patients. By sacrificing the exclusiveness of those at the top, it is felt that the morale of those at the bottom can be increased. A staid report of this process is given us by Maxwell Jones in his report on English experience with milieu therapy:

> In the unit we have attempted to develop the role of the doctor to meet our limited treatment goal and have tried to avoid pretense. This has meant a considerable break from hospital tradition. We do not dress to conform to the usual concept of the professional man. We have avoided the white coat, prominent stethoscope, and aggressive percussion hammer as extensions of our body image.[13]

Actually, when we study the interaction between two teams in everyday situations we find that often the super-ordinate team will be expected to unbend just a little. For one thing, such relaxation of front provides a basis for barter; the superordinate receives a service or good of some kind, while the subordinate receives an indulgent grant of intimacy. Thus, the reserve which upper-class people in Britain maintain during interaction with tradesmen and petty officials has been known to give way momentarily when a particular favor must be asked of these subordinates. Also, such relaxation of distance provides one means by which a feeling of spontaneity and involvement can be generated in the interaction. In any case, interaction between two teams often involves the taking of very small liberties, if only as a means of testing the ground to see if unexpected advantage might not be taken of the opposing side.

When a performer refuses to keep his place, whether it is of higher or lower rank than the audience, we may expect that the director, if there is one, and the audience may well become ill-disposed toward him. In many cases, the rank and file are also likely to object to him. As previously sug-

[13] Maxwell Jones, *The Therapeutic Community* (New York: Basic Books, 1953), p. 40.

gested in reference to rate-busters, any extra concession to the audience on the part of one member of the team is a threat to the stand the others have taken and a threat to the security they obtain from knowing and controlling the stand they will have to take. Thus, when one teacher in a school is deeply sympathetic to her charges, or enters into their play during recess, or is willing to come into close contact with the low-status ones among them, the other teachers will find that the impression they are trying to maintain of what constitutes appropriate work is threatened.[14] In fact, when particular performers cross the line that separates the teams, when someone becomes too intimate, or too indulgent, or too antagonistic, we may expect a circuit of reverberations to be set up which affects the subordinate team, the superordinate team, and the particular transgressors.

A hint of such reverberations may be cited from a recent study of merchant seamen, in which the author suggests that when officers quarrel in matters regarding ship duty, the seamen will avail themselves of the breach by offering their commiserations to the officer they feel has been wronged:

> In doing this [playing up to one of the disputants] the crewmen expected the officer to relax in his superior attitude and to allow the men a certain equality while discussing the situation. This soon led to their expecting certain privileges—such as standing in the wheel-house instead of on the wings of the bridge. They took advantage of the mates' dispute to ease their subordinate status.[15]

Recent trends in psychiatric treatment provide us with other examples; I would like to mention some of these.

One instance may be cited from the Maxwell Jones report, although his study purports to be an argument for easing status differences between staff levels and between patients and staff:

[14] Personal communication from Helen Blaw, schoolteacher.
[15] Beattie, *op. cit.*, pp. 25–26.

The integrity of the nurses' group can be upset by the indiscretion of any one member; a nurse who allows her sexual needs to be met in an overt way by the patient alters the patients' attitude towards the whole nursing group and makes the nurses' therapeutic role a less effective one.[16]

Another illustration is found in Bettelheim's comments on his experience in constructing a therapeutic milieu at the Sonia Shankman Orthogenic School at the University of Chicago:

Within the total setting of the therapeutic milieu, personal security, adequate instinctual gratification and group support all sensitize the child to inter-personal relations. It would, of course, defeat the purposes of milieu therapy if the children were not also safeguarded from the kind of disillusionment they have already experienced in their original settings. Staff coherency is therefore an important source of personal security to the children as the staff members remain impervious to the children's attempts to play off one staff member against another.

Originally, many children win the affection of one parent only at the cost of affectionate claims on the other. A child's means of controlling the family situation by pitting one parent against the other is often developed on this basis, but gives him no more than a relative security. Children who have used this technique with particular success are especially handicapped in their ability to form unambivalent relationships later on. In any case, as the children recreate oedipal situations in the school they also form positive, negative or ambivalent attachments to various staff members. It is essential that these relationships between children and individual staff members do not affect the relationships of staff members to each other. Without coherence in this area of the total milieu such attachments might deteriorate into neurotic relationships

16 Maxwell Jones, *op. cit.*, p. 38.

and destroy the basis of identification and sustained affectionate attachments.[17]

A final illustration may be taken from a group therapy project, in which suggestions are sketched in for handling recurrent interaction difficulties caused by troublesome patients:

> Attempts are made to establish a special relationship with the doctor. Patients often attempt to cultivate the illusion of a secret understanding with the doctor by, for example, trying to catch his eye if one patient brings up something that sounds "crazy." If they succeed in getting a response from the doctor which they can interpret as indicating a special bond, it can be very disrupting to the group. Since this type of dangerous byplay is characteristically non-verbal, the doctor must especially control his own non-verbal activity.[18]

Perhaps these citations tell us more about the partly hidden social sentiments of the writers than about the general processes that can occur when someone steps out of line, but recently, in the work of Stanton and Schwartz, we have

[17] Bruno Bettelheim and Emmy Sylvester, "Milieu Therapy," *Psychoanalytic Review*, XXXVI, 65.

[18] Florence B. Powdermaker and others, "Preliminary Report for the National Research Council: Group Therapy Research Project," p. 26.

Betrayal of one's team by catching the eye of a member of the other team is, of course, a common occurrence. It may be noted that in everyday life refusal to enter into momentary collusive communication of this kind when one has been invited to do so is itself a minor affront to the inviter. One may find oneself in a dilemma as to whether to betray the object of the requested collusion or to affront the person requesting the collusion. An example is provided by Ivy Compton-Burnett, *A Family and a Fortune* (London: Eyre & Spottiswoode, 1948), p. 13:

" 'But I was not snoring,' said Blanche, in the easier tone of losing grasp of a situation. 'I should have known it myself. It would not be possible to be awake and make a noise and not hear it.'

"Justine gave an arch look at anyone who would receive it. Edgar did so as a duty and rapidly withdrew his eyes as another."

been given a fairly detailed report of the circuit of consequences which arises when the line between two teams is crossed.[19]

It was suggested that at times of crisis lines may momentarily break and members of opposing teams may momentarily forget their appropriate places with respect to one another. It was also suggested that certain purposes can sometimes be served, apparently, when barriers between teams are lowered, and that to achieve these purposes superordinate teams may temporarily join with the lower ranks. It must be added, as a kind of limiting case, that interacting teams sometimes seem to be prepared to step out of the dramatic framework for their actions and give themselves up for extended periods of time to a promiscuous orgy of clinical, religious, or ethical analysis. We can find a lurid version of this process in evangelical social movements which employ the open confession. A sinner, sometimes admittedly not of very high status, stands up and tells to those who are present things he would ordinarily attempt to conceal or rationalize away; he sacrifices his secrets and his self-protective distance from others, and this sacrifice tends to induce a backstage solidarity among all present. Group therapy affords a similar mechanism for the building up of team spirit and backstage solidarity. A psychic sinner stands up and talks about himself and invites others to talk about him in a way that would be impossible in ordinary interaction. In-group solidarity tends to result, and this "social support," as it is called, presumably has therapeutic value. (By everyday standards, the only thing a patient loses in this way is his self-respect.) Perhaps an echo of this is also to be found in the nurse-doctor meetings previously mentioned.

It may be that these shifts from apartness to intimacy occur at times of chronic strain. Or perhaps we can view

---

[19] Alfred H. Stanton and Morris S. Schwartz, "The Management of a Type of Institutional Participation in Mental Illness," *Psychiatry*, XII, pp. 13–26. In this paper the writers describe nurse-sponsorship of particular patients in terms of its effects upon other patients, the staff, and the transgressors.

them as part of an anti-dramaturgical social movement, a cult of confession. Perhaps such lowering of barriers represents a natural phase in the social change which transforms one team into another: presumably opposing teams trade secrets so that they can start at the beginning to collect a new set of skeletons for a newly shared closet. In any case, we find that occasions arise when opposing teams, be they industrial, marital, or national, seem ready not only to tell their secrets to the same specialist but also to perform this disclosure in the enemy's presence.[20]

It may be suggested here that one of the most fruitful places to study realigning actions, especially temporary betrayals, may not be in hierarchically organized establishments but during informal convivial interaction among relative equals. In fact, the sanctioned occurrence of these aggressions seems to be one of the defining characteristics of our convivial life. It is often expected on such occasions that two persons will engage each other in a sparring conversation for the benefit of listeners and that each will attempt, in an unserious way, to discredit the position taken by the other. Flirting may occur in which males will try to destroy the females' pose of virginal unapproachability, while females may attempt to force from males a commitment of concern without at the same time weakening their own defensive position. (Where those who flirt are at the same time members of different connubial teams, relatively unserious betrayals and sellouts may also occur.) In conversational circles of five or six, basic alignments as between one conjugal pair and another, or between hosts and guests, or between men and women, may be lightheartedly set aside, and the participants will stand ready to shift and reshift team alignments with little provocation, jokingly joining their previous audience against their previous teammates by means of open betrayal of them or by mock collu-

---

[20] An example may be seen in the claimed role of the Tavistock group as therapists for "working through" the antagonism of labor and management in industrial establishments. See the consultation records reported in Eliot Jaques, *The Changing Culture of a Factory* (London: Tavistock Ltd., 1951).

sive communication against them. It may also be defined as
fitting if someone present of high status is made drunk and
made to drop his front and become intimately approachable
by his somewhat-lessers. The same aggressive tone is often
achieved in a less sophisticated way by playing games or
jokes in which the person who is the butt will be led, unseriously, into taking a position that is ludicrously untenable.

I would like to comment on a general point that seems
to emerge from these considerations of team behavior.
Whatever it is that generates the human want for social
contact and for companionship, the effect seems to take two
forms: a need for an audience before which to try out one's
vaunted selves, and a need for teammates with whom to
enter into collusive intimacies and backstage relaxation. And
here the framework of this report begins to be too rigid for
the facts that are pointed out by it. While the two functions
that others can perform for us are usually segregated (this
report being largely devoted to the reasons why this separa-
tion of function is necessary), there are no doubt times
when both functions are performed almost simultaneously
by the same others. As suggested, this may occur as a reciprocal license at convivial gatherings; but of course this dual
function is also found as an unreciprocated obligation, an
obligation enlarging the side-kick role so that its incumbent
will always be available either to witness the impression his
master makes or to help him convey it. Thus, on back-wards
in mental hospitals one can find attendant and patient who
have grown old together, and find that the patient is required to be the butt of the attendant's jokes at one moment, while receiving an aligning collusive wink from him
at another, this therapeutic support being given the attendant whenever he is pleased to demand it. Perhaps the
current military office of aide-de-camp can also be seen in
part in these side-kick terms, the incumbent providing his
general with a teammate who can be dispensed with at
will or used as a member of the audience. Some members
of street-corner gangs and some executive assistants in the
courts that form around Hollywood producers provide other
illustrations.

In this chapter four types of communication out of character have been considered: treatment of the absent; staging talk; team collusion; and realigning actions. Each of
these four types of conduct directs attention to the same
point: the performance given by a team is not a spontaneous, immediate response to the situation, absorbing all
of the team's energies and constituting their sole social reality; the performance is something the team members can
stand back from, back far enough to imagine or play out
simultaneously other kinds of performances attesting to
other realities. Whether the performers feel their official
offering is the "realest" reality or not, they will give surreptitious expression to multiple versions of reality, each version tending to be incompatible with the others.

Chapter VI

THE ARTS OF IMPRESSION MANAGEMENT

In this chapter I would like to bring together what has been said or implied about the attributes that are required of a performer for the work of successfully staging a character. Brief reference will therefore be made to some of the techniques of impression management in which these attributes are expressed. In preparation it may be well to suggest, in some cases for the second time, some of the principal types of performance disruptions, for it is these disruptions which the techniques of impression management function to avoid.

In the beginning of this report, in considering the general characteristics of performances, it was suggested that the performer must act with expressive responsibility, since many minor, inadvertent acts happen to be well designed to convey impressions inappropriate at the time. These events were called "unmeant gestures." Ponsonby gives an illustration of how a director's attempt to avoid an unmeant gesture led to the occurrence of another.

One of the Attachés from the Legation was to carry the cushion on which the insignia were placed, and in order to prevent their falling off I stuck the pin at the back of the Star through the velvet cushion. The Attaché, however, was not content with this, but secured the end of the pin by the catch to make doubly sure. The result was that when Prince Alexander, having made a suitable speech, tried to get hold of the Star, he found it firmly fixed to the cushion and spent some time in getting it loose. This rather spoilt the most impressive moment of the ceremony.[1]

It should be added that the individual held responsible for contributing an unmeant gesture may chiefly discredit his own performance by this, a teammate's performance, or the performance being staged by his audience.

When an outsider accidentally enters a region in which a performance is being given, or when a member of the audience inadvertently enters the backstage, the intruder is likely to catch those present *flagrante delicto*. Through no one's intention, the persons present in the region may find that they have patently been witnessed in activity that is quite incompatible with the impression that they are, for wider social reasons, under obligation to maintain to the intruder. We deal here with what are sometimes called "inopportune intrusions."

The past life and current round of activity of a given performer typically contain at least a few facts which, if introduced during the performance, would discredit or at least weaken the claims about self that the performer was attempting to project as part of the definition of the situation. These facts may involve well-kept dark secrets or negatively-valued characteristics that everyone can see but no one refers to. When such facts are introduced, embarrassment is the usual result. These facts can, of course, be brought to one's attention by unmeant gestures or inopportune intrusions. However, they are more frequently introduced by intentional verbal statements or non-verbal acts whose full significance is not appreciated by the individual who contributes them to the interaction. Following common usage such disruptions of projections may be called "faux pas." Where a performer unthinkingly makes an intentional contribution which destroys his own team's image we may speak of "gaffes" or "boners." Where a performer jeopardizes the image of self projected by the other team, we may speak of "bricks" or of the performer having "put his foot

[1] Ponsonby, *op. cit.*, p. 351.

in it." Etiquette manuals provide classic warnings against such indiscretions:

> If there is any one in the company whom you do not know, be careful how you let off any epigrams or pleasant little sarcasms. You might be very witty upon halters to a man whose father had been hanged. The first requisite for successful conversation is to know your company well.[2]

> In meeting a friend whom you have not seen for some time, and of the state and history of whose family you have not been recently or particularly informed, you should avoid making enquiries or allusions in respect to particular individuals of his family, until you have possessed yourself of knowledge respecting them. Some may be dead; others may have misbehaved, separated themselves, or fallen under some distressing calamity.[3]

Unmeant gestures, inopportune intrusions, and faux pas are sources of embarrassment and dissonance which are typically unintended by the person who is responsible for making them and which would be avoided were the individual to know in advance the consequences of his activity. However there are situations, often called "scenes," in which an individual acts in such a way as to destroy or seriously threaten the polite appearance of consensus, and while he may not act simply in order to create such dissonance, he acts with the knowledge that this kind of dissonance is likely to result. The common-sense phrase, "creating a scene," is apt because, in effect, a new scene is created by such disruptions. The previous and expected interplay between the teams is suddenly forced aside and a new drama forcibly takes its place. Significantly, this new scene often involves a sudden reshuffling and reapportioning of the previous team members into two new teams.

Some scenes occur when teammates can no longer coun-

---

[2] *The Laws of Etiquette* (Philadelphia: Carey, Lee and Blanchard, 1836), p. 101.

[3] *The Canons of Good Breeding*, p. 80.

tenance each other's inept performance and blurt out immediate public criticism of the very individuals with whom
they ought to be in dramaturgical co-operation. Such misconduct is often devastating to the performance which the
disputants ought to be presenting: one effect of the quarrel
is to provide the audience with a backstage view, and another is to leave them with the feeling that something is
surely suspicious about a performance when those who
know it best do not agree. Another type of scene occurs
when the audience decides it can no longer play the game
of polite interaction, or that it no longer wants to do so, and
so confronts the performers with facts or expressive acts
which each team knows will be unacceptable. This is what
happens when an individual screws up his social courage
and decides to "have it out" with another or "really tell him
off." Criminal trials have institutionalized this kind of open
discord, as has the last chapter of murder mysteries, where
an individual who has theretofore maintained a convincing
pose of innocence is confronted in the presence of others
with undeniable expressive evidence that his pose is only a
pose. Another kind of scene occurs when the interaction
between two persons becomes so loud, heated, or otherwise attention-getting, that nearby persons engaged in their
own conversational interaction are forced to become witnesses or even to take sides and enter the fray. A final type
of scene may be suggested. When a person acting as a
one-man team commits himself in a serious way to a claim
or request and leaves himself no way out should this be
denied by the audience, he usually makes sure that his
claim or request is the kind that is likely to be approved
and granted by the audience. If his motivation is strong
enough. however, an individual may find himself making a
claim or an assumption which he knows the audience may
well reject. He knowingly lowers his defenses in their presence, throwing himself, as we say, on their mercy. By such
an act the individual makes a plea to the audience to treat
themselves as part of his team or to allow him to treat himself as part of their team. This sort of thing is embarrassing enough, but when the unguarded request is refused to

the individual's face, he suffers what is called humiliation.

I have considered some major forms of performance disruption—unmeant gestures, inopportune intrusions, faux pas, and scenes. These disruptions, in everyday terms, are often called "incidents." When an incident occurs, the reality sponsored by the performers is threatened. The persons present are likely to react by becoming flustered, ill at ease, embarrassed, nervous, and the like. Quite literally, the participants may find themselves out of countenance. When these flusterings or symptoms of embarrassment become perceived, the reality that is supported by the performance is likely to be further jeopardized and weakened, for these signs of nervousness in most cases are an aspect of the individual who presents a character and not an aspect of the character he projects, thus forcing upon the audience an image of the man behind the mask.

In order to prevent the occurrence of incidents and the embarrassment consequent upon them, it will be necessary for all the participants in the interaction, as well as those who do not participate, to possess certain attributes and to express these attributes in practices employed for saving the show. These attributes and practices will be reviewed under three headings: the defensive measures used by performers to save their own show; the protective measures used by audience and outsiders to assist the performers in saving the performers' show; and, finally, the measures the performers must take in order to make it possible for the audience and outsiders to employ protective measures on the performers' behalf.

Defensive Attributes and Practices

1. DRAMATURGICAL LOYALTY. It is apparent that if a team is to sustain the line it has taken, the teammates must act as if they have accepted certain moral obligations. They must not betray the secrets of the team when between performances—whether from self-interest, principle, or lack of discretion. Thus, older members of a family must often exclude a child of the house from their gossip and self-

admissions, since one can never be sure to whom one's child will convey one's secrets. Hence it may only be when the child arrives at the age of discretion that the voices of his parents will cease to drop as he enters the room. Eighteenth-century writers on the servant problem cite a similar issue of disloyalty, but here in connection with persons who were old enough to know better:

> This lack of devotion [of servants to masters] gave rise to a multitude of petty annoyances from which few employers were entirely immune. Not the least harassing of these was the propensity of servants to retail their masters' business. Defoe takes notice of this, admonishing female domestics to "Add to your other Virtues PIETY, which will teach you the Prudence of *Keeping Family-Secrets;* the Want of which is a great Complaint. . . ."[1]

Voices are dropped at the approach of servants too, but in the early eighteenth century another practice was introduced as a means of keeping team secrets from servants:

> The dumb-waiter was a tier table, which, prior to the dinner hour, was stocked with food, drink, and eating utensils by the servants, who then withdrew, leaving the guests to serve themselves.[2]

Upon the introduction of this dramaturgical device in England, Mary Hamilton reported:

> "My cousin Charles Cathcart din'd with us at Lady Stormont's; we had dumb-waiters so our conversation was not under any restraint by ye Servants being in ye room."[3]

> "At dinner we had ye comfortable *dumb-waiters,* so our conversation was not obliged to be disagreeably *guarded* by ye attendance of Servants."[4]

---

[1] Hecht, *op. cit.,* p. 81, quoting from Defoe's *The Maid-Servant's Modest Defense.*

[2] Hecht, *op. cit.,* p. 208.

[3] *Ibid.,* p. 208.

[4] *Ibid.,* p. 208.

So, too, members of the team must not exploit their presence in the front region in order to stage their own show, as do, for example, marriageable stenographers who sometimes encumber their office surroundings with a lush undergrowth of high fashion. Nor must they use their performance time as an occasion to denounce their team. They must be willing to accept minor parts with good grace and perform enthusiastically whenever, wherever, and for whomsoever the team as a whole chooses. And they must be taken in by their own performance to the degree that is necessary to prevent them from sounding hollow and false to the audience.

Perhaps the key problem in maintaining the loyalty of team members (and apparently with members of other types of collectivities, too) is to prevent the performers from becoming so sympathetically attached to the audience that the performers disclose to them the consequences for them of the impression they are being given, or in other ways make the team as a whole pay for this attachment. In small communities in Britain, for example, the managers of stores will often be loyal to the establishment and will define the product being sold to a customer in glowing terms linked with false advice, but clerks can frequently be found who not only appear to take the role of the customer in giving buying-advice but actually do so. In Shetland Isle, for example, I heard a clerk say to a customer as the clerk was handing over a bottle of cherry pop: "I do not see how you can drink that stuff." No one present considered this to be surprising frankness, and similar comments could be heard every day in the shops on the island. So, too, filling station managers sometimes disapprove of tipping because it may lead attendants to give undue free service to the chosen few while other customers are left waiting.

One basic technique the team can employ to defend itself against such disloyalty is to develop high in-group solidarity within the team, while creating a backstage image of the audience which makes the audience sufficiently inhuman to allow the performers to cozen them with emotional and moral immunity. To the degree that teammates and their colleagues form a complete social community which offers each performer a place and a source of moral support regardless of whether or not he is successful in maintaining his front before the audience, to that degree it would seem that performers can protect themselves from doubt and guilt and practice any kind of deception. Perhaps we are to understand the heartless artistry of the Thugs by reference to the religious beliefs and ritual practices into which their depredations were integrated, and perhaps we are to understand the successful callousness of con men by reference to their social solidarity in what they call the "illegit" world and their well-formulated denigrations of the legitimate world. Perhaps this notion allows us to understand in part why groups that are alienated from or not yet incorporated into the community are so able to enter the dirty-work trades and the kind of service occupations which involve routine cheating.

A second technique for counteracting the danger of affective ties between performers and audience is to change audiences periodically. Thus filling station managers used to be shifted periodically from one station to another to prevent the formation of strong personal ties with particular clients. It was found that when such ties were allowed to form, the manager sometimes placed the interests of a friend who needed credit before the interests of the social establishment.[5] Bank managers and ministers have been routinely shifted for similar reasons, as have certain colonial administrators. Some female professionals provide another illustration, as the following reference to organized prostitution suggests:

> The Syndicate handles that these days. The girls don't stay in one place long enough to really get on speaking terms with anybody. There's not so much chance of a girl falling in love with some guy—you know, and causing

[5] Of course this betrayal is systematically faked in some commercial establishments where the customer is given a "special" cut price by a clerk who claims to be doing this in order to secure the buyer as a steady personal customer.

a squawk. Anyway, the hustler who's in Chicago this week is in St. Louis next, or moving around to half a dozen places in town before being sent somewhere else. And they never know where they're going until they're told.[6]

2. DRAMATURGICAL DISCIPLINE. It is crucial for the maintenance of the team's performance that each member of the team possess dramaturgical discipline and exercise it in presenting his own part. I refer to the fact that while the performer is ostensibly immersed and given over to the activity he is performing, and is apparently engrossed in his actions in a spontaneous, uncalculating way, he must none the less be affectively dissociated from his presentation in a way that leaves him free to cope with dramaturgical contingencies as they arise. He must offer a show of intellectual and emotional involvement in the activity he is presenting, but must keep himself from actually being carried away by his own show lest this destroy his involvement in the task of putting on a successful performance.

A performer who is disciplined, dramaturgically speaking, is someone who remembers his part and does not commit unmeant gestures or faux pas in performing it. He is someone with discretion; he does not give the show away by involuntarily disclosing its secrets. He is someone with "presence of mind" who can cover up on the spur of the moment for inappropriate behavior on the part of his teammates, while all the time maintaining the impression that he is merely playing his part. And if a disruption of the performance cannot be avoided or concealed, the disciplined performer will be prepared to offer a plausible reason for discounting the disruptive event, a joking manner to remove its importance, or deep apology and self-abasement to reinstate those held responsible for it. The disciplined performer is also someone with "self-control." He can suppress his emotional response to his private problems, to his teammates when they make mistakes, and to the audience when

[6] Charles Hamilton, *Men of the Underworld* (New York: Macmillan, 1952), p. 222.

they induce untoward affection or hostility in him. And he can stop himself from laughing about matters which are defined as serious and stop himself from taking seriously matters defined as humorous. In other words, he can suppress his spontaneous feelings in order to give the appearance of sticking to the affective line, the expressive *status quo,* established by his team's performance, for a display of proscribed affect may not only lead to improper disclosures and offense to the working consensus but may also implicitly extend to the audience the status of team member. And the disciplined performer is someone with sufficient poise to move from private places of informality to public ones of varying degrees of formality, without allowing such changes to confuse him.[7]

Perhaps the focus of dramaturgical discipline is to be found in the management of one's face and voice. Here is the crucial test of one's ability as a performer. Actual affective response must be concealed and an appropriate affective response must be displayed. Teasing, it often seems, is an informal initiation device employed by a team to train and test the capacity of its new members to "take a joke," that is, to sustain a friendly manner while perhaps not feeling it. When an individual passes such a test of expression-control, whether he receives it from his new teammates in a spirit of jest or from an unexpected necessity of playing in a serious performance, he can thereafter venture forth as a player who can trust himself and be trusted by others. A very nice illustration of this is given in a forthcoming paper by Howard S. Becker on marijuana-smoking. Becker reports that the irregular user of the drug has a great fear of finding himself, while under the influence of the drug, in the immediate presence of parents or work associates who will expect an intimate undrugged performance from him. Apparently the irregular user does not become a confirmed regular user until he learns he can be "high" and yet carry off a performance before non-smokers without betraying himself. The same issue arises, perhaps in a less dramatic

[7] For an example see Page, *op. cit.,* pp. 91–92.

form, in ordinary family life, when a decision has to be reached as to the point in their training at which young members of the team can be taken to public and semipublic ceremonies, for only when the child is ready to keep control of his temper will he be a trustworthy participant on such occasions.

3. DRAMATURGICAL CIRCUMSPECTION. Loyalty and discipline, in the dramaturgical sense of these terms, are attributes required of teammates if the show they put on is to be sustained. In addition, it will be useful if the members of the team exercise foresight and design in determining in advance how best to stage a show. Prudence must be exercised. When there is little chance of being seen, opportunities for relaxation can be taken; when there is little chance of being put to a test, the cold facts can be presented in a glowing light and the performers can play their part for all it is worth, investing it with full dignity. If no care and honesty are exercised, then disruptions are likely to occur; if rigid care and honesty are exercised, then the performers are not likely to be understood "only too well" but they may be misunderstood, insufficiently understood, or greatly limited in what they can build out of the dramaturgical opportunities open to them. In other words, in the interests of the team. performers will be required to exercise prudence and circumspection in staging the show. preparing in advance for likely contingencies and exploiting the opportunities that remain. The exercise or expression of dramaturgical circumspection takes well-known forms; some of these techniques for managing impressions will be considered here.

Obviously, one such technique is for the team to choose members who are loyal and disciplined, and a second one is for the team to acquire a clear idea as to how much loyalty and discipline it can rely on from the membership as a whole for the degree to which these attributes are possessed will markedly affect the likelihood of carrying off a performance and hence the safety of investing the performance with seriousness, weight, and dignity.

The circumspect performer will also attempt to select the

kind of audience that will give a minimum of trouble in terms of the show the performer wants to put on and the show he does not want to have to put on. Thus it is reported that teachers often favor neither lower-class pupils nor upper-class ones, because both groups may make it difficult to maintain in the classroom the kind of definition of the situation which affirms the professional teacher role.[8] Teachers will transfer to middle-class schools for these dramaturgical reasons. So, too, it is reported that some nurses like to work in an operating room rather than on a ward because in the operating room measures are taken to ensure that the audience, whose members number only one, is soon oblivious to the weaknesses of the show, permitting the operating team to relax and devote itself to the technological requirements of actions as opposed to the dramaturgical ones.[9] Once the audience is asleep it is even possible to bring in a "ghost surgeon" to perform the tasks that others who were there will later claim to have done.[10] Similarly, given the fact that husband and wife are required to express marital solidarity by jointly showing regard for those whom they entertain, it is necessary to exclude from their guests those persons about whom they feel differently.[11] So also, if a man of influence and power is to make sure that he can take a friendly role in office interactions, then it will be useful for him to have a private elevator and protective circles of receptionists and secretaries so that no one can get in to see him whom he might have to treat in a heartless or snobbish fashion.

It will be apparent that an automatic way of ensuring that no member of the team or no member of the audience

[8] Becker, "Social Class Variations . . ." *op. cit.*, pp. 461–62.

[9] Unpublished research report by Edith Lentz. It may be noted that the policy sometimes followed of piping music by earphones to the patient who is undergoing an operation without a general anesthetic is a means of effectively removing him from the talk of the operating team.

[10] Solomon, *op. cit.*, p. 108.

[11] This point has been developed in a short story by Mary McCarthy, "A Friend of the Family," reprinted in Mary McCarthy, *Cast a Cold Eye* (New York: Harcourt Brace, 1950).

acts improperly is to limit the size of both teams as much as possible. Other things being equal, the fewer the members, the less possibility of mistakes, "difficulties," and treacheries. Thus salesmen like to sell to unaccompanied customers, since it is generally thought that two persons in the audience are much more difficult to "sell" than one. So, too, in some schools there is an informal rule that no teacher is to enter the room of another teacher while the other is holding a class; apparently the assumption is that it will be likely the new performer will do something that the waiting eyes of the student audience will see as inconsistent with the impression fostered by their own teacher.[12] However, there are at least two reasons why this device of limiting the number of persons present has limitations itself. First, some performances cannot be presented without the technical assistance of a sizable number of teammates. Thus, although an army general staff appreciates that the more officers there are who know the plans for the next phase of action, the more likelihood that someone will act in such a way as to disclose strategic secrets, the staff will still have to let enough men in on the secret to plan and arrange the event. Secondly, it appears that individuals, as pieces of expressive equipment, are more effective in some ways than non-human parts of the setting. If, then, an individual is to be given a place of great dramatic prominence, it may be necessary to employ a sizable court-following to achieve an effective impression of adulation around him.

I have suggested that by keeping close to the facts it may be possible for a performer to safeguard his show, but this may prevent him from staging a very elaborate one. If an elaborate show is to be safely staged it may be more useful to remove oneself from the facts rather than stick to them. It is feasible for an official of a religion to conduct a solemn, awesome presentation, because there is no recognized way by which these claims can be discredited. Similarly, the professional takes the stand that the service he performs is not to be judged by the results it achieves but by the degree

[12] Becker, "The Teacher in the Authority System of the Public School," *op. cit.*, p. 139.

to which available occupational skills have been proficiently
applied; and, of course, the professional claims that only the
colleague group can make a judgment of this kind. It is
therefore possible for the professional to commit himself
fully to his presentation, with all his weight and dignity,
knowing that only a very foolish mistake will be capable
of destroying the impression created. Thus the effort of
tradesmen to obtain a professional mandate can be understood as an effort to gain control over the reality they present to their customers; and in turn we can see that such
control makes it unnecessary to be prudently humble in the
airs one assumes in performing one's trade.

There would appear to be a relation between the amount
of modesty employed and the temporal length of a performance. If the audience is to see only a brief performance,
then the likelihood of an embarrassing occurrence will be
relatively small, and it will be relatively safe for the performer, especially in anonymous circumstances, to maintain
a front that is rather false.[18] In American society there is
what is called a "telephone voice," a cultivated form of
speech not employed in face-to-face talk because of the
danger in doing so. In Britain, in the kinds of contact between strangers that are guaranteed to be very brief—the
kinds involving "please," "thank you," "excuse me," and
"may I speak to"—one hears many more public-school accents than there are public-school people. So also, in Anglo-
American society, the majority of domestic establishments
do not possess sufficient staging equipment to maintain a
show of polite hospitality for guests who stay more than a
few hours; only in the upper-middle and upper classes do
we find the institution of the weekend guest, for it is only
here that performers feel they have enough sign-equipment

13 In brief anonymous service relations, servers become skilled
at detecting what they see as affectation. However, since their
own position is made clear by their service role they cannot
easily return affectation with affectation. At the same time,
customers who are what they claim to be often sense that the
server may not appreciate this. The customer may then feel
ashamed because he feels as he would feel were he as false as he
appears to be.

to bring off a lengthy show. Thus, on Shetland Isle, some crofters felt they could sustain a middle-class show for the duration of a tea, in some cases a meal, and in one or two cases even a weekend; but many islanders felt it only safe to perform for middle-class audiences on the front porch, or, better still, in the community hall, where the efforts and responsibilities of the show could be shared by many teammates.

The performer who is to be dramaturgically prudent will have to adapt his performance to the information conditions under which it must be staged. Aging prostitutes in nineteenth-century London who restricted their place of work to dark parks in order that their faces would not weaken their audience appeal were practicing a strategy that was even older than their profession.[14] In addition to reckoning with what can be seen, the performer will also have to take into consideration the information the audience already possesses about him. The more information the audience has about the performer, the less likely it is that anything they learn during the interaction will radically influence them. On the other hand, where no prior information is possessed, it may be expected that the information gleaned during the interaction will be relatively crucial. Hence, on the whole, we may expect individuals to relax the strict maintenance of front when they are with those they have known for a long time, and to tighten their front when among persons who are new to them. With those whom one does not know, careful performances are required.

Another condition associated with communication may be cited. The circumspect performer will have to consider the audience's access to information sources external to the interaction. For example, members of the Thug tribe of India are said to have given the following performances during the early nineteenth century:

As a general rule they pretended to be merchants or soldiers, traveling without weapons in order to disarm sus-

14 Mayhew, *op. cit.*, Vol. 4, p. 90.

picion, which gave them an excellent excuse for seeking permission to accompany travelers, for there was nothing to excite alarm in their appearance. Most Thugs were mild looking and peculiarly courteous, for this camouflage formed part of their stock-in-trade, and well-armed travelers felt no fear in allowing these knights of the road to join them. This first step successfully accomplished, the Thugs gradually won the confidence of their intended victims by a demeanor of humility and gratitude, and feigned interest in their affairs until familiar with details of their homes, whether they were likely to be missed if murdered, and if they knew anyone in the vicinity. Sometimes they traveled long distances together before a suitable opportunity for treachery occurred; a case is on record where a gang journeyed with a family of eleven persons for twenty days, covering 200 miles, before they succeeded in murdering the whole party without detection.[15]

Thugs could give these performances in spite of the fact that their audiences were constantly on the watch for such performers (and quickly put to death those identified as Thugs) partly because of the informational conditions of travel; once a party set out for a distant destination, there was no way for them to check the identities claimed by those whom they encountered, and if anything befell the party on the way it would be months before they would be considered overdue, by which time the Thugs who had performed for and then upon them would be out of reach. But in their native villages, the members of the tribe, being known, fixed, and accountable for their sins, behaved in an exemplary fashion. Similarly, circumspect Americans who would ordinarily never chance a misrepresentation of their social status may take such a chance while staying for a short time at a summer resort.

If sources of information external to the interaction constitute one contingency the circumspect performer must take into consideration, sources of information internal to

15 Sleeman, *op. cit.*, pp. 25-26.

the interaction constitute another. Thus the circumspect performer will adjust his presentation according to the character of the props and tasks out of which he must build his performance. For example, clothing merchants in the United States are required to be relatively circumspect in making exaggerated claims, because customers can test by sight and touch what is shown to them; but furniture salesmen need not be so careful, because few members of the audience can judge what lies behind the front of varnish and veneer that is presented to them.[16] In Shetland Hotel, the staff had great freedom in regard to what was put in soups and puddings, because soups and puddings tend to conceal what is contained in them. Soups, especially, were easy to stage; they tended to be additive—the remains of one, plus everything lying around, served as the beginnings of another. With meats, the true character of which could be more easily seen less leeway was possible; in fact here the standards of the staff were stiffer than those of mainland guests, since what smelt "high" to natives could smell "well hung" to outsiders. So, also, there is a tradition on the island which allows aging crofters to retire from the arduous duties of adult life by feigning illness, there being little conception otherwise of a person becoming too old to work. Island doctors—although the current one was not cooperative in this regard—are supposed to recognize the fact that no one can be sure whether or not illness lies hidden within the human body, and are expected tactfully to restrict their unequivocal diagnoses to externally visible complaints. Similarly, if a housewife is concerned with showing that she maintains cleanliness standards she is likely to focus her attention upon the glass surfaces in her living room, for glass shows dirt all too clearly: she will give less attention to the darker and less revealing rug which may well have been chosen in the belief that "dark colors do not show the dirt." So, too, an artist need take little care with the décor of his studio—in fact, the artist's studio has become stereotyped as a place where those who work backstage do

16 Conant, *op. cit.*, p. 169, makes this point.

not care who sees them or the conditions in which they are seen—partly because the full value of the artist's product can, or ought to be, immediately available to the senses; portrait painters, on the other hand, must promise to make the sittings satisfactory and tend to use relatively prepossessing rich-looking studios as a kind of guarantee for the promises they make. Similarly, we find that confidence men must employ elaborate and meticulous personal fronts and often engineer meticulous social settings, not so much because they lie for a living but because, in order to get away with a lie of that dimension, one must deal with persons who have been and are going to be strangers, and one has to terminate the dealings as quickly as possible. Legitimate businessmen who would promote an honest venture under these circumstances would have to be just as meticulous in expressing themselves, for it is under just such circumstances that potential investors scrutinize the character of those who would sell to them. In short, since a con merchant must swindle his clients under those circumstances where clients appreciate that a confidence game could be employed the con man must carefully forestall the immediate impression that he might be what in fact he is, just as the legitimate merchant, under the same circumstances, would have to forestall carefully the immediate impression that he might be what he is not.

It is apparent that care will be great in situations where important consequences for the performer will occur as a result of his conduct. The job interview is a clear example. Often the interviewer will have to make decisions of far-reaching importance for the interviewee on the sole basis of information gained from the applicant's interview-performance The interviewee is likely to feel, and with some justice that his every action will be taken as highly symbolical. and he will therefore give much preparation and thought to his performance. We expect at such times that the interviewee will pay much attention to his appearance and manner, not merely to create a favorable impression, but also to be on the safe side and forestall any unfavorable impression that might be unwittingly conveyed.

Another example may be suggested: those who work in the field of radio broadcasting and, especially, television keenly appreciate that the momentary impression they give will have an effect on the view a massive audience takes of them, and it is in this part of the communication industry that great care is taken to give the right impression and great anxiety is felt that the impression given might not be right. The strength of this concern is seen in the indignities that high-placed performers are willing to suffer in order to come off well: congressmen allow themselves to be made up and to be told what to wear; professional boxers abase themselves by giving a display, in the manner of wrestlers, instead of a bout.[17]

Circumspection on the part of performers will also be expressed in the way they handle relaxation of appearances. When a team is physically distant from its inspectorial audience and a surprise visit is unlikely, then great relaxation becomes feasible. Thus we read that small American Navy installations on Pacific islands during the last war could be run quite informally, whereas a readjustment in the direction of spit and polish was required when the outfit moved to places that members of the audience were more likely to frequent.[18] When inspectors have easy access to the place where a team carries on its work, then the amount of relaxation possible for the team will depend on the efficiency and reliability of its warning system. It is to be noted that thoroughgoing relaxation requires not only a warning system but also an appreciable time lapse between warning and visit, for the team will be able to relax only to the degree that can be corrected during such a time lapse. Thus, when a schoolteacher leaves her classroom for a moment, her charges can relax into slovenly postures and whispered conversations, for these transgressions can be corrected in the few seconds' warning the pupils will have that the teacher is about to re-enter; but it is unlikely that it will

[17] See John Lardner's weekly column in *Newsweek*, February 22, 1954, p. 59.
[18] Page, *op. cit.*, p. 92.

be feasible for the pupils to sneak a smoke, for the smell of smoke cannot be got rid of quickly. Interestingly enough, pupils, like other performers, will "test the limits," gleefully moving far enough away from their seats so that when the warning comes they will have to dash madly back to their proper places so as not to be caught off base. Here, of course, the character of the terrain can become important. In Shetland Isle, for example, there were no trees to block one's view and little concentration of dwelling units. Neighbors had a right to drop in upon each other whenever happening to be close by, but it was usually possible to see them coming for a good few minutes before actual arrival. Ever-present croft dogs would usually accentuate this visible warning by, as it were, barking the visitor in. Extensive relaxation was therefore possible because there were always minutes of grace to put the scene in order. Of course, with such a warning, knocking on the door no longer served one of its main functions, and fellow crofters did not extend this courtesy to one another, although some made a practice of scraping their feet a little in entering as an extra, final warning. Apartment hotels, the front door of which opens only when a resident presses a button from the inside, provide a similar guarantee of ample warning and allow a similar depth of relaxation.

I would like to mention one more way in which dramaturgical circumspection is exercised. When teams come into each other's immediate presence, a host of minor events may occur that are accidentally suitable for conveying a general impression that is inconsistent with the fostered one. This expressive treacherousness is a basic characteristic of face-to-face interaction. One way of dealing with this problem is, as previously suggested, to select teammates who are disciplined and will not perform their parts in a clumsy, gauche, or self-conscious fashion. Another method is to prepare in advance for all possible expressive contingencies. One application of this strategy is to settle on a complete agenda before the event, designating who is to do what and who is to do what after that. In this way confusions and lulls can be avoided and hence the impressions that such hitches in the proceedings might convey to the audience can be avoided too. (There is of course a danger here. A completely scripted performance, as found in a staged play, is very effective providing no untoward event breaks the planned sequence of statements and acts; for once this sequence is disrupted, the performers may not be able to find their way back to the cue that will enable them to pick up where the planned sequence had been disrupted. Scripted performers, then, can get themselves into a worse position than is possible for those who perform a less organized show.) Another application of this programming technique is to accept the fact that picayune events (such as who is to enter a room first or who is to sit next to the hostess, etc.) will be taken as expressions of regard and to apportion these favors consciously on the basis of principles of judgment to which no one present will take offense, such as age, gross seniority in rank, sex, temporary ceremonial status, etc. Thus in an important sense protocol is not so much a device for expressing valuations during interaction as a device for "grounding" potentially disruptive expressions in a way that will be acceptable (and uneventful) to all present. A third application is to rehearse the whole routine so that the performers can become practiced in their parts and so that contingencies that were not predicted will occur under circumstances in which they can be safely attended to. A fourth is to outline beforehand for the audience the line of response they are to take to the performance. When this kind of briefing occurs, of course, it becomes difficult to distinguish between performers and audience. This type of collusion is especially found where the performer is of highly sacred status and cannot trust himself to the spontaneous tact of the audience. For example, in Britain, women who are to be presented at court (whom we may think of as an audience for the royal performers) are carefully schooled beforehand as to what to wear, what kind of limousine to arrive in, how to curtsy, and what to say.

Protective Practices

I have suggested three attributes that team members must have if their team is to perform in safety: loyalty, discipline, and circumspection. Each of these capacities is expressed in many standard defensive techniques through which a set of performers can save their own show. Some of these techniques of impression management were reviewed. Others, such as the practice of controlling access to back regions and front regions, were discussed in earlier chapters. In this section I want to stress the fact that most of these defensive techniques of impression management have a counterpart in the tactful tendency of the audience and outsiders to act in a protective way in order to help the performers save their own show. Since the dependence of the performers on the tact of the audience and outsiders tends to be underestimated, I shall bring together here some of the several protective techniques that are commonly employed although, analytically speaking, each protective practice might better be considered in conjunction with the corresponding defensive practice.

First, it should be understood that access to the back and front regions of a performance is controlled not only by the performers but by others. Individuals voluntarily stay away from regions into which they have not been invited. (This kind of tact in regard to place is analagous to "discretion," which has already been described as tact in regard to facts.) And when outsiders find they are about to enter such a region, they often give those already present some warning, in the form of a message, or a knock, or a cough, so that the intrusion can be put off if necessary or the setting hurriedly put in order and proper expressions fixed on the faces of those present.[1] This kind of tact can become nicely

---

[1] Maids are often trained to enter a room without knocking, or to knock and go right in, presumably on the theory that they are non-persons before whom any pretense or interaction readiness on the part of those in the room need not be maintained.

elaborated. Thus, in presenting oneself to a stranger by means of a letter of introduction, it is thought proper to convey the letter to the addressee before actually coming into his immediate presence; the addressee then has time to decide what kind of greeting the individual is to receive, and time to assemble the expressive manner appropriate to such a greeting.[2]

We often find that when interaction must proceed in the presence of outsiders, outsiders tactfully act in an uninterested, uninvolved, unperceiving fashion, so that if physical isolation is not obtained by walls or distance, effective isolation can at least be obtained by convention. Thus when two sets of persons find themselves in neighboring booths in a restaurant, it is expected that neither group will avail itself of the opportunities that actually exist for overhearing the other.

Etiquette regarding tactful inattention, and the effective privacy it provides, varies, of course, from one society and subculture to another. In middle-class Anglo-American society, when in a public place, one is supposed to keep one's nose out of other people's activity and go about one's own business. It is only when a woman drops a package, or when a fellow motorist gets stalled in the middle of the road, or when a baby left alone in a carriage begins to scream, that middle-class people feel it is all right to break down momentarily the walls which effectively insulate them. In Shetland Isle different rules obtained. If any man happened to find himself in the presence of others who were engaged in a task, it was expected that he would lend a hand, especially if the task was relatively brief and relatively strenuous. Such casual mutual aid was taken as a matter of course and was an expression of nothing closer than fellow-islander status.

Once the audience has been admitted to a performance, the necessity of being tactful does not cease. We find that there is an elaborate etiquette by which individuals guide

---

Friendly housewives will enter each other's kitchens with similar license, as an expression of having nothing to hide from each other.

[2] *Esquire Etiquette, op. cit.,* p. 73.

themselves in their capacity as members of the audience. This involves: the giving of a proper amount of attention and interest; a willingness to hold in check one's own performance so as not to introduce too many contradictions, interruptions, or demands for attention; the inhibition of all acts or statements that might create a faux pas; the desire, above all else, to avoid a scene. Audience tact is so general a thing that we may expect to find it exercised even by individuals, famous for their misbehavior, who are patients in mental hospitals. Thus one research group reports:

> At another time, the staff, without consulting the patients, decided to give them a Valentine party. Many of the patients did not wish to go, but did so anyway as they felt that they should not hurt the feelings of the student nurses who had organized the party. The games introduced by the nurses were on a very childish level; many of the patients felt silly playing them and were glad when the party was over and they could go back to activities of their own choosing.[3]

> In another mental hospital it was observed that when ethnic organizations gave hostess dances for patients in the hospital Red Cross house, providing thereby some charity work-experience for a few of their less-favored daughters, the hospital representative would sometimes prevail on a few of the male patients to dance with these girls in order that the impression might be sustained that the visitors were bestowing their company on persons more needful than themselves.[4]

When performers make a slip of some kind, clearly exhibiting a discrepancy between the fostered impression and a disclosed reality, the audience may tactfully "not see" the slip or readily accept the excuse that is offered for it. And at moments of crisis for the performers, the whole audience

[3] William Caudill, Frederick C. Redlich, Helen R. Gilmore and Eugene B. Brody, "Social Structure and Interaction Processes on a Psychiatric Ward," *American Journal of Orthopsychiatry*, XXII, pp. 321–22.

[4] Writer's study, 1953–54.

may come into tacit collusion with them in order to help them out. Thus we learn that in mental hospitals when a patient dies in a manner that reflects upon the impression of useful treatment that the staff is attempting to maintain, the other patients, ordinarily disposed to give the staff trouble, may tactfully ease up their warfare and with much delicacy help sustain the quite false impression that they have not absorbed the meaning of what has happened.[5] Similarly, at times of inspection, whether in school, in barracks, in the hospital, or at home, the audience is likely to behave itself in a model way so that the performers who are being inspected may put on an exemplary show. At such times, team lines are apt to shift slightly and momentarily so that the inspecting superintendent, general, director, or guest will be faced by performers and audience who are in collusion.

A final instance of tact in handling the performer may be cited. When the performer is known to be a beginner, and more subject than otherwise to embarrassing mistakes, the audience frequently shows extra consideration, refraining from causing the difficulties it might otherwise create.

Audiences are motivated to act tactfully because of an immediate identification with the performers, or because of a desire to avoid a scene, or to ingratiate themselves with the performers for purposes of exploitation. Perhaps this latter is the favorite explanation. Some successful women of the street, it seems, are ones who are willing to enact a lively approval of their clients' performance, thus demonstrating the sad dramaturgical fact that sweethearts and wives are not the only members of their sex who must engage in the higher forms of prostitution:

Mary Lee says she does no more for Mr. Blakesee than she does for her other rich customers.

"I do what I know they want, make believe I'm ga-ga

---

[5] See Taxel, *op. cit.*, p. 118. When two teams know an embarrassing fact, and each team knows the other team knows it, and yet neither team openly admits its knowledge, we get an instance of what Robert Dubin has called "organizational fictions." See Dubin, *op. cit.*, pp. 341–45.

over them. Sometimes they act like little boys playing games. Mr. Blakesee always does. He plays the cave man. He comes to my apartment and sweeps me in his arms and holds me till he thinks he's taken my breath away. It's a howl. After he's finished making love to me, I have to tell him, 'Darling, you made me so happy I could just cry.' You wouldn't believe a grown-up man would want to play such games. But he does. Not only him. Most of the rich ones."

Mary Lee is so convinced that her prime stock in trade with her wealthy customers is her ability to act spontaneously that she recently submitted to an operation for prevention of pregnancy. She considered it an investment in her career.[6]

But here again the framework of analysis employed in this report becomes constrictive: for these tactful actions on the part of the audience can become more elaborate than is the performance for which they are a response.

I would like to add a concluding fact about tact. Whenever the audience exercises tact, the possibility will arise that the performers will learn that they are being tactfully protected. When this occurs, the further possibility arises that the audience will learn that the performers know they are being tactfully protected. And then, in turn, it becomes possible for the performers to learn that the audience knows that the performers know they are being protected. Now when such states of information exist, a moment in the performance may come when the separateness of the teams will break down and be momentarily replaced by a communion of glances through which each team openly admits to the other its state of information. At such moments the whole dramaturgical structure of social interaction is suddenly and poignantly laid bare, and the line separating the teams momentarily disappears. Whether this close view of things brings shame or laughter, the teams are likely to draw rapidly back into their appointed characters.

[6] Murtagh and Harris, *op. cit.*, p. 165. See also pp. 161–67.

Tact Regarding Tact

It has been argued that the audience contributes in a significant way to the maintenance of a show by exercising tact or protective practices on behalf of the performers. It is apparent that if the audience is to employ tact on the performer's behalf, the performer must act in such a way as to make the rendering of this assistance possible. This will require discipline and circumspection, but of a special order. For example, it was suggested that tactful outsiders in a physical position to overhear an interaction may offer a show of inattention. In order to assist in this tactful withdrawal, the participants who feel it is physically possible for them to be overheard may omit from their conversation and activity anything that would tax this tactful resolve of the outsiders, and at the same time include enough semi-confidential facts to show that they do not distrust the show of withdrawal presented by the outsiders. Similarly, if a secretary is to tell a visitor tactfully that the man he wishes to see is out, it will be wise for the visitor to step back from the interoffice telephone so that he cannot hear what the secretary is being told by the man who is presumably not there to tell her.

I would like to conclude by mentioning two general strategies regarding tact with respect to tact. First, the performer must be sensitive to hints and ready to take them, for it is through hints that the audience can warn the performer that his show is unacceptable and that he had better modify it quickly if the situation is to be saved. Secondly, if the performer is to misrepresent the facts in any way, he must do so in accordance with the etiquette for misrepresentation; he must not leave himself in a position from which even the lamest excuse and the most co-operative audience cannot extricate him. In telling an untruth, the performer is enjoined to retain a shadow of jest in his voice so that, should he be caught out, he can disavow any claim to seriousness and say that he was only joking. In misrepresenting his physical appearance, the performer is enjoined to use a method which allows of an innocent excuse. Thus balding men who affect a hat indoors and out are more or less excused, since it is possible that they have a cold, that they merely forgot to take their hat off, or that rain can fall in unexpected places; a toupee, however, offers the wearer no excuse and the audience no excuse for excuse. In fact there is a sense in which the category of impostor, previously referred to, can be defined as a person who makes it impossible for his audience to be tactful about observed misrepresentation.

In spite of the fact that performers and audience employ all of these techniques of impression management, and many others as well, we know, of course, that incidents do occur and that audiences are inadvertently given glimpses behind the scenes of a performance. When such an incident occurs, the members of an audience sometimes learn an important lesson, more important to them than the aggressive pleasure they can obtain by discovering someone's dark, entrusted, inside, or strategic secrets. The members of the audience may discover a fundamental democracy that is usually well hidden. Whether the character that is being presented is sober or carefree, of high station or low, the individual who performs the character will be seen for what he largely is, a solitary player involved in a harried concern for his production. Behind many masks and many characters, each performer tends to wear a single look, a naked unsocialized look, a look of concentration, a look of one who is privately engaged in a difficult, treacherous task. De Beauvoir, in her book on women, provides an illustration:

And in spite of all her prudence, accidents will happen: wine is spilled on her dress, a cigarette burns it; this marks the disappearance of the luxurious and festive creature who bore herself with smiling pride in the ballroom, for she now assumes the serious and severe look of the housekeeper; it becomes all at once evident that her toilette was not a set piece like fireworks, a transient burst of splendor, intended for the lavish illumination of a mo-

ment. It is rather a rich possession, capital goods, an
investment; it has meant sacrifice; its loss is a real disas-
ter. Spots, rents, botched dressmaking, bad hairdo's are
catastrophes still more serious than a burnt roast or a
broken vase; for not only does the woman of fashion
project herself into things, she has chosen to make herself a thing, and she feels directly threatened in the
world. Her relations with dressmaker and milliner, her
fidgeting, her strict demands—all these manifest her serious attitude and her sense of insecurity.[1]

Knowing that his audiences are capable of forming
bad impressions of him, the individual may come to feel
ashamed of a well-intentioned honest act merely because
the context of its performance provides false impressions
that are bad. Feeling this unwarranted shame, he may feel
that his feelings can be seen; feeling that he is thus seen,
he may feel that his appearance confirms these false conclusions concerning him. He may then add to the precari-
ousness of his position by engaging in just those defensive
maneuvers that he would employ were he really guilty. In
this way it is possible for all of us to become fleetingly for
ourselves the worst person we can imagine that others
might imagine us to be.

And to the degree that the individual maintains a show
before others that he himself does not believe, he can come
to experience a special kind of alienation from self and a
special kind of wariness of others. As one American college
girl has said:

I sometimes "play dumb" on dates, but it leaves a bad
taste. The emotions are complicated. Part of me enjoys
"putting something over" on the unsuspecting male. But
this sense of superiority over him is mixed with feelings
of guilt for my hypocrisy. Toward the "date" I feel some
contempt because he is "taken in" by my technique, or
if I like the boy, a kind of maternal condescension. At
times I resent him! Why isn't he my superior in all ways

[1] De Beauvoir, op. cit., p. 536.

in which a man should excel so that I could be my
natural self? What am I doing here with him, anyhow?
Slumming?

And the funny part of it is that the man, I think, is
not always so unsuspecting. He may sense the truth and
become uneasy in the relation. "Where do I stand? Is
she laughing up her sleeve or did she mean this praise?
Was she really impressed with that little speech of mine
or did she only pretend to know nothing about politics?"
And once or twice I felt that the joke was on me; the boy
saw through my wiles and felt contempt for me for stoop-
ing to such tricks.[2]

Shared staging problems; concern for the way things appear; warranted and unwarranted feelings of shame; ambivalence about oneself and one's audience: these are some
of the dramaturgic elements of the human situation.

[2] Komarovsky, *op. cit.*, p. 188.

Chapter VII

CONCLUSION

The Framework

A social establishment is any place surrounded by fixed barriers to perception in which a particular kind of activity regularly takes place. I have suggested that any social establishment may be studied profitably from the point of view of impression management. Within the walls of a social establishment we find a team of performers who co-operate to present to an audience a given definition of the situation. This will include the conception of own team and of audience and assumptions concerning the ethos that is to be maintained by rules of politeness and decorum. We often find a division into back region, where the performance of a routine is prepared, and front region, where the performance is presented. Access to these regions is controlled in order to prevent the audience from seeing backstage and to prevent outsiders from coming into a performance that is not addressed to them. Among members of the team we find that familiarity prevails, solidarity is likely to develop, and that secrets that could give the show away are shared and kept. A tacit agreement is maintained between performers and audience to act as if a given degree of opposition and of accord existed between them. Typically, but not always, agreement is stressed and opposition is underplayed. The resulting working consensus tends to be contradicted by the attitude toward the audience which the performers express in the absence of the audience and by carefully controlled communication out of character conveyed by the performers while the audience is present.

We find that discrepant roles develop: some of the individuals who are apparently teammates, or audience, or outsiders acquire information about the performance and relations to the team which are not apparent and which complicate the problem of putting on a show. Sometimes disruptions occur through unmeant gestures, faux pas, and scenes, thus discrediting or contradicting the definition of the situation that is being maintained. The mythology of the team will dwell upon these disruptive events. We find that performers, audience, and outsiders all utilize techniques for saving the show, whether by avoiding likely disruptions or by correcting for unavoided ones, or by making it possible for others to do so. To ensure that these techniques will be employed, the team will tend to select members who are loyal, disciplined, and circumspect, and to select an audience that is tactful.

These features and elements, then, comprise the framework I claim to be characteristic of much social interaction as it occurs in natural settings in our Anglo-American society. This framework is formal and abstract in the sense that it can be applied to any social establishment; it is not, however, merely a static classification. The framework bears upon dynamic issues created by the motivation to sustain a definition of the situation that has been projected before others.

The Analytical Context

This report has been chiefly concerned with social establishments as relatively closed systems. It has been assumed that the relation of one establishment to others is itself an intelligible area of study and ought to be treated analytically as part of a different order of fact -the order of institutional integration. It might be well here to try to place the perspective taken in this report in the context of other perspectives which seem to be the ones currently employed, implicitly or explicitly, in the study of social establishments as closed systems. Four such perspectives may be tentatively suggested.

An establishment may be viewed "technically," in terms of its efficiency and inefficiency as an intentionally organized system of activity for the achievement of predefined objectives. An establishment may be viewed "politically," in terms of the actions which each participant (or class of participants) can demand of other participants, the kinds of deprivations and indulgences which can be meted out in order to enforce these demands, and the kinds of social controls which guide this exercise of command and use of sanctions. An establishment may be viewed "structurally," in terms of the horizontal and vertical status divisions and the kinds of social relations which relate these several groupings to one another. Finally, an establishment may be viewed "culturally," in terms of the moral values which influence activity in the establishment—values pertaining to fashions, customs, and matters of taste, to politeness and decorum, to ultimate ends and normative restrictions on means, etc. It is to be noted that all the facts that can be discovered about an establishment are relevant to each of the four perspectives but that each perspective gives its own priority and order to these facts.

It seems to me that the dramaturgical approach may constitute a fifth perspective, to be added to the technical, political, structural, and cultural perspectives.[1] The dramaturgical perspective, like each of the other four, can be employed as the end-point of analysis, as a final way of ordering facts. This would lead us to describe the techniques of impression management employed in a given establishment, the principal problems of impression management in the establishment, and the identity and interrelationships of the several performance teams which operate in the establishment. But, as with the facts utilized in each of the other perspectives, the facts specifically pertaining to impression management also play a part in the matters that

[1] Compare the position taken by Oswald Hall in regard to possible perspectives for the study of closed systems in his "Methods and Techniques of Research in Human Relations" (April, 1952), reported in E. C. Hughes et al., Cases on Field Work (forthcoming).

are a concern in all the other perspectives. It may be useful
to illustrate this briefly.

The technical and dramaturgical perspectives intersect
most clearly, perhaps, in regard to standards of work. Important for both perspectives is the fact that one set of
individuals will be concerned with testing the unapparent
characteristics and qualities of the work-accomplishments
of another set of individuals, and this other set will be concerned with giving the impression that their work embodies
these hidden attributes. The political and dramaturgical
perspectives intersect clearly in regard to the capacities of
one individual to direct the activity of another. For one
thing, if an individual is to direct others, he will often find
it useful to keep strategic secrets from them. Further, if
one individual attempts to direct the activity of others by
means of example, enlightenment, persuasion, exchange,
manipulation, authority, threat, punishment, or coercion, it
will be necessary, regardless of his power position, to convey
effectively what he wants done, what he is prepared to do
to get it done and what he will do if it is not done. Power of
any kind must be clothed in effective means of displaying
it, and will have different effects depending upon how it is
dramatized. (Of course, the capacity to convey effectively
a definition of the situation may be of little use if one is not
in a position to give example, exchange, punishment, etc.)
Thus the most objective form of naked power, i.e., physical
coercion, is often neither objective nor naked but rather
functions as a display for persuading the audience; it is
often a means of communication, not merely a means of
action. The structural and dramaturgical perspectives seem
to intersect most clearly in regard to social distance. The
image that one status grouping is able to maintain in the
eyes of an audience of other status groupings will depend
upon the performers' capacity to restrict communicative
contact with the audience. The cultural and dramaturgical
perspectives intersect most clearly in regard to the maintenance of moral standards. The cultural values of an establishment will determine in detail how the participants are
to feel about many matters and at the same time establish

a framework of appearances that must be maintained, whether or not there is feeling behind the appearances.

Personality-Interaction-Society

In recent years there have been elaborate attempts to bring into one framework the concepts and findings derived from three different areas of inquiry: the individual personality, social interaction, and society. I would like to suggest here a simple addition to these inter-disciplinary attempts.

When an individual appears before others, he knowingly and unwittingly projects a definition of the situation, of which a conception of himself is an important part. When an event occurs which is expressively incompatible with this fostered impression, significant consequences are simultaneously felt in three levels of social reality, each of which involves a different point of reference and a different order of fact.

First, the social interaction, treated here as a dialogue between two teams, may come to an embarrassed and confused halt; the situation may cease to be defined, previous positions may become no longer tenable, and participants may find themselves without a charted course of action. The participants typically sense a false note in the situation and come to feel awkward, flustered, and, literally, out of countenance. In other words, the minute social system created and sustained by orderly social interaction becomes disorganized. These are the consequences that the disruption has from the point of view of social interaction.

Secondly, in addition to these disorganizing consequences for action at the moment, performance disruptions may have consequences of a more far-reaching kind. Audiences tend to accept the self projected by the individual performer during any current performance as a responsible representative of his colleague-grouping, of his team, and of his social establishment. Audiences also accept the individual's particular performance as evidence of his capacity to perform the routine and even as evidence of his capacity to perform any routine. In a sense these larger social units—teams, establishments, etc.—become committed every time the individual performs his routine; with each performance the legitimacy of these units will tend to be tested anew and their permanent reputation put at stake. This kind of commitment is especially strong during some performances. Thus, when a surgeon and his nurse both turn from the operating table and the anesthetized patient accidentally rolls off the table to his death, not only is the operation disrupted in an embarrassing way, but the reputation of the doctor, as a doctor and as a man, and also the reputation of the hospital may be weakened. These are the consequences that disruptions may have from the point of view of social structure.

Finally, we often find that the individual may deeply involve his ego in his identification with a particular part, establishment, and group, and in his self-conception as someone who does not disrupt social interaction or let down the social units which depend upon that interaction. When a disruption occurs, then, we may find that the self-conceptions around which his personality has been built may become discredited. These are consequences that disruptions may have from the point of view of individual personality.

Performance disruptions, then, have consequences at three levels of abstraction: personality, interaction, and social structure. While the likelihood of disruption will vary widely from interaction to interaction, and while the social importance of likely disruptions will vary from interaction to interaction, still it seems that there is no interaction in which the participants do not take an appreciable chance of being slightly embarrassed or a slight chance of being deeply humiliated. Life may not be much of a gamble, but interaction is. Further, in so far as individuals make efforts to avoid disruptions or to correct for ones not avoided, these efforts, too, will have simultaneous consequences at the three levels. Here, then, we have one simple way of articulating three levels of abstraction and three perspectives from which social life has been studied.

Comparisons and Study

In this report, use has been made of illustrations from societies other than our Anglo-American one. In doing this I did not mean to imply that the framework presented here is culture-free or applicable in the same areas of social life in non-Western societies as in our own. We lead an indoor social life. We specialize in fixed settings, in keeping strangers out, and in giving the performer some privacy in which to prepare himself for the show. Once we begin a performance, we are inclined to finish it, and we are sensitive to jarring notes which may occur during it. If we are caught out in a misrepresentation we feel deeply humiliated. Given our general dramaturgical rules and inclinations for conducting action, we must not overlook areas of life in other societies in which other rules are apparently followed. Reports by Western travelers are filled with instances in which their dramaturgical sense was offended or surprised, and if we are to generalize to other cultures we must consider these instances as well as more favorable ones. We must be ready to see in China that while actions and décor may be wonderfully harmonious and coherent in a private tea-room, extremely elaborate meals may be served in extremely plain restaurants, and shops that look like hovels staffed with surly, familiar clerks may contain within their recesses, wrapped in old brown paper, wonderfully delicate bolts of silk.[1] And among a people said to be careful to save each other's face, we must be prepared to read that:

> Fortunately the Chinese do not believe in the privacy of a home as we do. They do not mind having the whole details of their daily experience seen by everyone that cares to look. How they live, what they eat, and even the family jars that we try to hush up from the public are things that seem to be common property, and not to belong exclusively to this particular family who are most concerned.[2]

[1] Macgowan, *op. cit.*, pp. 178–79.
[2] *Ibid.*, pp. 180–81.

And we must be prepared to see that in societies with settled inequalitarian status systems and strong religious orientations, individuals are sometimes less earnest about the whole civic drama than we are, and will cross social barriers with brief gestures that give more recognition to the man behind the mask than we might find permissible.

Furthermore, we must be very cautious in any effort to characterize our own society as a whole with respect to dramaturgical practices. For example, in current management-labor relations, we know that a team may enter joint consultation meetings with the opposition with the knowledge that it may be necessary to give the appearance of stalking out of the meeting in a huff. Diplomatic teams are sometimes required to stage a similar show. In other words, while teams in our society are usually obliged to suppress their rage behind a working consensus, there are times when teams are obliged to suppress the appearance of sober opposition behind a demonstration of outraged feelings Similarly, there are occasions when individuals, whether they wish to or not, will feel obliged to destroy an interaction in order to save their honor and their face. It would be more prudent, then, to begin with smaller units, with social establishments or classes of establishments, or with particular statuses, and document comparisons and changes in a modest way by means of the case-history method. For example, we have the following kind of information about the shows that businessmen are legally allowed to put on:

> The last half-century has seen a marked change in the attitude of the courts toward the question of justifiable reliance. Earlier decisions, under the influence of the prevalent doctrine of "caveat emptor," laid great stress upon the plaintiff's "duty" to protect himself and distrust his antagonist, and held that he was not entitled to rely even upon positive assertions of fact made by one with whom he was dealing at arm's length. It was assumed that anyone may be expected to overreach another in a bargain if he can, and that only a fool will expect common

honesty. Therefore the plaintiff must make a reasonable investigation, and form his own judgment. The recognition of a new standard of business ethics, demanding that statements of fact be at least honestly and carefully made, and in many cases that they be warranted to be true, has led to an almost complete shift in this point of view.

It is now held that assertions of fact as to the quantity or quality of land or goods sold, the financial status of the corporations, and similar matters inducing commercial transactions, may justifiably be relied on without investigation, not only where such investigation would be burdensome and difficult, as where land which is sold lies at a distance, but likewise where the falsity of the representation might be discovered with little effort by means easily at hand.[8]

And while frankness may be increasing in business relations, we have some evidence that marriage counselors are increasingly agreed that an individual ought not to feel obliged to tell his or her spouse about previous "affairs," as this might only lead to needless strain. Other examples may be cited. We know, for example, that up to about 1830 pubs in Britain provided a backstage setting for workmen, little distinguishable from their own kitchens, and that after that date the gin palace suddenly burst upon the scene to provide much the same clientele with a fancier front region than they could dream of.[4] We have records of the social history of particular American towns, telling us of the recent decline in the elaborateness of domestic and avocational fronts of the local upper classes. In contrast, some material is available which describes the recent increase in elaborateness of the setting that union organizations employ,[5] and the increasing tendency to "stock" the setting with academically-trained experts who provide an aura of

---

[8] Prosser, *op. cit.*, pp. 749–50.
[4] M. Gorham and H. Dunnett, *Inside the Pub* (London: The Architectural Press, 1950), pp. 23–24.
[5] See, for example, Hunter, *op. cit.*, p. 19.

thought and respectability.[6] We can trace changes in the plant layout of specific industrial and commercial organizations and show an increase in front, both as regards the exterior of the head-office building and as regards the conference rooms, main halls, and waiting rooms of these buildings. We can trace in a particular crofting community how the barn for animals, once backstage to the kitchen and accessible by a small door next the stove, has lately been removed a distance from the house, and how the house itself, once set down in an unprotected way in the midst of garden, croft equipment, garbage, and grazing stock, is becoming, in a sense, public-relations oriented, with a front yard fenced off and kept somewhat clean, presenting a dressed-up side to the community while debris is strewn at random in the unfenced back regions. And as the connected byre disappears, and the scullery itself starts to become less frequent, we can observe the up-grading of domestic establishments, wherein the kitchen, which once possessed its own back regions, is now coming to be the least presentable region of the house while at the same time becoming more and more presentable. We can also trace that peculiar social movement which led some factories, ships, restaurants, and households to clean up their backstages to such an extent that, like monks, Communists, or German aldermen, their guards are always up and there is no place where their front is down, while at the same time members of the audience become sufficiently entranced with the society's id to explore the places that had been cleaned up for them. Paid attendance at symphony orchestra rehearsals is only one of the latest examples. We can observe what Everett Hughes calls collective mobility, through which the occupants of a status attempt to alter the bundle of tasks performed by them so that no act will be required which is expressively inconsistent with the image of self that these incumbents are attempting to establish for themselves. And

6 See Wilensky, *op. cit.*, chap. iv, for a discussion of the "window-dressing" function of staff experts. For reference to the business counterpart of this movement see Riesman, *op. cit.*, pp. 138–39.

we can observe a parallel process, which might be called "role enterprise," within a particular social establishment, whereby a particular member attempts not so much to move into a higher position already established as to create a new position for himself, a position involving duties which suitably express attributes that are congenial to him. We can examine the process of specialization, whereby many performers come to make brief communal use of very elaborate social settings, being content to sleep alone in a cubicle of no pretension. We can follow the diffusion of crucial fronts—such as the laboratory complex of glass, stainless steel, rubber gloves, white tile, and lab coat—which allow an increasing number of persons connected with unseemly tasks a way of self-purification. Starting with the tendency in highly authoritarian organizations for one team to be required to spend its time infusing a rigorously ordered cleanliness in the setting the other team will perform in, we can trace, in establishments such as hospitals, air force bases, and large households, a current decline in the hypertrophic strictness of such settings. And finally, we can follow the rise and diffusion of the jazz and "West Coast" cultural patterns, in which terms such as bit, goof, scene, drag, dig, are given currency, allowing individuals to maintain something of a professional stage performer's relation to the technical aspects of daily performances.

The Role of Expression Is Conveying
Impressions of Self

Perhaps a moral note can be permitted at the end. In this report the expressive component of social life has been treated as a source of impressions given to or taken by others. Impression, in turn, has been treated as a source of information about unapparent facts and as a means by which the recipients can guide their response to the informant without having to wait for the full consequences of the informant's actions to be felt. Expression, then, has been treated in terms of the communicative role it plays during social interaction and not, for example, in terms of consummatory or tension-release function it might have for the expresser.[1]

Underlying all social interaction there seems to be a fundamental dialectic. When one individual enters the presence of others, he will want to discover the facts of the situation. Were he to possess this information, he could know, and make allowances for, what will come to happen and he could give the others present as much of their due as is consistent with his enlightened self-interest. To uncover fully the factual nature of the situation, it would be necessary for the individual to know all the relevant social data about the others. It would also be necessary for the individual to know the actual outcome or end product of the activity of the others during the interaction, as well as their innermost feelings concerning him. Full information of this order is rarely available; in its absence, the individual tends to employ substitutes—cues, tests, hints, expressive gestures, status symbols, etc.—as predictive devices. In short, since the reality that the individual is concerned with is unperceivable at the moment, appearances must be relied upon in its stead. And, paradoxically, the more the individual is concerned with the reality that is not available to perception, the more must he concentrate his attention on appearances.

The individual tends to treat the others present on the basis of the impression they give now about the past and the future. It is here that communicative acts are translated into moral ones. The impressions that the others give tend to be treated as claims and promises they have implicitly made, and claims and promises tend to have a moral character. In his mind the individual says: "I am using these impressions of you as a way of checking up on you and your activity, and you ought not to lead me astray." The peculiar thing about this is that the individual tends to take

[1] A recent treatment of this kind may be found in Talcott Parsons, Robert F. Bales, and Edward A. Shils, *Working Papers in the Theory of Action* (Glencoe, Ill.: The Free Press, 1953), Chap. II, "The Theory of Symbolism in Relation to Action."

this stand even though he expects the others to be uncon-
scious of many of their expressive behaviors and even
though he may expect to exploit the others on the basis of
the information he gleans about them. Since the sources of
impression used by the observing individual involve a multitude of standards pertaining to politeness and decorum,
pertaining both to social intercourse and task-performance,
we can appreciate afresh how daily life is enmeshed in
moral lines of discrimination.

Let us shift now to the point of view of the others. If they
are to be gentlemanly, and play the individual's game, they
will give little conscious heed to the fact that impressions
are being formed about them but rather act without guile
or contrivance, enabling the individual to receive valid impressions about them and their efforts. And if they happen
to give thought to the fact that they are being observed,
they will not allow this to influence them unduly, content
in the belief that the individual will obtain a correct impression and give them their due because of it. Should they
be concerned with influencing the treatment that the individual gives them, and this is properly to be expected, then
a gentlemanly means will be available to them. They need
only guide their action in the present so that its future
consequences will be the kind that would lead a just individual to treat them now in a way they want to be treated;
once this is done, they have only to rely on the perceptive-
ness and justness of the individual who observes them.

Sometimes those who are observed do, of course, employ
these proper means of influencing the way in which the
observer treats them. But there is another way, a shorter
and more efficient way, in which the observed can influence
the observer. Instead of allowing an impression of their activity to arise as an incidental by-product of their activity,
they can reorient their frame of reference and devote their
efforts to the creation of desired impressions. Instead of
attempting to achieve certain ends by acceptable means,
they can attempt to achieve the impression that they are
achieving certain ends by acceptable means. It is always

possible to manipulate the impression the observer uses as a substitute for reality because a sign for the presence of a thing, not being that thing, can be employed in the absence of it. The observer's need to rely on representations of things itself creates the possibility of misrepresentation.

There are many sets of persons who feel they could not stay in business, whatever their business, if they limited themselves to the gentlemanly means of influencing the individual who observes them. At some point or other in the round of their activity they feel it is necessary to band together and directly manipulate the impression that they give. The observed become a performing team and the observers become the audience. Actions which appear to be done on objects become gestures addressed to the audience. The round of activity becomes dramatized.

We come now to the basic dialectic. In their capacity as performers, individuals will be concerned with maintaining the impression that they are living up to the many standards by which they and their products are judged. Because these standards are so numerous and so pervasive, the individuals who are performers dwell more than we might think in a moral world. But, *qua* performers, individuals are concerned not with the moral issue of realizing these standards, but with the amoral issue of engineering a convincing impression that these standards are being realized. Our activity, then, is largely concerned with moral matters, but as performers we do not have a moral concern with them. As performers we are merchants of morality. Our day is given over to intimate contact with the goods we display and our minds are filled with intimate understandings of them; but it may well be that the more attention we give to these goods, then the more distant we feel from them and from those who are believing enough to buy them. To use a different imagery, the very obligation and profitability of appearing always in a steady moral light, of being a socialized character, forces one to be the sort of person who is practiced in the ways of the stage.

Staging and the Self

The general notion that we make a presentation of ourselves to others is hardly novel; what ought to be stressed in conclusion is that the very structure of the self can be seen in terms of how we arrange for such performances in our Anglo-American society.

In this report, the individual was divided by implication into two basic parts: he was viewed as a *performer*, a harried fabricator of impressions involved in the all-too-human task of staging a performance; he was viewed as a *character*, a figure, typically a fine one, whose spirit, strength, and other sterling qualities the performance was designed to evoke. The attributes of a performer and the attributes of a character are of a different order, quite basically so, yet both sets have their meaning in terms of the show that must go on.

First, character. In our society the character one performs and one's self are somewhat equated, and this self-as-character is usually seen as something housed within the body of its possessor, especially the upper parts thereof, being a nodule, somehow, in the psychobiology of personality. I suggest that this view is an implied part of what we are all trying to present, but provides, just because of this, a bad analysis of the presentation. In this report the performed self was seen as some kind of image, usually creditable, which the individual on stage and in character effectively attempts to induce others to hold in regard to him. While this image is entertained *concerning* the individual, so that a self is imputed to him, this self itself does not derive from its possessor, but from the whole scene of his action, being generated by that attribute of local events which renders them interpretable by witnesses. A correctly staged and performed scene leads the audience to impute a self to a performed character, but this imputation—this self —is a *product* of a scene that comes off, and is not a *cause* of it. The self, then, as a performed character, is not an organic thing that has a specific location, whose fundamental fate is to be born, to mature, and to die; it is a dramatic effect arising diffusely from a scene that is presented, and the characteristic issue, the crucial concern, is whether it will be credited or discredited.

In analyzing the self then we are drawn from its possessor, from the person who will profit or lose most by it, for he and his body merely provide the peg on which something of collaborative manufacture will be hung for a time. And the means for producing and maintaining selves do not reside inside the peg; in fact these means are often bolted down in social establishments. There will be a back region with its tools for shaping the body, and a front region with its fixed props. There will be a team of persons whose activity on stage in conjunction with available props will constitute the scene from which the performed character's self will emerge, and another team, the audience, whose interpretive activity will be necessary for this emergence. The self is a product of all of these arrangements, and in all of its parts bears the marks of this genesis.

The whole machinery of self-production is cumbersome, of course, and sometimes breaks down, exposing its separate components: back region control; team collusion; audience tact; and so forth. But, well oiled, impressions will flow from it fast enough to put us in the grips of one of our types of reality—the performance will come off and the firm self accorded each performed character will appear to emanate intrinsically from its performer.

Let us turn now from the individual as character performed to the individual as performer. He has a capacity to learn, this being exercised in the task of training for a part. He is given to having fantasies and dreams, some that pleasurably unfold a triumphant performance, others full of anxiety and dread that nervously deal with vital discreditings in a public front region. He often manifests a gregarious desire for teammates and audiences, a tactful considerateness for their concerns; and he has a capacity for deeply felt shame, leading him to minimize the chances he takes of exposure.

These attributes of the individual *qua* performer are not

merely a depicted effect of particular performances; they are psychobiological in nature, and yet they seem to arise out of intimate interaction with the contingencies of staging performances.

And now a final comment. In developing the conceptual framework employed in this report, some language of the stage was used. I spoke of performers and audiences; of routines and parts; of performances coming off or falling flat; of cues, stage settings and backstage; of dramaturgical needs, dramaturgical skills, and dramaturgical strategies. Now it should be admitted that this attempt to press a mere analogy so far was in part a rhetoric and a maneuver.

The claim that all the world's a stage is sufficiently commonplace for readers to be familiar with its limitations and tolerant of its presentation, knowing that at any time they will easily be able to demonstrate to themselves that it is not to be taken too seriously. An action staged in a theater is a relatively contrived illusion and an admitted one; unlike ordinary life, nothing real or actual can happen to the performed characters—although at another level of course something real and actual can happen to the reputation of performers *qua* professionals whose everyday job is to put on theatrical performances.

And so here the language and mask of the stage will be dropped. Scaffolds, after all, are to build other things with, and should be erected with an eye to taking them down. This report is not concerned with aspects of theater that creep into everyday life. It is concerned with the structure of social encounters—the structure of those entities in social life that come into being whenever persons enter one another's immediate physical presence. The key factor in this structure is the maintenance of a single definition of the situation, this definition having to be expressed, and this expression sustained in the face of a multitude of potential disruptions.

A character staged in a theater is not in some ways real, nor does it have the same kind of real consequences as does the thoroughly contrived character performed by a confidence man; but the *successful* staging of either of these types of false figures involves use of *real* techniques—the same techniques by which everyday persons sustain their real social situations. Those who conduct face to face interaction on a theater's stage must meet the key requirement of real situations; they must expressively sustain a definition of the situation: but this they do in circumstances that have facilitated their developing an apt terminology for the interactional tasks that all of us share.

INDEX

Hamilton, Mary, 213
Harris, Sara, 148 n., 233 n.
Hart, C. W. M., ix
Hartog, Jan de, 198 n.
Hecht, J. J., 104 n., 189 n.,
    213 n.
Henrey, Mrs. Robert, 184 n.
Hilton, John, 32 n.
Hirsch, Louis, 192 n.
Holcombe, Chester, 89 n.
Hughes, E. C., ix, 44, 62 n.,
    90, 124, 156, 161 n., 164,
    247
Hughes, Helen M., 156 n.,
    161 n., 164 n.
Hunter, Floyd, 87 n., 246 n.

Ichheiser, Gustav, 2

James, William, 48–49
Jaques, Eliot, 205 n.
Joad, C. E. M., 50 n.
Johnson, Charles, 38 n., 79
Jones, Maxwell, 200, 201–2
Jones, Mervyn, 26 n.

Kafka, Franz, 95
Kahn, E. J., Jr., 26 n.
Kincaid, Dennis, 171–72
King, Joe, 30 n.
Kinsey, Alfred C., 42, 131
Komarovsky, Mirra, 39 n.,
    237 n.
Kornhauser, William, 48 n.
Kroeber, A. L., 21
Kuper, Leo, 120 n.

LaCroix, Paul, 125 n.
Lang, K. and G., 62 n.
Lardner, John, 226 n.
Lentz, Edith, 32 n., 219 n.
Lindzey Gardener, 73 n.
Littlejohn, James, ix
Lortie, Dan C., 28 n.

McCarthy, Mary, 219 n.
McDowell, Harold D., 64 n.
Macgowan, J., 25 n., 244 n.

Macgregor, F. C., 61 n.
Mannheim, Karl, 81 n.
Marriott, McKim, 157 n.
Martin, Clyde E., 131 n.
Maurer, David W., 146 n.,
    174 n.
Mayhew, Henry, 41 n., 222 n.
Melville, Herman, 136–37
Mencken, H. L., 61 n.
Merton R. K., 72 n.
Métraux, Alf d, 74 n., 112 n.
Miller Charles, 180 n.
Miller Warren, 97 n.
Moore, Gerald, 87 n., 181 n.,
    182 n.
Morgenstein, Oscar, 16 n.
Murtagh, J. M., 148 n., 233 n.

Orwell, George, 122 n., 123

Page, Charles Hunt, 46 n.,
    217 n., 226 n.
Park, Robert Ezra, 19, 20 n.
Parsons Talcott, 249 n.
Peterson, Warren, 49 n.
Pinelli, Babe, 30 n., 66 n.,
    98 n, 197 n.
Plant, Marjorie, 38 n.
Pomeroy Wardell B., 131 n.
Posonby, Sir Frederick, 15 n.,
    54, 68, 120 n., 133–34, 183,
    208–9
Potter, Stephen, 8 n., 191 n.
Powdermaker, Florence B.,
    203 n.
Prosser, William L., 63 n.,
    246 n.

Radcliffe-Brown, A. R., 26,
    27 n., 35
Ralph J. B., 40 n.
Redlich Frederick C., 231 n.
Rencke, Richard, 126 n.
Riesman, David, 102 n., 142 n.,
    247 n.
Riezler, Kurt, 70, 159
Roethlisberger, Fritz, 99 n.,
    150 n.

ABOUT THE AUTHOR

ERVING GOFFMAN was born in Canada in 1922. He received his B.A. from the University of Toronto in 1945 and then studied at the University of Chicago, receiving his M.A. in 1949 and his Ph.D. in 1953. For a year he resided on one of the smaller of the Shetland Isles while he gathered material for a dissertation on that community, and later he served as a visiting scientist at the National Institute of Mental Health in Washington. Dr. Goffman is the author of several articles and book reviews which have appeared in such periodicals as *Psychiatry* and the *American Journal of Sociology*.

The Presentation of Self in Everyday Life was first published as a monograph at the Social Sciences Research Centre at the University of Edinburgh in 1956. Dr. Goffman has revised and expanded it for the Anchor edition.